D1569814

THE NEXT
PROGRESSIVE
ERA

THE NEXT
PROGRESSIVE
ERA

A BLUEPRINT FOR
BROAD PROSPERITY

Phillip Longman
and **Ray Boshara**

PoliPointPress

The Next Progressive Era: A Blueprint for Broad Prosperity

Copyright © 2009 by Phillip Longman and Ray Boshara

Production management: Michael Bass Associates
Book design: Michael Bass Associates
Cover design: Charles Kreloff

Library of Congress Cataloging-in-Publication Data

Longman, Phillip.
  The next Progressive Era : a blueprint for broad prosperity / by Phillip Longman and Ray Boshara ; foreword by Steve Coll.
       p. cm.
    Includes bibliographical references and index.
    ISBN 978-0-9815769-4-7 (alk. paper)
    1. United States—Social conditions—21st century. 2. United States—Economic conditions—21st century. I. Boshara, Ray. II. Title.
  HN59.2.L66 2009
  306.0973'09051—dc22   2008049527

Published by:
PoliPointPress, LLC
P.O. Box 3008
Sausalito, CA 94966-3008
(415) 339-4100
www.p3books.com

Distributed by Ingram Publisher Services

Printed in the USA

CONTENTS

THE ELECTION of President Barack Obama has been greeted by many of his supporters as the dawn of a "new Progressive Era." This is a label derived from American history but often used to connote the present—a label rich with implication but not so well endowed with specificity. The longest and most expensive presidential campaign in history clearly produced a result that was transformative, at least in its relation to America's founding vision of equality. Yet what an Obama presidency portends for modern-day progressivism—and what policy agendas this label suggests—is far from clear.

The questions begin with the tactics and strategies of electoral politics. Is this new Progressive Era, for example, postpartisan, or is it hyperpartisan? Among the earliest to claim the mantle of twenty-first-century progressivism were members of the so-called netroots community—as exemplified by the Daily Kos and Moveon.org. Their partisanship extended to attacking, with exceptional conviction, moderate Democrats such as Joe Lieberman, Hillary Clinton, Harold Ford Jr. and the Democrat Leadership Council, who had also started calling themselves progressives, as opposed to liberals. Yet the candidate around whom these self-styled progressives eventually rallied, Barack Obama, propelled himself to victory with a political message that was strikingly postpartisan, using formulations like "disagree without being disagreeable," "bring people together," and "working with those we don't agree with." Obama even went so far as to praise Ronald Reagan's leadership.

Another confusion centers on the intertwined meanings of race, class, and gender in this new Progressive Era. Did the election of the nation's first African-American president signal a new postracial America? Certainly it did in the limited sense that millions of Americans voted for a man their parents and grandparents would have rejected on the basis of skin color alone. Yet African-Americans voted almost monolithically, while Obama attracted only 41 percent of the white male vote and a mere 39 percent of the white female vote. Meanwhile, an infusion of Hispanics and African-Americans into the voting booths of California, Arizona, and Florida brought with it a rejection of gay marriage through statewide ballot initiatives. So if the election signaled a new politics of inclusion, that politics remains incomplete.

Many feminists were forced to consider the meaning and limits of sisterly solidarity when they encountered Sarah Palin. At the same time, the ceilings shattered by both Obama and Hillary Clinton have tended to undermine in many people's minds the case for such progressive causes as affirmative action. As never before, the value of "personal responsibility" now confronts the progressive mind-set, even as progressives confront a world that is still beset by prejudice and inequality of opportunity.

The progressive movement also evinces some confusion about class. Obama's electoral coalition was broad and diverse, but many of his core supporters are, like himself, well educated, upscale, thoughtful—drawn from, or aiming for, professions such as the media, law, academia, foundations, and financial services. As Obama's contest against Hillary Clinton forecasted, his coalition remains vulnerable to rebellion from "below" because of its struggle to connect with or even tolerate the views of some middle- and working-class Americans, as exemplified by Palin. Obama drew stronger support from people making over $250,000, for whom he proposed a tax hike, than he did among middle-income Americans for whom he proposed a tax cut.

There is debate, too, about how much of the progressive movement's agenda the country can afford. The financial crisis is enough to bring out the inner New Dealer in all of us. But one difference between the start of Great Depression and now is that American people were not deeply encumbered by credit card debt and exploding mortgages going in. Also, the federal government itself carried almost no debt. In the 1930s, the challenge was to boost consumer spending at a time of great fear. Now the challenge is to do that again, but at the same time to encourage a new ethos of thrift—a paradoxical goal, and a difficult one.

These weaknesses and tensions within the progressive movement might not be so serious were it not for the nature of the issues facing the broad country it now must attempt to govern. At their core, nearly all these issues—health care, climate change, energy, repair of the credit markets, infrastructure investment, sustainable fiscal policy—augur a substitute of investment for consumption, if not a permanent new thrift ethos. They also necessarily involve broad expansion of government control over the economy, and in many instances over personal behavior, in a country deeply suspicious of concentrated political power, let alone any lurch toward true socialism.

What, for example, is to be the progressive movement's solution to the health care crisis? The accumulating failures in the country's health care system are a cause of profound weakness in the American economy; unaddressed, this weakness will exacerbate the current recession and crimp its aftermath. A large number of the country's housing foreclosures in recent years appear to be related to medical problems and health care expenses. American businesses often can't afford to hire as many employees as they would like because of rising health insurance costs; employees often can't afford to quit to chase their "better mousetrap" dreams because they can't risk going without coverage. Add to this the system's moral failings: about twenty-two thousand people die in this country annually because they lack health insurance. That is more than the number of Americans who are murdered in a year.

On this much all progressives can agree. But reform of the health care system must involve far more than just universal access to an already-broken system. It must address the provision of health care itself—the actual practice of medicine—which, for the insured and uninsured alike, has become extraordinarily expensive, wasteful, uncoordinated, and even dangerous. About a third of all medical spending in the United States goes for treatments that are unnecessary at best, harmful at worst. Meanwhile, the single largest driver of inflating health care costs is not improvement in the effectiveness of medical technology but spreading chronic disease due to environmental and lifestyle factors. The spread of obesity among children is so profound that they may become the first generation of Americans that does not outlive its parents.

Overcoming America's health care crisis is achievable, but it will require policies that will impinge on the individual autonomy, particularly of doctors and specialists, as we seek to inject more science into the practice of medicine and reduce unnecessary treatment. It will also involve the use of electronic medical records, which will be a great aide in diagnosis and coordination of care, but which also comes at some cost in personal privacy. And it will involve policies that at least nudge Americans into taking better care of themselves. Have today's progressives confronted these realities, let alone figured out how to sell the necessary solutions to a country steeped in individualism?

Another question facing progressives in power is their stand on the so-called democratization of credit. Since the New Deal and particularly after the 1960s, liberalism was committed to extending access to credit, especially home mortgages, to people of modest means. These policies helped create a nation of homeowners and a broad, asset-owning middle class. Yet now we have reached a moment where more people are falling out of the middle class than rising into it due to the debts they have taken on. Progressives are thus left to confront another set of questions that go against the grain of American individualism. What, if any, constraints should be placed on the amount and terms of consumer borrowing? How much should Americans be forced or nudged into saving, whether for homeownership, college, or retirement?

My colleagues at the New America Foundation, Phillip Longman and Ray Boshara, have been pondering these questions for many years, including during their work on New America's Next Social Contract project. In writing this book, they have employed a unique approach that offers much promise to today's newly empowered progressives as they search for politically feasible and sustainable solutions to a bewildering array of problems. In surveying the major domestic policy issues facing the nation, Longman and Boshara ask first, what would the original Progressives have done?

It is a question well worth asking. In the early years of the twentieth century, Americans faced many of the same problems we do today, ranging from deepening income inequality, concentrated corporate power, and an increasingly global economy prone to financial panics, to problems with tainted foods, dangerous drugs, and a health care system falling far short of its potential. Yet Progressives, working across deep cultural and class divides, achieved supermajorities in election after election, as both parties competed to adopt their agenda.

Preserving capitalism while rejecting socialism, the Progressives built their winning coalition, Longman and Boshara argue, by tapping into America's long-standing "yeoman" tradition, which pays special deference to the interests of small-scale producers and calls for broad-scale ownership of assets—from small farms in Thomas Jefferson's time, to suburban homesteads and home office start-ups more recently. This yeoman ideal may at first seem archaic, yet in an economy marked more and more by free agency and dwindling middle-class wages and benefits, it is gaining new relevancy. Many Americans recoil at the thought that government should just "spread the wealth around." But the idea that government should bend its efforts toward providing the striving yeoman protection against monopoly and other forms of predatory economic power, as well as from destructive social forces that threaten the yeoman's hearth and home, has deep roots in American political tradition and, as such, provides a political theme whose revival could help steer today's progressives.

Longman and Boshara also unpack the meaning of thrift as the original Progressives understood it. Today, progressives still talk in a language of conservation when it comes to the use of natural resources. But long forgotten is how original Progressives also applied thrift and conversation to preventive health care, personal finance, and even the use of one's time. The authors also show how the original Progressives anticipated the findings of today's behavioral economics in crafting programs to encourage thrift in realms as diverse as personal hygiene, asset building, and temperance. Properly understood, thrift was an ideal that tied together many of the original Progressives' most promising ideas and policy agendas, and it could again today.

Of course, there is much in this tradition that we justifiably reject today. The original Progressives clearly overreached, for example, in adopting social control measures such as Prohibition, even if they did so largely in the name of preventive health and financial independence for the working class. Many Progressives also embraced eugenics and other pseudosciences to justify deepening repression of blacks and other minority groups.

Still, their past constructively informs our present. The original Progressives blended populist sentiment with true scientific expertise in the formulation of public policy—and all in the name of preserving the yeoman ideal of economic and political independence from both Big Government and Big Business. The value of this book arises from its analysis of contemporary policy issues through the lens of the original Progressives, revealing forgotten lessons about what it takes to unite individualistic Americans around bold collective plans of action. It also offers concrete policy proposals likely to appeal across a broad center of American politics. History doesn't repeat itself, but if there is truly to be a new Progressive Era, we need to understand our relationship with the deeper patterns of reform and reaction in American history and learn from them.

Steve Coll
President and CEO, New America Foundation
Washington, DC
November 17, 2008

I T WAS AN ERA of dazzling scientific advance, and of rising religious fundamentalism. It was an age that produced great concentrations of wealth for some, but deepening indebtedness for most. It was time of rising personal freedom, but also of spreading anonymity, anarchy, terrorism, segregation, contagion, prohibitions, and abridged civil rights. And it was a great age of reform—one that called itself, and is called today, "the Progressive Era."

In little more than a decade, the innovations included the first automobiles, the first airplanes, the mass production of electricity, wireless communication, and a plethora of consumer items that transformed day-to-day life: fans, phonographs, telephones, vacuum cleaners, refrigerators, motion pictures, and above all the electric lightbulb.

Gains in pure science were even more impressive. In 1905, Albert Einstein experienced his bewildering Annus Mirabilis, confirming atomic reality but also calling into question the reality of time and space, as well as, for some, conventional morality. At around the same time, biologists isolated the hereditary function of chromosomes and terms like gene, genotype, and phenotype came into use (and severe misuse).

Meanwhile, millions of Americans left mainline churches to embrace End Times prophesy. Baptist preacher William Bell Riley, and the *Fundamentals* series of premillennial religious tracts to which he contributed, gave today's fundamentalism its name. Darwinism went from being a curious theory in the late nineteenth century that some used to justify laissez-faire government, to a subject seen by cultural conservatives as a threat to civilization itself.

The era began with the depression of the early 1890s, which was caused in part by the crash of what we would today call "subprime mortgages" that were bundled up, "securitized," and sold to unwitting foreign investors.[1] Eventually, the unemployment rate reached as high as 18.4 percent before the economy started to grow again. But the nation's financial architecture, manipulated by what Teddy Roosevelt called "the predatory man of wealth," remained under great strain and beset by panics. The worst came in 1907, when the failure of the Knickerbocker Trust set off wave and wave of investment bank failures and the 37 percent fall in share prices—a perfect storm that could have ended in a Great Depression but instead led to creation of the Federal Reserve System and vastly expanded federal control of credit markets.[2]

Over the era, gains in industrial efficiency and scientific management were staggering, while inflation was growing but manageable. Yet the fragile middle and working classes struggled with mounting debt to what we today call "payday lenders" and to mortgage finance companies even as "the octopus of monopoly" devoured small-scale merchants, farmers, and producers.

Today we tend to remember the turn of the last century through the nostalgic lens of Thornton Wilder's *Our Town*—a time of bicycles built for two and Sousa bands playing in the park during the good old summertime. Yet it was also a time of fearsome economic change and economic insecurity. Between 1894 and 1904, more than 1,800 companies consolidated into just 93 giant corporations—Standard Oil, International Harvester, and Northern Securities among the most notorious for their tentacles. Globalization of trade and finance, on a scale that would not be seen again until the 1990s, put Americans of all classes at the mercy of distant foreign markets. Meanwhile, from the coalfields of Pennsylvania to the docks of San Francisco, union organizers struggled, and mostly failed, as wave after wave of immigrants gave employers a surplus of low-cost workers to exploit. Steel magnate Andrew Carnegie would refer to them as "a Golden Stream."

Fear of the outsider became a hallmark of the age. A Polish-named anarchist assassinated President William McKinley. Another immigrant fired a bullet into the chest of Teddy Roosevelt, who was saved only by the thickness of a speech he was carrying in his breast pocket. Waves of terrorist bombings attributed to the foreign born, including a massive explosion near the sight of what would become the World Trade Center, made Americans as fearful of Eastern European and Sicilian immigrants as they would later become of Islamic fundamentalists.

As the era reached its climax just before World War I, five hundred Mexican bandits/terrorists/revolutionaries (take your choice) attacked the border town of Columbus, New Mexico, killing ten American civilians and fourteen soldiers. In reaction, the U.S. military set in motion a highly mechanized "Punitive Expeditionary Force" of ten thousand men to hunt down their charismatic leader. As with Osama bin Laden, Pancho Villa kept hidden in mountain redoubts. After a year of asymmetrical warfare, the manhunt ended in failure as troops were redeployed to fight a greater war no one saw coming.

History doesn't repeat itself. But as Mark Twain is said to have observed, it often rhymes. Along with rapid technological change, rising fundamentalism, increasing inequality, and a big problem with networks of violent nonstate actors, other parallels between today and the turn of the last century are also striking.

For example, one hundred years ago, as today, mothers fretted over the quality and safety of the food they served their families—and for the same reason: more and more of it was carelessly processed or adulterated in distant packing plants by giant, underregulated agribusinesses. Then the processors were mostly in Chicago, Minneapolis, or Pittsburgh and had still familiar names like Swift, National Biscuit Company, and H. J. Heinz. Now, an even more concentrated food processing industry imports tainted food from as far away as China, and nobody is sure just who is responsible for what ingredients. Researchers estimate food-borne diseases cause approximately 76 million illnesses, 325,000 hospitalizations, and 5,000 deaths in the United States each year.[3]

During the Progressive Era, the health care system was also widely perceived to be in crisis. Faith in doctors and the drug industry collapsed. More and more of the "patent medicines" they dispensed were exposed as ineffective or dangerous. The modern cliché about "snake oil salesmen" comes from Stanley Snake Oil, a once popular cure-all that government investigators discovered in 1917 contained no snake oil but mostly turpentine. Today's equivalent is the long line of popular prescription drugs—Vioxx, Celebrex, Rezulin, Baycol, Butazolidin, phenformin, Seldane, and dozens more—that despite approval by a now broken legacy of the Progressive Era, the Food and Drug Administration, have killed Americans in the hundreds of thousands. Vioxx alone killed more Americans than died in the Vietnam War before it was finally withdrawn from the market.

In the Progressive Era, as now, experts pointed to the expanding vectors for infectious disease, such as the so-called Spanish flu, which killed an estimated 2 to 5 percent of world population in the late teens, including some 675,000 mostly young adult Americans. Fear of tuberculosis, influenza, syphilis, and other pathogens (many now reemerging in more virulent forms) led to both sound and extreme public health measures, ranging from pasteurization, improved sanitation, and a safer water supply to the quarantining without trial of Mary Mallon, aka "Typhoid Mary."

It all seemed so quaint by the late 1960s, when the apparent success of antibiotics would prompt the surgeon general to advise Congress, "It is time to close the book on infectious diseases."[4] Since then, however, the rapid evolution of microbes resistant to antibiotics, combined with increased global travel and trade, global warming, the spread of sexually transmitted diseases, and other factors has created an infectious environment very much like that faced by the Progressives, if not worse. When combined with the explosive growth of chronic illness, the resurgence of infectious disease has cut the rate of improvement in life expectancy at birth to roughly half of what it was during the Progressive Era, despite Americans committing more than 17 percent of their economy to health care.

During the Progressive Era, millions of Americans also struggled to throw off their addictions to alcohol, cocaine, absinthe, and other mind-altering substances or called for laws to make others to do so. Eventually, reformers succeeded in criminalizing alcohol, recreational use of narcotics, and, in Washington State, even cigarettes. Many made a cult of exercise while extolling thinness, especially for women. Nearly everyone recognized the need for improved physical fitness and better diets. Bennarr MacFadden made millions promoting muscle building and "physical culture." Horace Fletcher, "the Great Masticator," made a fad of long, slow chewing to avoid excess calories, attracting followers ranging from John D. Rockefeller to Henry James. "Dr." John Harvey Kellogg stressed the purported relationship between meat and masturbation, while writers like Upton Sinclair popularized vegetarianism. What you ate and what you weighed became a political statement.

Meanwhile, much as with today's Internet, children and young Americans suddenly gained cheap and easy access to violent and obscene moving images through the spread a powerful new medium. Its "platform" included newfangled mutoscopes, kinetescopes, cinematographs, and nickelodeons. And its most commercially successful "content" turned out to be "peep shows"—sometimes featuring extreme pornography—whose most ardent viewers were untended children in poor and working-class neighborhoods.

During an era in which thinking people commonly saw themselves as part of a so-called "Child" Saving movement—whose expressions included first federal Child Bureau (1912), the Boy Scouts (1910), and the Girl Scouts (1912)—the spread of peep shows provoked deep fears and outrage. This was particularly true for Progressives who were learning from the new social sciences the profound effect of the environment on human development.

Feminists, fundamentalists, and outraged parents of all stripes campaigned for a government crackdown and eventually succeeded. Pennsylvania established the first state censor board targeting the fledging movie industry in 1911. Access to pornography would not become so widespread again until the introduction of the World Wide Web in the 1990s.

Another eerie parallel between today and the Progressive Era is the sharply rising, politically untouchable, and unsustainable levels of spending on the well-organized elderly. By 1894, a staggering 38 percent of all federal spending went just to pay pensions to Union Civil War veterans and their dependents. (By comparison, in 2008, Social Security and Medicare consumed 42 percent of federal spending.) Though the Union pensions were originally promised only to veterans with service-related disabilities, eligibility gradually came to be based on age alone as pressure groups like the Grand Army of the Republic (which evolved into the country's first institutionalized gray lobby) intimidated dissenting politicians. "I hold it an insidious wrong inflicted upon the Republic," fumed Harvard president Charles Eliot, "that the pension system instituted for the benefit of soldiers and sailors of the United States has been prosecuted and degraded."[5]

Paying for this runaway entitlement program required Americans to endure regressive tariffs on imports that, while protecting key Northern industries, ran as high as 50 percent. Resentment against the misadministration Civil War pensions and their financing was a deep spur to Progressive Era civil service reform, the adoption of the "progressive" income tax as the major source of federal finance, and early state and local initiatives to build a sounder pension system.

America a century ago was also wracked by energy shortages, transportation deadlocks, and mounting concerns about the environment. By 1911, the country was devouring twenty-three billion cubic feet of wood a year, while the natural growth of the remaining timberland amounted to only one-third as much.[6] Having already depleted eastern forests as a source of energy, Americans shivered in the dark during repeated coal shortages caused by speculators, strikes, inadequate infrastructure, and ever-mounting demand.

Experts called for, and the country rapidly pulled off, a massive conversion to low-cost, alternative energy sources, specifically to then-abundant and comparatively clean petroleum. The era also saw massive investment in infrastructure, including paved roads, the wiring of cities for electricity, and the construction of tens of thousands of miles of now sorely missed "interurban" lines, some of which are today being rebuilt at tremendous cost as light rail systems. Most Progressives enthusiastically embraced the automobile but saw it as just one mode in a truly integrated road and rail system.

Meanwhile, Progressives passed the first zoning laws to deal with runaway development and urban sprawl. Thoughtful Americans abhorred the waste of both money and natural resources that produced the emerging modern lifestyle, bemoaned the threats to country's vanishing wilderness and wildlife, and called for conservation and stewardship under what came to be known as the "thrift movement."

Yet one important parallel is still lacking, at least for now, between the America of the early twentieth century and today. For the Progressive Era was an age of unprecedented reform rivaled only by the New Deal and in many ways more impressive.

The New Deal, as Franklin Roosevelt famously put it, was a series of ad hoc, experimental measures designed to end the Great Depression. "It is common sense to take a method and try it," FDR said in 1932. "If it fails, admit it frankly and try another. But above all, try something." The New Deal had many enduring accomplishments, including Social Security and much needed regulation of Wall Street and banks. But along the way came an alphabet soup of new agencies and programs, most of which, it is generally agreed, had little effect in ending the Depression and only passed because voters were in a panic.

By contrast, most Progressive Era reforms resulted from decades of rising, populist demand combined with long, careful expert study and advocacy. Moreover, the conditions facing Progressive Era reformers were more analogous to our own than those faced by New Dealers. The Great Depression of the 1930s, most people thought at the time and most economists would still agree, was caused by lack of effective consumer demand. The challenge of the 1930s was to match a well-developed system of mass production with a commensurate new system of mass consumption. By contrast, the next Great Depression, if it comes to that, will have been caused by a consumer-driven economy that eventually exhausted its ability to borrow. The original Progressives, as we'll see, made a cult of thrift, while the New Dealers viewed it as antisocial, which suggests that the Progressives may have much more to teach us.

Also unlike New Deal reformers, the Progressives lived during a period of relative if also very uneven economic growth, when conservatives were well funded and very well organized. Karl Rove, President George W. Bush's would-be mastermind, has often expressed his admiration for Mark Hanna, the Republican machine politician who nearly derailed the emerging Progressive Era in 1896 by seeing to it that conservative William McKinley prevailed over populist William Jennings Bryan.

In these ways as well, the Progressives faced political and economic conditions similar to those faced by Americans over the last twenty years, yet there is no comparison in results. Imagine that, beginning early in this decade, Americans had earnestly and thoughtfully reduced the role of money in politics, reformed the health care system, dramatically reduced rates of infectious disease, tamed the drug industry, and created a regulatory regime for Wall Street and the banking sector that prevented any need for massive taxpayer bailouts.

Imagine as well that they busted the Microsoft monopoly and effectively regulated Enron and modern-day loan sharks, such as payday lenders and subprime mortgage brokers. Imagine that they had forestalled the growth of terrorism, rationalized immigration, deconsolidated oil companies, clamped down on sex trafficking and child access to pornography, engineered a massive conversion to cleaner, cheaper, more efficient forms of energy, while also launching an entirely new transportation system that transformed American life as much as the internal combustion engine did.

Imagine, finally, that they had dramatically improved the quality and independence of journalism, restored public trust in government and the professions, revamped the public schools, and ended reliance on foreign sweatshops and child labor, all while instilling an ethic of thrift, conservation, and public service and leaving no legacy of public debt. That would have been an age approximating the accomplishments of the first Progressive Era.

Also unlike the New Deal, Progressive Era reforms emerged during a time of harsh cultural, religious, racial, and sectional divides exacerbated by high levels of immigration and a weak, fragmented labor movement. These divisions, though still strong in the 1930s, were much reduced by then. Under pressure from Progressives among others, immigration had long since come to a halt, and the labor movement was consequently stronger. The widespread lynching of southern blacks that marked the Progressive age had given way during the 1930s to less violent race relations after millions of African-Americans moved north to take advantage of jobs that previously would have been filled by immigrants.

Yet even though the Progressives had to work with an electorate singularly lacking in social solidarity and yearning for segregation, they built a bipartisan, almost postpartisan, supermajority movement, drawing support from all regions of the country and from nearly all walks of life—yeoman farmers and trade unionists, German-trained social engineers and maternal feminists crusading against child labor and ardent spirits. In both absolute numbers and proportion, the greatest concentration of support for Progressive legislation in Congress came from southern and midwestern members representing states that after 1968 would vote solidly for conservative Republicans.[7]

Prairie populists like Williams Jennings Bryan made common cause with Ivy League eggheads like Woodrow Wilson, who appointed Bryan to be his secretary of state. Assorted earnest "goo goos" (good government types) and "Miss Nancys," reminiscent in their idealism and civic-mindedness with today's rising college-educated "millennial" generation, didn't dismiss yeoman farmers as anti-intellectual, racist rubes but instead worked tirelessly to preserve the yeoman's way of life from predatory capitalists and corrupt legislators.

Both parties contained and were dominated by strong progressive wings opposed to the "stand patters" and old-time machine politicians. In Teddy Roosevelt's eyes, there was nothing the matter with Kansas much less Montana, except that the western frontier was slowly coming to a close. Inheriting a corrupt, ultraconservative party too long in power, Roosevelt used progressivism to renew the GOP and fit it to new conditions. And with this broad bipartisan coalition, Progressives in both parties worked together to solve many of the most pressing problems of their day.

The movement's apogee came in 1912 when three presidential candidates—incumbent Republican William Taft, Democrat Woodrow Wilson, and insurgent, Progressive Party "Bull Moose" candidate Teddy Roosevelt—all competed in the general election over who was biggest "Progressive." Taft, perceived to be the most conservative among them, would exclaim, "I am not a reactionary. I'm a progressive." And indeed, as he liked to point out, he had busted more trusts during his one term in office than Roosevelt had during his previous two. In the election of 1912, Socialist Eugene Debs and these three self-styled Progressives received 100 percent of the vote.

Before the era was over, circa 1920, both American government, at all its levels, and the U.S. economy had become transformed. Primaries and direct election of U.S. senators eroded the power of political machines and special interest money. Civil servants replaced political hacks. Antitrust suits had broken up monopolies, creating a space for entrepreneurs. Government regulators insured the safety of the food and drug supply, and closely regulated prices in key industries like railroads, which the federal government nationalized for the duration of World War I. Reform legislation also brought an end to child labor and gave women the right to vote. Government for the first time took on responsibility for enforcing product safety, job safety, insurance against on-the-job accidents, public health, conservation, and environmental protection.

Some major reforms of the Progressive Era, such as Prohibition, failed in practice. Others, such as "scientific management" of transportation under the Interstate Commerce Commission, crippled railroads and set in motion today's auto dependency and many other problems. Progressive Era reform brought science to medicine and dramatically improved public health, but it also led the commercialization of medicine that is at the heart of our current health care crisis. Yet of this there can be no doubt: Americans at the turn of the last century faced many of the same economic, environmental, cultural, demographic, and social challenges Americans once again face today, and they crafted a progressive politics that could do something about them. Could today's self-styled progressives do the same?

CHAPTER 1

Present Progressive

I N RECENT YEARS, it has become common among people who used to call themselves liberals to call themselves progressives. "I prefer the word 'progressive,'" Hillary Clinton announced in 2007, "which has a real American meaning, going back to the Progressive era at the beginning of the twentieth-century. I consider myself a modern progressive."[1]

Also taking up the progressive banner these days are folks who rallied for Howard Dean in 2004, joined Moveon.org, and spent the remaining Bush years posting on *Daily Kos, Huffington Post*, or MyDD.com. Most are sure that neither Clinton nor her husband is one of them. After characterizing her as "viciously opportunistic," *Huffington Post* blogger Norman Soloman asked in 2007, "In the interests of truth-in-labeling, shouldn't Hillary Clinton be described as anti-progressive?" Many like-minded bloggers and "progressive" activists are equally contemptuous of the Democratic Leadership Council, once chaired by Bill Clinton, and its think tank, the pointedly named Progressive Policy Institute.

Many other folks who describe themselves as progressives hold an admixture of views that often to seem to swim together, however uneasily. In modern usage, for example, it's "progressive" to be for multiculturalism and against patriarchy—a stance that makes criticism of the subjugation of women in the Islamic world, for example, seem contradictory. Are all cultural values equally valid, or are some, such as those supporting clitoridectomy, polygamy, and arranged marriages of teenage girls morally regressive? The original Progressives certainly knew where they stood. "There is moral progress," wrote the influential Progressive Era philosophers John Dewey and James Hayden Tufts, "and there is a moral order."[2] If we do not truly believe in moral progress and a moral order, can we be truly "progressives"?

Similarly, it is "progressive" to have sympathy for the "common man" and to have a deep faith in democracy with no abridgments on free speech or thought. Yet for years self-styled progressives pushed for hate speech codes on campus while also condemning vast swaths of the electorate as irredeemably racist. If America is essentially a racist society, what's so great about democracy or free speech? Alternatively, if we are committed to cultural pluralism, by what standard do we condemn the racial attitudes of some folk or another? Are we truly for tolerance and understanding, or simply intolerant of intolerance?

Today's progressives also typically harbor a deep commitment to expanded civil rights, for blacks, women, gays, and, more recently, illegal (undocumented) aliens. But where do these rights come from? Today's progressives reject appeals to divine right, natural law, or custom and point to the Constitution as the lodestone from which new individual and minority rights can be extracted. By contrast, the original Progressives rarely engaged in "rights talk" but embraced pragmatism, social control, and popular recall of federal judges. "The people themselves must be the ultimate makers of their own Constitution," thundered Teddy Roosevelt at the Progressive Party Convention in 1912, "and where their agents differ in their interpretations of the Constitution the people themselves should be given the chance . . . to settle what interpretation it is that their representatives shall thereafter adopt as binding."[3]

Faith in science, including economics and other social sciences, is also a hallmark of progressivism and always has been. "The scientific spirit is the discipline of democracy, the escape from drift, the outlook of a free man," wrote Walter Lippmann in *Drift and Mastery*, published to wide acclaim in 1914.[4] Yet many of today's progressives, much more so than their forebears, are conflicted about the course of scientific progress. Stem cell research is good, but genetically modified food is not. Darwinism is established fact but not social Darwinism, much less any form of eugenics. Solar power is good, but nuclear power is bad. Broad prosperity is good, but pollution and materialism are bad.

Today's progressives of course have their different reasons, good and bad, for making these distinctions, but in doing so we reveal that our adherence to the ideal of material progress is selective and conditional. Material progress, after all, is what brought us the auto culture, the sprawling suburbs, oil wars, obesity and ultimately global warming. There is, of course, no necessary contradiction between environmentalism and progressivism. But it remains true that many of us no longer see progress as the "one true and only heaven" as the original Progressives did. Instead, we hope to roll back the march of progress to a more "wholesome," "sustainable" "ecofriendly" past, with some even praising the virtues of hunter-gatherer societies. Are we truly "progressives"?

Then there is John McCain, who during the last election compared himself, and was compared by many others on both the Left and Right, to Progressive Party candidate Teddy Roosevelt. By extension, would not McCain himself also be a progressive? Just as liberalism went from meaning pro–free market/small government in the nineteenth century, to pro–Big Government/Big Labor in the 1930s, the meaning of the term *progressive* is clearly shifting. Yet shifting to what?

In the person of Barack Obama, modern progressives discovered a transcendent new vocabulary that spoke of the audacity of hope, change you can believe in, overcoming differences, postpartisanship, and putting the 1960s (and the baby boomers) behind us. Yet Jimmy Carter, too, was once a transcendent new voice in American politics, who, like Obama, drew much of his strength from a combination of personal appeal to the young, high idealism, and popular revulsion against eight years of Republican misrule and incompetence. It was not enough. Not only did Carter barely win against the hapless Gerald Ford, but his inability to unify and govern even his own party set up the long era of triumphant, movement conservatism and YOYO (You're On Your Own) economics.[5]

Is there a coherent vision of what progressivism could and should mean in our time, one that could, as in the original Progressive Era, unite Americans, from moose burger eaters to those who favor arugula? Is there a specific agenda that will attract enduring majority support for solutions to America's well-recognized but long-neglected chronic conditions, from increasing indebtedness and energy dependence, to a broken health care system, crumbling transportation infrastructure, and a shrinking middle class?

What happens now that George Bush has ridden off into the Texas sunset? What exactly unites today's self-styled progressives beyond contempt for Bush misrule and religious fundamentalism? As described by *New York Times Magazine* writer Matt Bai in his book *The Argument*, assorted left-wing billionaires have spent years pouring hundreds of millions of dollars into funding an infrastructure of so-called progressive think tanks devoted to putting just the right "frame" on progressive messages. Yet, as Bai quotes a fretting John Podesta of the Center for American Progress, "We still haven't gotten it into people's minds a picture of what a progressive America would look like."[6]

That would not be such a problem were not the stakes so high. After decades of drift and denial, America is now desperately in need of vast changes in its social contract, including deep reforms in high and low finance, health care, infrastructure, trade, energy independence, carbon emissions, and other areas that necessarily involve expansion in the size and regulatory role of government. This book is not about how Democrats can vanquish Republicans with some new "frame" or another. Frankly, given the GOP's intellectual exhaustion, Republicans are more desperately in need of rediscovering their own substantial record of Progressive Era reform than are Democrats. We hope they do and predict they will. For there is no other way to put America's domestic policies on course for a new century.

The book takes its inspiration and its title from Americans who did just that one hundred years ago and who were the first to call themselves progressives, whether they were Republicans, Democrats, or members of the short-lived Progressive Party itself. And as we shall see, the key to their political and substantive success was a common adherence to an ancient American Dream—the dream of sustainable self-sufficiency that then, as now, had become deeply threatened by global forces beyond the control of any individual.

The original Progressive Era contained two seeming paradoxes. First, it sought to preserve the independence of a hardy, freedom-loving, populist American yeomanry, mostly comprising small-scale property owners and producers inherently suspicious of government—and it did so by mobilizing scientifically informed, expert-designed collective action. Second, it embraced the value of thrift, conservation, and family life while also endorsing patriotism, capitalism, and material progress.

These inherent tensions within progressivism are not easy to manage in day-to-day politics and administration. Progressivism, unlike socialism or communism, is committed to markets, private property, and individual rights, and it wants no part of government for its own sake. Yet it also understands that collective action and social control are needed to preserve these all-American values. "It is . . . essential to recognize," wrote Herbert Croly in *The Promise of American Life* (1911), "that the individual American will never obtain a sufficiently complete chance of self-expression, until the American nation has earnestly undertaken and measurably achieved the realization of its collective purpose."[7]

This is not an easy balance to maintain. From roughly the time of the Scopes "Monkey Trial" in the 1920s until today, the exploitation of cultural and religious divisions between elites and yeomen has prevented the reemergence of a true progressive politics. But the growing seriousness of the issues now threatening us as a nation make it imperative that we learn what we can from the original Progressives about how to bridge these divides and make the best use of our collective intelligence.

The Forgotten Legacy

To be sure, much in the record of the last Progressive Era is repulsive by today's standards. Many reforms also were taken to excess and failed so spectacularly as to rekindle the forces of apathy and reaction. The temperance movement's transformation from advocating moderation to advocating prohibition comes to mind. So does the era's faith in eugenics, which rationalized segregation and eventually led to the Supreme Court's embrace of forced sterilization of "imbeciles."[8] Yet the original Progressives also have much to teach us about how to overcome the special challenges presented to effective government by

America's extraordinary diversity, inherent individualism, dynamic capitalism, and instinctive distrust of collective action.

Aside from a commitment to conservation, many of today's progressives hold comparatively few political views in common with their namesakes of one hundred years ago. The original Progressives' primary focus was not on individual or constitutional rights, for example, of which they tended to be suspicious. Nor did they have any time for "bohemians." Instead, their focus was on protecting children, the family, and small-scale producers of all kinds from the ravages of monopoly capitalism and a degraded culture—specifically, corporate plutocrats, political bosses, stock jobbers, predatory lenders, liquor dealers, pornographers, white slavers, assassins, Wobblies, quack doctors, "snake oil" salesmen, corrupt judges, shady lawyers, polluters, disease carriers, communist agitators, and bomb-throwing anarchists.

In his 1925 memoir, *Confessions of a Reformer*, Frederic Howe explained the mind-set behind the seeming contradictions of his own life and times. "Missionaries and battleships, anti-saloon leagues and Ku Klux Klans, Wilson and Santo Domingo are all part of that evangelistic psychology that makes America what it is."[9]

It's an era that's very poorly remembered, to say the least. That's true for many reasons beyond just contemporary America's general innocence of history. Americans who came of age in the late teens and 1920s, for example, tended to look back at the Progressives as hopeless moralizers who put their "lost" generation into the trenches of a war that didn't end all wars, offered them few veterans' benefits, and took away their beer and gin. No hagiographic histories of the era came from them. In a 1920 *Atlantic Monthly* article entitled "'These Wild Young People' by One of Them," a young writer named John Carter observed with typical truculent cynicism, "The older generation has certainly pretty well ruined this world before passing it on to us."[10]

Succeeding generations of Marxists and socialists, meanwhile, have depicted Progressives as middle-class reactionaries who not only suppressed their revolution by sometimes extreme measures but committed the United States to imperialism in Cuba, Panama, the Philippines, and Santo Domingo. As reflected in the thinking of the radical American socialist William English Walling, there was no reason to give Progressives credit for taming capitalism when capitalism itself was doomed. The "essential or practical difference," Walling thought, between reform and revolution, was that reformers expected "to work, on the whole, with the capitalists who are to be done away with, while socialists expect to work against them."[11]

New Deal liberals also had their issues with Progressives. The New Deal embraced gigantism, seeking to harmonize Big Business, Big Government, and Big Labor. Though many of the architects of the New Deal were themselves aging Progressives—or "New Deal Isaiahs," in the mocking phrase of H. L. Mencken—they were men and women of a different time and generation whose highest ideal had been to preserve the values and economic independence of yeoman farmers and small-town America. To the rising generation of liberals, the Progressives seemed quaint and committed to a vanishing way of life that could never compete with mass production and the rising forces of totalitarianism.

By the 1950s, liberal historians tended to paint Progressives as a collection of privileged do-gooders suffering from "status anxiety" and nostalgia for "Americana." This is the theme of what is still the best-known history of the era, Richard Hofstadter's *Age of Reform*, published in 1955, which describes Progressives accurately but disapprovingly as clinging to the Jeffersonian vision of a nation of yeoman farmers.[12]

As liberalism became increasingly committed to secularism, focusing its energy on banning school prayers and other issues involving the separation of church and state, liberals discovered something else not to like about the Progressive Era. "Liberals might applaud Progressives' turn-of-the-century efforts to create a welfare state," historian Eldon J. Eisenach has observed, "but are mystified and even angered by all their talk of social justice as the collective achievement of an American 'Christ ideal.'"[13]

New Left historians of the 1960s heaped on further scorn, chastising Progressives for insufficient radicalism. Joining in were libertarians and communitarians, who in the 1970s and 1980s denounced the Progressive legacy of an expanded welfare state controlled by a "new class" of meddling experts.[14] As intellectuals of the Left and Right tore at the very idea of progressivism, the shallow, popular memory was of a musty era that produced ragtime and "Reds." Aging ragtime pianist Eubie Blake, who received the Medal of Honor in 1981 from Ronald Reagan, became the living face of the age, joined by Warren Beatty depicting the dashing communist John Reed in the movie *Reds* of the same year.

Meanwhile, scholarship focusing on the history of minority groups brought long overdue attention to the phenomenon of lynching that marked the Progressive Era and further tarnished its memory. Seemingly for reasons of political correctness, many academic historians since the 1970s have denied that a coherent Progressive movement even existed or had much effect. Better to deny there was a Progressive Era than to admit that its key ideas and reforms were largely the product of white, Anglo-Saxon Protestants.[15]

Given these many different vantage points over succeeding generations, it is startling how blithely erstwhile liberals began reaching a few years ago for the progressive label. Yet there is a common heritage and a common experience—one that today's self-styled progressive must instinctively sense, if not fully understand. Fortunately, it is possible to see the Progressives with all their faults and still appreciate how much they have to teach us about achieving difficult reforms in a deeply divided and individualistic nation.

The Search for Order

Most Progressives clearly were racists by today's highly charged, if underdefined, meaning of the term. Most believed unswervingly in the superiority of Western, particularly Anglo-Saxon, Christian civilization, and they viewed America as having a special mission to spread its social and religious gospel to less evolved people. Among elites, such chauvinism seemed to be confirmed by the findings of the newly formed social sciences, for which Progressives had great respect.

"At college," notes historian David W. Southern, "budding progressives not only read exposés of capitalistic barons and attacks on laissez-faire economics by muckraking journalists, they also read racist tracts that drew on the latest anthropology, biology, psychology, sociology, eugenics, and medical science."[16]

The first Intelligence Quotient (IQ) tests, for example, were developed during the Progressive Era, and they showed (or appeared to show) that native-born whites possessed superior intelligence. Most Progressives viewed blacks, southern Europeans, and other "swarthy" races as backward and undisciplined, though not as—and this is key—*inherently irredeemable.* For why else put so much effort into missionary work, settlement houses, public education, and Negro and Indian colleges designed to instill "the American way of life"?

This is another point missing from many accounts of the era. What can look to us like racism pure and simple was, for many Progressives, well-intended, reluctant social engineering. The Reverend Washington Gladden, for example, was a prominent champion of the Progressive Era's social gospel movement and, after meeting with the "radical" black leader W. E. B. DuBois in the early 1900s and reading his book *The Soul of Black Folks*, spoke out against racial discrimination. Yet by 1907, Gladden was so distraught by the nation's mounting racial tensions that he advocated setting aside three or four southern states for blacks.[17]

Many of the Progressives who went along with Jim Crow did so after reluctantly concluding that "separate but equal," while a blight on democracy, was the only realistic response to the volatile, self-reinforcing spiral of white racism and black criminality in both the rapidly urbanizing South and the industrial North. In upholding the constitutionality of Jim Crow laws, U.S. Supreme Court justice Henry Billings Brown wrote in *Plessy v. Ferguson* (1896) that they were necessary for the "the preservation of the public peace and good order." Brown would later go on to uphold the constitutionality of the progressive income tax.[18] In 1915, the *New York Times* would refer in a matter-of-fact tone to "the legacy of crime and violence left behind by the misguided 'statesmen' of reconstruction" whose "best intentions had become a curse to the country."[19]

Separate waiting rooms, schools, and other forms of segregation would at least help ease the racial tensions that were producing hundreds of lynchings year after year. A white woman was less likely to accuse a black man of an inappropriate stare or remark, and thereby set off a white race riot, if the two simply never occupied the same public space. As Booker T. Washington, who should be thought of as a leading voice of turn-of-the-century black progressivism, put it: "In all things that are purely social we can be as separate as the fingers, yet one as the hand in all things essential to mutual progress."[20]

Yet even the excesses of the era provide an important lesson. They show how progressive change in the United States has tended to require broad, unswerving faith not just in progress itself but in the existence and the superiority of distinctly American ideas and values. For if a true American people does not exist, and we are instead just a random, multicultural mix of populations on their way to different destinations, then why go through all the turmoil and upheaval of forcing wholesale reform on society?

What is most striking about the original Progressives was their success in co-opting and coordinating populist, reactionary, chauvinistic, and patriotic sentiments, instead of railing against them. They would never speak casually of a need to "spread the wealth around" but stressed the need to protect striving, small-scale proprietors from the predations of Wall Street financiers and monopolists—using a language that even Joe the Plumber could understand. They also completely rejected what we today call multiculturalism, would never be caught "blaming America first" or belittling organized religion, and had no concept of "liberal guilt." Many, like Jane Addams and other settlement house activists, had deep sympathy for immigrants and devoted their lives to helping them. But the Progressives had a deep, clear, proud sense of a unique American civilization, and they demanded allegiance to its core political principles and cultural traditions. "There is no room in this country for hyphenated Americanism," proclaimed Teddy Roosevelt, addressing the Knights of Columbus in 1915. At a time when the Civil War was still within living memory, Progressives fostered and championed a distinctly American national identity that was, and is, a precondition to collective action in this deeply diverse and individualistic nation.

Nationalism, of a kind deeply and organically connected to the country's enduring political traditions, was the key to the Progressives' political success. They created an era in which both "tillers and toilers"—the yeoman farmer in Kansas and the steel worker Pittsburgh, as well as

"Professor Tweezer" at Madison or Johns Hopkins, the small store-owner, the suffragette, the liberal theologian, the Bible-thumping itin-erate preacher, the WASPy "club" woman, the German-trained social engineer—all could find vast areas of common ground based on a sim-ple principle. It was to preserve the best of nation's long-standing moral and political values—including preeminently self-sufficiency but also equal opportunity, self-governance, stewardship, and commitment to wholesome family life—in the face of rapid economic and demographic changes that were trampling those traditions.

The result was that, under crosscutting conditions eerily parallel to our own, the Progressive movement achieved bipartisan, supermajor-ity support for difficult reforms that preserved the American Dream for a new century. That is why, in this book, as we look at the major domes-tic issues of our time—ranging from health care, conservation, and immigration, to the shrinking middle class and the growing ranks of self-employed Americans—we always ask first, "What would the Pro-gressives have done?" In many areas, we must reject their example. But it would be folly to ignore the Progressive legacy of reform if we hope to achieve positive solutions to our problems, which are in so many ways like their own.

For the mass of Americans who today feel let down by orthodox-ies of Left and Right, and who sense that the country's political system is failing to address the essential needs and purposes of their lives, the Progressive Era offers many positive as well as cautionary lessons. We offer this book as a road map for the next Progressive Era, a time in which Americans will once again, in the face of rapidly changing con-ditions, come together to adjust and modernize the American social contract.

CHAPTER 2

Progressivism and the Yeoman Ideal

A progressive is someone who understands that it is the people of our country who make it great, and unless we take care of the people first, we'll never be successful in maintaining our greatness. Taking care of the people means providing health care for everyone. It means keeping the environment clean, safe and preserved. It means great schools and great jobs. It means improving the lives of families, rather than lining the pockets of big business, or big politicians. It means taking care of each other here, and around the world. We're all in this together.

> —Carol S., Amherst, MA, winning entry, "What Is a Progressive?" online contest, Campaign for America's Future, 2006

Legislation . . . must proceed upon the principle of aiming to get for each man a fair chance to allow him to show the stuff there is in him. No legislation can make some men prosperous; no legislation can give wisdom to the foolish, courage to the timid, strength to the shiftless. All that legislation can do, and all that honest and fearless administration of the laws can do is to give each man as good a chance as possible to develop the qualities he has in him, and to protect him so far as is humanly possible against wrong of any kind at the hands of his fellows.

> —President Theodore Roosevelt, Jamestown, ND, April 7, 1903

REFLECT ON the differences in these two conceptions of what progressive government is. The first is a fair description of how many of today's progressives state their values and vision. In the contest held by Campaign for America's Future to define modern progressivism, the winning entry, like the nine finalists', emphasizes caring (mentioned three times), togetherness, and the provision of public goods, seemingly for their own sake.

By contrast, Teddy Roosevelt, in describing his vision of Progressive government, stressed anything but caring. His emphasis was on creating a world in which striving, deserving individuals get the opportunity to realize their full potential. He does not presume a world in which everyone cares for strangers out of the goodness of their hearts. Instead, he recognizes a world of vicious competition in which the role of government is to assure that no one gets an unfair advantage over anyone else and everyone has an equal opportunity (but not an entitlement) to thrive.

This is a crucial distinction, and it goes a long way toward explaining the stunning electoral success of the original Progressive movement. TR and other Progressives of his generation cared as much or more about the environment, health care, good schools, and good jobs as any progressive today. They were outraged as much, if not more, by the ravages of Big Business, Wall Street, and corrupt political machines. But in advancing their movement, they didn't appeal to altruism or feel-good, one-world togetherness. Nor did they presume or advocate anything like complete equality of result, since there was nothing to be done for those who were too "foolish" or "timid" or "shiftless" to help themselves. Rather, they tapped deep into the genes of America's distinctive political DNA by emphasizing the need to preserve self-sufficiency, economic independence, and equal opportunity—even if it required, paradoxically enough, an enormous increase in the size and power of government to achieve these ends.

This was the genius of the original Progressive movement. It didn't work against the grain of America's tradition of individualism. Instead, it used it to advance collective action. Nor did it mock those who tended to hold their economic independence most dear—the yeoman farmer or artisan, the small store owner or mechanic. Instead, it paid special honor to the yeoman tradition in American life and went to war with stand-pat conservatism in its name.

This is the all-American "meme" that is missing from most progressive discourse these days and one of the reasons today's self-styled progressives strike so many of their compatriots as disconnected and vaguely un-American. The American creed has always had much to say about "caring" and "sharing" among family members, neighbors, fellow congregationalists, unionists, brethren in fraternal orders, and mutual aid societies. But it has always been suspicious of sharing and caring with distant strangers, unless it be to share the light of Jesus Christ.

The Return of Yeomanry

The stunning failures of the Bush administration, of Wall Street, of American automakers, of free markets and libertarianism generally—all have brought us to a moment when even many iconic conservatives, such as Alan Greenspan, are calling for more dramatic stimulus spending and reregulation. Yet the financial panic will pass, perhaps sooner rather than later if the Obama Administration proves its competence. And even before it does, an enlarged government will become more liable (fairly or unfairly) to real and perceived boondoggles and to widening resentments of its expanding powers. This is not a moment to be smug about the center of American politics having shifted permanently in favor of Big Government, much less to a Big Government that is using much of its power to shore up Big Business and Big Finance.

This is why we need to look especially closely now at the lessons of the last Progressive Era, with its concentration on the economic interests of small-scale producers. For progressivism to become an enduring majority movement, it must not ridicule but speak on behalf of and make common cause with America's yeomanry, whose ranks are continually expanding. Today, few yeomen farmers are left, to be sure, though their numbers are again growing after generations of decline. But the ranks of small business owners, entrepreneurs, "mompreneurs," consultants, contract employees, and free agents of all kinds are exploding as secure employment in large corporations fades away.

Between 1995 and 2005, the ranks of the self-employed increased by 13.1 percent. Nearly 13 percent of men and 7.2 percent of women now work for themselves.[1] According to the latest available IRS data, in 2003 there were 19.7 million nonfarm sole proprietorships, a 120 percent increase since 1980.[2] If one counts independent contractors and contingent work-ers, such as agency temps, nearly a third of the workforce is engaged in independent employment.[3] These numbers would no doubt be much higher were it not for the millions of Americans now forced to work for wages because of the lack of affordable, individual health insurance.

More so than at any time since the Progressive Era, Americans are discovering the virtues and the risks of independent employment, as well as the lack of security offered by wage "slavery." Despite record increases in productivity, hourly compensation for the median worker has not grown at all in this decade. In 2007, nearly a third of all female workers and more than a fifth of all male workers earned poverty-level wages.[4]

This is what connects our own times with the Progressive Era more than any other feature and what causes liberalism by contrast to seem stale and spent. New Deal liberalism was about Big Government and Big Labor leaning on Big Business to offer good wages and benefits. Yet today, the assumptions behind the New Deal social contract—of a one-paycheck, married family norm, of health care, unemployment insurance, and pension systems geared to wage workers moving steadily up the seniority scale of a single corporation—are all passing away fast. And so more and more of us are thrown back to some form of yeo-manry whether we like it or not. In this way, we are returning to the future, only without a political vocabulary to describe our experience or connect it with American political tradition.

The Yeoman Tradition

As Progressives well knew and pounded into the heads of immigrant schoolchildren, that tradition began with the unique circumstances of America's origins. From the earliest days, a distinctive feature of the American experience has been the high proportion of small-scale prop-erty owners among the population. In one of the first works describing the American character, published in the late eighteenth century, J. Hector St. John de Crèvecoeur drew this contrast between the old world and the new: "Europe contains hardly any other distinctions but lords and tenants; this fair country alone is settled by freeholders, the possessors of the soil they cultivate, members of the government they obey, and the framers of their own laws."[5]

In the mid-1700s, two-thirds of all white men in America owned property. Among the third who did not, many were young apprentices and indentured servants who soon would. In England, by contrast, the ratio of those with property to those without was reversed. Thomas Jefferson's "yeoman farmer" was not just an ideal of political imagination in early American life; he was a typical white man of the era.

The yeoman ideal today seems archaic because we conflate it with agrarianism, for understandable reasons. As Jefferson famously wrote in his *Notes on the State of Virginia*, "Those who labour in the earth are the chosen people of God, if ever he had a chosen people, whose breasts he has made his peculiar deposit for substantial and genuine virtue."[6]

Yet the yeoman ideal is not per se about the virtues of rural life; it is about the virtues of small-scale property ownership and the social and civic benefits most American still believe flow from it. Jefferson, for example, did not imagine that slaves or tenants working the soil obtained any particular virtue thereby, and he had deep doubts about the morality of his own slaveholding planter class. Indeed, in his later years, Jefferson regretted denigrating urban labor and came around to the idea that the continued expansion of the country's industrial base was no threat to liberty so long as workers had the option to become property owners, which is the essence of the yeoman ideal. "As yet our manufacturers [i.e., industrial workers] are as much at their ease, as independent and moral as our agricultural inhabitants," he wrote in 1805. "And they will continue so as long as there are vacant lands for them to resort to; because whenever it shall be attempted by the other classes to reduce them to the minimum of subsistence, they will quit their trades and go to laboring the earth."[7]

Jefferson's yeoman was thus only incidentally a farmer. If he farmed, it was because farming was then, for many, a good business. He was, far more importantly, a small-scale, entrepreneurial, family-oriented property holder; and from this, Jefferson and other defenders of the yeoman ideal have always believed, all sorts of benefits flow.

Such benefits are easily summarized. One is a stake hold in society that serfs, tenants, slaves, and urban proletarians lack. This long-standing American view finds expression today in the settled opinion of most Americans that homeownership makes for stronger communities, while public housing, even if necessary to meet immediate practical needs, breeds crime and dependency. Sadly, in recent years, this commitment to homeownership caused politicians of both parties to look the other way as millions of Americans became encumbered by predatory mortgage lenders. Yet here again it is back to the future. The abuse of yeoman by creditors, and what to do about it, is an unending tension in American politics and one that particularly animated the Progressives, who responded by cracking down on abusive lenders, creating new savings institutions for farmers and working-class Americans, and committing themselves to the ideal of thrift.

The tradition also holds that widespread yeomanry improves politics. We no longer limit the vote to property owners, but the assumptions the Founders used to justify that policy are still with us. Informed participation in civic life, we still believe, requires time, education, and judgment. This in turn requires (many quietly believe) some measure of economic independence.

Another tenet of the yeoman ideal is that small-scale proprietors (whether farmers, artisans, or store owners) exhibit such virtues—sobriety, commitment to work, thrift, craftsmanship, and belief in the future—that are too often lacking in the idle rich and the idle poor. The yeoman also, so goes the tradition, has a propensity to marry and raise children in a wholesome environment, whether a farm or suburban homestead—which is again a characteristic often held to be lacking in both the urban underclass and decadent, sterile elites.

For all these reasons, the yeoman also, it has long been held, makes a good defender of liberty. Arguing in favor of the Homestead Act in 1852, Representative Galusha A. Grow of Pennsylvania exclaimed:

> Man, in defense of his hearthstone and fireside, is an invincible against a world of mercenaries. In battling for his home, and all that is dear to him on earth, he never was conquered save with his life. . . . In such a struggle every pass becomes a Thermopylae, every plain a Marathon. With an independent yeomanry scattered over your vast domain, the young eagle may bid defiance to the world in arms.[8]

The yeoman ideal thus reflects a perceived golden mean in society, comprising citizens unmoved by demagogues, naturally opposed to despots, engaged in productive labor, and quick to defend their land and wholesome families from any threat. It is the essence of the American creed.

Wagons Ho

Early America's abundant frontier not only provided for the creation of a large class of remarkably prosperous freehold farmers but also vastly improved the economic condition and political power of industrial workers compared to their European counterparts, just as Jefferson predicted. So long as the frontier remained open to settlers, as it did until the late nineteenth century, employers had to deal with the reality that laborers could, quite literally, like Huckleberry Finn at the end of Twain's tale, "light out for the territories ahead of the rest."

This was the theme of Frederick Jackson Turner's Progressive Era masterwork, *The Frontier in American History.* Turner noted that in Boston during the 1630s, officials laying out the city felt it necessary to offer lowly workers generous plots of land. As Governor Winthrop explained in 1634, the policy was "partly to prevent the neglect of trades."[9] Winthrop knew that if Boston's workers were not well provided for in town, they would just walk west, as many did throughout American history until the dawn of the Progressive Era when, in 1890, the Census Bureau declared the frontier officially closed.

Along the way came the Civil War. It, too, was largely about preserving the yeoman tradition, and its lessons deeply informed many Progressive Era reformers. Among the arguments most frequently employed by John C. Calhoun, George Fitzhugh, and other apologists for slavery was that northern workers, facing ever-greater competition in the labor markets, were (or soon would be) worse off than those in bondage. Northern workers were "slaves without masters," Fitzhugh argued in his notorious book by that title. They were oppressed by capitalists who, unlike slaveholders, had no equity stake in the well-being of their workers. The prospect of men who were supposed to be "wage slaves" prospering instead as yeomen in Missouri, Kansas, and elsewhere in what was then "the West" thus undermined the planter class's view of itself and the world.

White settlers, meanwhile, viewed the prospect of having to compete with African slaves and an expanding plantation system led by decadent aristocrats with horror. Southern "Slave Power," declared Senator Thomas Morris of Ohio, was even worse than northern "Bank Power." Morris vowed to take on not only the banks but also the "Goliath of all monopolies," the slave system. The result of this collision between slave power and the yeoman ideal was, to say the least, a serious rewrite of the nation's social contract—one that involved far more than freeing the slaves, and one that has deepening relevance today as the modern wage system comes under stress.

The passage of the Homestead Act in 1862 is a prime example of how much the Civil War was about preservation of the yeoman ideal. Because of the political opposition from slaveholders, Congress debated the act but could not pass it for more than a decade. But once the South seceded, the act's promise of 160 acres of western land to any citizen was quickly realized. In practice, the Homestead Act would not live up to its champions' expectations, but it was an important expression of the nation's commitment to, in the words of Senator Samuel Pomeroy of Kansas, "the hearts, the bones, the sinews, of an independent, loyal, free yeomanry, who have the comforts of home, the fear of a God, the love of mankind and the inspiration of a good cause."[10]

With the South out of the Union, Congress was also able to pass the Morrill Act. It offered all northern states land grants of at least ninety thousand acres, which they could sell to finance the creation of so-called land grant colleges, as they became known. These were originally agricultural and mechanical schools, designed to further the independence of yeomen. During the inaugural ceremonies for one of the first land grant colleges—the institution that eventually became the University of Illinois—its new president heaped praise on the leading champion of the bill, Jonathan Baldwin Turner, for having "plowed and plunged and ricocheted through these prairies with an energy and vehemence that no bulwarks of ignorance or apathy could withstand, and which brought nearly every farmer and artisan hurrying to his standard from far and near, and put in motion the imperial columns of our freeborn yeomanry."[11]

Also in 1862, President Abraham Lincoln signed into law a bill establishing the United States Department of Agriculture. Its intent was to serve the nation's yeoman farmers or, as the president approvingly put it, "the largest interest [group] of the nation that . . . is so independent in its nature as to not have demanded and extorted more from the government."[12]

The Civil War was about slavery. It was also about states' rights. And it was very much about whether the average American would be an independent, educated property owner or a servile, ignorant tenant. Since the Civil War, the question has at times seemed settled. But it was the dominant underlying issue of the last Progressive Era, and it will be that of the Next Progressive Era as well.

Busted in Kansas

The Homestead Act, though it was the clearest expression of the yeoman ideal in American politics, turned out to be a disappointment to most who took up its offer. One reason was that the frontier had moved into territories that were so arid—Nebraska, Oklahoma, and the Dakotas—that they could not support small family farms. Meanwhile, land grants to railroads consumed much of the most promising real estate. Speculators gobbled up still more.

A separate Southern Homestead Act, passed in 1866 and specifically designed to benefit African-Americans, had no chance of success. Like General William Tecumseh Sherman's Special Field Order No. 15, with its promise of "forty acres of tillable ground" to newly freed slaves, it fell victim to white backlash and sectional compromise during Reconstruction and was rescinded in 1876. Along with more and more of their white counterparts in the South and elsewhere, black farmers would be tenant farmers and sharecroppers, or slaves without masters.

There were exceptions, and their example underscores how crucial small-scale asset ownership has long been in American life. Harvard scholar Henry Louis Gates Jr. studied the family trees of twenty successful African-American families, including Oprah Winfrey's and track star Jackie Joyner-Kersee's. Gates was astonished to find that most shared a long family history of property ownership: fifteen of the twenty successful families descended from former slaves who managed to obtain property by 1920—something only one-quarter of black families had managed to do by that time. Oprah's great-grandfather, Constantine

Winfrey, bartered cotton he had picked on his own time on eighty acres in Mississippi, while Whoopi Goldberg's great-great grandparents were among the few who, as she says, "got its forty acres and a mule" through the Southern Homestead Act before its repeal in 1876.[13]

The Gilded Age

By the 1870s, the yeoman ideal was under deep strain for both blacks and whites. In the cities, immigrants faced squalor as bad or worse as the conditions they had fled in Europe, even as stockjobbers and monopolists like Jay Gould and Cornelius Vanderbilt amassed vast fortunes. Mark Twain labeled it "the Gilded Age" and remarked of the typical American, "In our day he is always some man's slave for wages, and does that man's work."

Arguably the most famous American of this era after Twain was a journalist-turned-economist named Henry George, who would have a deep influence on the fast-approaching Progressive Era. He wrote a book, *Progress and Poverty*, which became a runaway best seller and inspired discussion groups around the country, some of which still exist today. George advocated a tax on land that would compensate the landless for the loss of their birthright. Academic economists quarreled with George's analysis, but to millions of Americans steeped in the yeoman tradition, it seemed to explain everything. Farmers and workers created value, using land and other natural resources that were God's gift to mankind. Landlords, bankers, speculators, and monopoly capitalists, by contrast, produced no value. Everything this expanding, rent-seeking class consumed from morning to night—their bonbons, their cigars, their silk top hats—was produced by the hand of labor. Take away that hand and all fortunes would be revealed as worthless, because there would be nothing for the rich to buy.

Many Americans turned to socialism, led by such figures as the union leader and political activist Eugene V. Debs, who ran unsuccessfully for president five times—including once from prison. But the main currents of the emerging populist, labor, and progressive movements rejected common ownership of the means of production, instead favoring government action to preserve the yeoman from predatory trusts and banks.

The major currents of the labor movement in this era also reveal the influence of the yeoman tradition. The dominant labor leader, Samuel Gompers, founder of the American Federation of Labor, opposed socialism and preached instead a social gospel that stressed strong family life, self-improvement, and "working-class thrift" or what we would today call "asset building." When asked, amid the economic depression of the early 1890s, what labor wanted, Gompers famously said one word: "More." But more what? More wages and more time off, certainly. But specifically, more economic independence. As Gompers later elaborated, "We tacitly declare that political liberty with[out] economic independence is illusory and deceptive, and that . . . only . . . as we gain economic independence can our political liberty become tangible and important."[14]

This is the language of civic republicanism, only now spoken on behalf of a yeoman who is no longer a farmer but a unionized craft tradesman and who retains his aspirations to own his own home, raise and educate his family, and in these and other ways rise up as a free man in a free republic. The images of the early American labor movement that come down through history are mostly red—that is, both bloody and associated with leftist anarchy: the Mollie Maguires up against the Pinkertons; the Wobblies vandalizing box cars with "silent agitator" stickers, or Eugene Debs and the Pullman strikers battling federal troops amid the flames of the torched World Columbian Exposition. But the earliest and, over time, the most politically influential strain of the labor movement rejected socialism, rejected communism, rejected anarchy, and aligned itself with a distinctly American, "progressive" approach to preserving the American Dream.

This approach embraced the yeoman ideal, and in so doing it also embraced what we would today call the "traditional family values" that went with it. Specifically, Progressives emphasized the need for a "family wage" that would pay a reasonably sober, thrifty man enough to keep his wife and children out of the mills and the mines and preserve their home. The famous labor leader Mary Harris (Mother) Jones, is today remembered as a Leftist feminist icon. She even has a muckraking, Left-leaning magazine named after her, which in 1995 published a special issue on how exporting women's liberation to the Third World would control overpopulation.[15] The real Mother Jones certainly was a woman who knew how to raise hell. But she believed so strongly in the yeoman values of hearth and home that she championed what we would today call "wage discrimination" against women so that a "family wage" might be possible. Speaking of the "average working woman" of her day, Jones thundered, "Home training of the child should be her task, and it is the most beautiful of tasks. Solve the industrial problem and the men will earn enough so that women can remain at home and learn it."[16]

Opposing her, and all the many other like-minded "maternal feminists" of her age, were business interests such as the National Association of Manufacturers (NAM), whose members wanted to continue exploiting cheap female labor. NAM therefore threw its weight behind legislation outlawing wage discrimination against women or what amounted to the same thing: a "family wage" for married men.[17]

In this era, everyone recognized that some women had to work for wages before they married or after they became widows. But the idea that capitalists might be able to employ working-class wives and thereby drive down everyone's wages to the point that children had to work as well was anathema to the Progressive labor movement. Historian Linda Gordon has identified seventy-six women who were national leaders of welfare reform movements from 1890 to 1935. She was surprised to find that even the majority of women who were single "did not . . . contradict the prevailing premises that children and women needed breadwinning husbands, that children needed full-time mothers, that women should choose between family and career."[18] One of those women, a settlement house activist who would later become the first female cabinet member and a major architect of Social Security, was FDR's labor secretary Frances Perkins. She typified Progressive thinking on work and family issues as it endured into the 1930s, when she denounced the working middle-class woman with an employed husband as a "pin money worker, a menace to society, [and] a selfish shortsighted creature who ought to be ashamed of herself."[19]

Why did Progressive Era women demand suffrage? Mostly it was to advance causes like promoting Prohibition, ending child labor, and preserving and restoring the single wage-earning, intact "patriarchal" family in the face of withering assault by capitalism.

Today's rising younger generation, many of whose members now find themselves unable to start families or spend much time with their children, due to the necessity of two or more paychecks, might well ask themselves whether they, too, have been exploited by an unbridled capitalism that cannibalizes family life. The Next Progressive Era is unlikely to see the return of legal wage discrimination against women. But if it is to meet the needs of young families now under assault by resurgent market forces, it is likely, as we'll see in chapter 12, to seek a restoration of the "family wage" by other means.

The Octopus of Monopoly

Like today, the Progressive Era was a time of deep conflicts and confusion over how best to preserve the yeoman tradition under rapidly changing conditions. One hallmark of the age was a very high faith among American elites in science and "scientific" government. The creation of a civil service, Teddy Roosevelt and other high-minded Progressives believed, would purify politics and professionalize administration. Progressives also believed that bureaucrats at the newly empowered Interstate Commerce Commission could protect small-scale producers from the monopoly power of railroads by scientifically determining with their slide rules the exact right price for transporting, say, a pig, as opposed to a ham, from Dubuque to Chicago. Another great Progressive Era cause was "scientific management" of business, informed by Frederick Taylor's "time and motion" studies of assembly line workers, which figures like the jurist Louis Brandeis cited in hammering against the waste and inefficiency of monopolistic enterprises.

Yet it was also an era of deep fear, irrationality, and rejection of science. The writer Henry Adams was appalled by the forty-foot electric dynamos he encountered at the World Columbian Exposition because they made "the planet itself seem . . . less impressive." Teddy Roosevelt was deeply troubled by the closing of the American frontier, fretted over the declining fertility of America's original Puritan stock, and pined for a more heroic way of life than he saw coming under industrialism. Like most of his followers, William Jennings Bryan, a leading Progressive Era figure, rejected Darwin and put literal faith in the Bible.

Yet despite these contradictions and contrasts, one broadly shared priority united populist farmers and urban professionals, Bible thumpers and secular social engineers. It was that government should preserve the promise of American life by using its powers to protect small-scale producers from the predations of monopoly capital—and do so without resorting to any radical socialist schemes that would threaten the yeoman's ideal of liberty.

"Which do you want?" Woodrow Wilson asked a campaign audience in 1912:

> Do you want to live in a town patronized by some great combination of capitalists who pick it out as a suitable place to plant their industry and draw you into their employment? Or do you want to see your sons and your brothers and your husbands build up business for themselves under the protection of laws which make it impossible for any giant, however big, to crush them and put them out of business?[20]

No talk about "caring" for your fellow man from Wilson, either. Instead, the stress is on how to preserve equal opportunity and the yeoman ideal in the face of rapidly changing industrial conditions. For Progressives, neither laissez-faire policy nor the collective ownership of property was the right answer. The state's proper role was actively to promote strong families and small-scale enterprise threatened by monopoly and consolidation. How to achieve this goal—whether by busting all trusts or just "bad trusts," with federal power or state power, with rule by experts or through direct primaries, short ballots, and trade unionism, or closing the door to immigrants—was hotly contested. But outside the dark-paneled offices of Standard Oil, Northern Securities, and the other giant trusts, the goal of self-sufficiency wasn't.

Beyond Caring and Sharing

Today, it is not so different. Even if that word *yeomanry* itself has almost entirely disappeared from America's political lexicon, even if few college graduates could tell you its meaning in American history, we all carry with us, with pride or repudiation, the values and mind-set it denotes. Americans acquire the yeoman tradition's values and attitudes just as they acquire their accents, not by formal study of previous generations but by casual contact with all who surround them.

This explains the jolt that went through the country when it first encountered Sarah Palin's frontier persona. It explains why Ronald Reagan and George W. Bush were always eager to be photographed chopping wood or clearing brush on their respective ranches, no matter how phony the image. And it explains why Bill Clinton, when his political fortunes sagged in 1995, decided to give up vacationing on Martha's Vineyard and, based on focus group input, chose to summer in Wyoming instead.

These are superficial expressions of a much deeper truth. When the yeoman ideal is truly threatened, as it was in the Progressive Era and again during the Great Depression, the majority of Americans will demand, or can be led to demand, large expansions of government to protect it, and they won't see any contradiction in doing so. The New Dealers who crafted the Social Security Act, for example, were careful to give deference to the yeoman idea of self-sufficiency by financing it with a payroll tax that made it seem as if family breadwinners paid for their own benefits. And they were also careful to foster the yeoman values of hearth and home by crafting those benefits to encourage marriage, homemaking, and a "family wage." Much has changed in American society in the last seventy years, but not Social Security's treatment of married, stay-at-home mothers, who collect spousal benefits from the system whether or not they directly contributed payroll taxes.

A modern-day progressive movement that neglects to tap into the yeoman ideal will seem to most Americans as utopian at best and foreign, unpatriotic, illegitimate, elitist, socialistic, and relativistic at worst. Without shrewd use of the yeoman ideal, progressivism may have its occasional pyrrhic victories—the partial integration of public schools, expanding Medicaid coverage to more children, the establishment of gay marriage in some states. But unless connected to the yeoman ideal, these accomplishments will either set in motion powerful forces of reaction or be partial and fleeting.

This is not an accident of history but a natural outgrowth of how the country first came to be settled, and most of the time governed, by coalitions of small-scale property holders. Nor is it an anachronism. After a generation of falling real wages, never before has "freehold" property ownership, whether of homes or business and financial assets, been so determinative of who gets ahead in American life and who in effect remains a wage slave. Even before the great financial crisis of 2008, we were living with an economy in which the gross national product increased year after year and unemployment was low by historical standards, yet real wages and salaries of most Americans fell year after year. The era in which the mass of Americans could count on their standard of living rising dramatically just through higher wages and not through increases in capital died in the 1970s.

As the Economic Policy Institute has pointed out, "For the first time since the Census Bureau began tracking such data back in the mid-1940s, the real incomes of middle-class families are lower at the end of this business cycle than they were when it started. This fact stands as the single most compelling piece of evidence that prosperity is eluding working families." Data going back to 1913 show that income inequality today is even steeper than it was then—indeed, steeper than any year save one, 1928.[21]

Americans don't need to read studies to know this. Yeoman farmers may constitute a vanishingly small fraction of the American population, even after counting the rapidly increasing numbers of small-scale organic farmers and other niche producers. But the percentage of Americans who own or aspire to own their own independent business is large and increasingly rapidly. So is the percentage of Americans whose economic independence is threatened by corporate consolidation, declining real wages, predatory lending, the collapse of employer-provided health care and pension systems, competition from foreign labor, age discrimination, crumbling infrastructure, tainted food, unsafe drugs, and consumer products.

Nor, since the Progressive Era, have we seen such deep threats to the economic viability and social cohesion of the family. All the conditions for the Next Progressive Era are set, but only if today's reformers truly know their history and their country, as did the original Progressives.

CHAPTER 3

Thrift

With riches have come inexcusable waste. We have squandered a great part of what we might have used, and have not stopped to conserve the exceeding bounty of nature, without which our genius for enterprise would have been worthless and impotent, scorning to be careful, shamefully prodigal as well as admirably efficient.

—Woodrow Wilson, first inaugural address, March 4, 1913

I believe we are at the threshold of a fundamental change in popular economic thought . . . in the future we are going to think less about the producer and more about the consumer.

—Franklin D. Roosevelt, address at Oglethorpe University, May 22, 1932

YEOMANRY was one musty word at the heart of the first Progressive Era. Another was thrift, used in a rich and subtle sense that is forgotten today but that applies handsomely to so many of our most pressing contemporary problems, from health care and climate change to mounting financial indebtedness.

Unless you are more than about a hundred years old, thrift probably strikes you as a crimped, downscale word. There's thrift as in thrift shop—a place where maybe your grandfather went to buy worn cloths and dented toys. There's thrift as in old Auntie Mae who once scolded you for removing the wrap on her sofa and spent her whole life saving up Green Stamps, convinced that another Great Depression was just around the corner.

And as every economics major knows, there's thrift as in "the paradox of thrift," the doctrine at the heart of the Keynesian economics, or "the fundamental change in popular economic thought" to which FDR refers in the chapter-opening quote. Under this doctrine, which deeply informed the economic policies of the New Deal, Keynes acknowledged that thrift could bring personal advantage. But he condemned it as a social vice because it reduced the consumer spending that he, and so many economists since, have thought was needed to keep the economy humming. It's been a long time since thrift had truly positive connotations for most Americans, progressive or otherwise. "We're all Keynesians now," Richard Nixon said in the 1970s—a truth President Bush and Congress reaffirmed in 2008 by sending out "stimulus" checks to every American in hopes, unrealized, that we would spend it fast.

Yet for the original Progressives, thrift was a powerful word, full of life, full of hope, the very point of progress. Thrift didn't just apply to money. It applied to conservation of natural resources and inspired the early environmental movement. It applied to health. It even applied to the very use of one's time on Earth, which could be wasted or which could be conserved and made more meaningful and bountiful with thrift.

Long before the Progressive Era, Benjamin Franklin and many others, of course, promoted thrift as a secret of success. "'Tis hard for an empty bag to stand upright," Franklin typically warned. Yet Progressives gave thrift uniquely deeper, moral meaning, more akin to "wise use."

Some sense of just how powerful this word thrift became during the Progressive Era, both here and in England, comes from Joseph Conrad, who, being a modernist far ahead of his time, thought it was all a crock. In his novel *Chance*, Conrad writes,

> Just about that time the word Thrift was to the fore. You know the power of words. We pass through periods dominated by this or that word. . . . Well just then it was the word Thrift which was out in the streets walking arm in arm with righteousness, the inseparable companion and backer-up of all such national catchwords, looking everybody in the eye as it were.[1]

A more sympathetic account of the thrift movement that pervaded the Progressive Era comes from Arthur Henry and James Franklin Chamberlain, authors of *Thrift and Conservation: How to Teach It*, published in 1919.

> During the few years past, and especially from the beginning of the Great War, the term "thrift" has been much more in the public mind and on the public tongue than heretofore. Men and women are talking thrift and economy; children are writing essays on thrift and are earning and saving as never before. There are lectures and published plans and outlines telling how to earn and invest and save; how to avoid waste; how to make best use of time and talents and money; how to preserve and improve the health; how to conserve our natural resources of soil and water and forest, so that they may remain the inheritance of peoples for all time to come.[2]

Underscoring the Progressives' preoccupation with thrift was the launch, in 1917, of Thrift Week, under the sponsorship of a broad coalition led by the YMCA. Pegged to Benjamin Franklin's birthday on January 17, each day of the week drew attention to specific aspects of thrift, such as "Pay your bills promptly day," "Make a will day," and "Share with others day." What does sharing with others have to do with thrift? As one YMCA official explained, "Thrift is not alone putting in, but is also giving out, in a wise program of spending."[3] Thrift, in the sense of wise use, empowered parents to care for themselves, for their children, for other people's children, and, through conservation of resources, for children not yet born. For Progressives, thrift thus became a high moral principle without which their program of life cannot be understood.

Thrift and the Yeoman Ideal

In the eyes of Progressives, thrift was also closely related to the yeoman ideal. We can see this, for example, in the writing of William Hannibal Thomas, a freeborn African-American writer and self-described champion of Negro rights active at the turn of the century. Criticized by many as an Uncle Tom, Thomas did indeed reflect the values of the majority culture of his time—and of many contemporary African-Americans as well when it came to value of thrift and property owner-ship. Thomas celebrated the African-Americans who "by dint of skill and rare frugality become a small landowner and prosperous propri-etor." He also praised the spirit of

> thrifty Negro mechanics and plodding all-sorts, who on the out-skirts of some sleepy village or drowsing town or piney crossroads, own a few acres of land and live contentedly in humble cottages. The man who owns the soil he tills, and is conscious that he alone is the rightful and exclusive possessor thereof, has a sense of manly independence which landless classes lack; and these sentiments are not only the life-springs that build up fresh, healthy, noble char-acters in individuals, but constitute, as well, the bulwarks of solid national development.[4]

The ideal of thrift connects with and makes sense of many other Progressive Era causes and obsessions. These range from home eco-nomics, temperance, and the stress on healthy living, to conservation, efficiency, and the creation of a vast new network of small-scale finan-cial institutions designed to protect the working class from loan sharks, usurious "salary lenders," and Ponzi schemers.

Today, many of these subjects—financial institution architecture, environmental protection, physical fitness—may seem only distantly related, if at all. But to Progressives they were all of a piece under their broad concept of thrift, which encompassed self-sufficiency, steward-ship, and sustainability.

In their *History of the Thrift Movement*, published in 1920, S. W. Straus and Rollin Kirby captured the creed: "There must be thrift of health—thrift of time—thrift of energy—as well as thrift of money." The two authors went on to applaud Teddy Roosevelt's "gigantic thrift program" to conserve water and topsoil. They also approvingly quoted his archrival in Progressive politics. "We are in this world not to pro-vide for ourselves alone," said Woodrow Wilson, "but for others, and that is the basis of economy—so that thrift and economy and everything that administers to thrift and economy, supply the foundation of our national life."[5]

For the Progressives, thrift was not just a personal virtue but a moral imperative. "Every penny wasted is a direct injury to the community," wrote one apostle of the thrift movement in 1918. ". . . For instance a wanton waste of coal must tend to impoverish a neighbor as well as one's self. Every ton unnecessarily consumed must lessen the supply and raise the price."[6]

Progressives similarly railed against the wasted manpower caused by profligate consumption, particularly of energy. "We must first understand that every commodity we use is based on manpower," wrote another apostle. "We must understand that every minute an electric light is turned up is just that much consumption of manpower in the power station, on the railroad that brought the coal to the station, and in the mine where the coal was dug. We must realize that manpower is sorely needed."[7]

Wasting food was an even greater offense, as even the Chamber of Commerce could agree. "It takes four years to raise a porterhouse steak, and to send half of it back to the kitchen is an economic crime," read one pamphlet, simply entitled "Thrift."

> If you waste money you will have no more to waste; but you can keep on wasting food until you eat no more and wonder why you are poor. Better take inventory of what goes out in the garbage basket and see how much you contribute toward this enormous sum, so big in its proportions that you fail to grasp its magnitude.[8]

"Thrift of time" creates an odd ring in modern ears, however much we may squander time in long commutes, surfing the Internet, or watching reality TV. But for Progressives, the folly of wasting time was even more obvious than the folly of wasting money, coal, or food. Indeed, like all forms of thriftlessness, wasting time, in the Progressive view, bred not just poverty but criminality. According to the book *Thrift and Conservation*:

> A habit of doing nothing, of dawdling, of standing on the street corners, of moping in school, of sneaking away from the bench in

the shop, of gossiping, idling, persistent and regular card playing, of perpetual play of any sort, soon has a reactionary effect upon the individual and upon those with whom he comes in contact. Those who habitually waste time soon become indolent and lazy. In the final analysis, our criminal classes are recruited in no small degree from the ranks of the habitual time-wasters.[9]

Routing the Salary Lenders

Besides the energy, food, and time shortages that marked the Progressive Era, another large reason the thrift movement took hold then was that, just as today, ordinary Americans (including not just farmers but city dwellers) were becoming deeply encumbered by debt. Salary lenders, or what we today call "payday" lenders, date back to shortly after the Civil War. But by the Progressive Era they had expanded into nearly every city, often as multistate chains, offering "advances" on paychecks at interest rates up to 300 percent. According a survey in 1911, in each city over thirty thousand in population, one in five wage earners took out a salary loan over the course of a year.[10] In Manhattan alone, according to a "muckraking" investigation by a young Columbia University graduate named Clarence W. Wassam, there were more than thirty salary lenders, most clustered on Nassau Street and lower Broadway, making loans or renewing loans to thirty thousand individuals every day. In New York City, more than three out of ten workers owed money to the salary lenders.

In his exposé *The Salary Loan Business in New York City* (1908), Wassam told tale after tale of the misery created by this illegal but rarely prosecuted industry. "For $150 in cash," Wassam related, "one borrower paid about $665 to ten different companies over the course of 19 months before he became destitute and sought charity. And the loan companies continued to dun him for the $150."[11] Though such lending practices violated state usury laws, the burgeoning industry had the temerity to advertise in newspapers and billboards until Progressive reformers shut them down. "Money! Money! Money!" screamed one ad. "There is no disgrace in being in need of money. . . . We procure loans for EVERY ONE—railroad men, clerks, factory employes, street car men, office employees, and all salaried people."

Progressive reformers were also alarmed that most working-class people were, as we would say today, "unbanked"—that is, unable to find a financial institution that would deign to hold their meager savings and allow them to begin to accumulate enough to buy a home, farm, or small business. This violated the Progressives' ideals of thrift and yeomanry alike. Thus, in this era came the first "thrift" institutions and credit unions, where a working-class man or woman would be spared the high-hat treatment. Said one early champion of the credit union movement, "We take the bank to the member; we make it simple; we do not wait in dignified silence behind a fretted grill in a mosaic paved, high vaulted banking room, condescending, willing to accept custody of what the timid depositor brings to us."[12]

Before these institutions were deregulated and taken over by the fast-buck crowd in the 1980s, they provided a staid but reliable vehicle for building a nation of "freeholding" middle-class homeowners and small-scale entrepreneurs. Most Americans understood, until the triumph of the anti-thrift institutions, that their own freedom from wage slavery—and, indeed, the civic health and wealth of the republic—depended on the savings habit and the widespread ownership of unencumbered small properties that it makes possible.

Today we face, in the words of a recent report entitled *For a New Thrift*, "an almost identical crisis" to that faced by the original Progressives. Its features are, in words of the report, "low savings, large and growing numbers of Americans over their heads in debt, and the return with a vengeance of payday lending and other anti-thrift institutions."[13] Even before the credit crunch and housing meltdown of 2008, one in seven families was dealing with a debt collector. Children today are more likely to live through their parents' bankruptcy than their parents' divorce. Even with unemployment at historically low levels, Americans spent more than they earned between 2005 and 2007—and charged the difference. Household debt, not including mortgages, now eats up nearly 15 percent of disposable income—more than food and gasoline combined.

Indeed, the reforms made during the Progressive Era to encourage small savers and to protect against predatory lenders lay mostly in tatters today. Deregulation of thrift institutions during the Reagan years opened the door to profiteers who looted the industry. Preemption of state usury laws has led to a roaring comeback of salary or payday lenders. Just between 2000 and 2004, the number of payday lenders more than doubled, from ten thousand to over twenty thousand. Nationwide, there are more payday lender franchisees than Starbucks and McDonald's combined.[14]

Along with the return of payday lenders have come new, more vicious species of loan sharks: subprime credit card issuers, auto title lenders, private student loan companies charging up to 20 percent APR, check-cashing outlets, and subprime mortgage brokers and lenders. Debt, both their own and their neighbors', now threatens American homeowners as much or more as it threatened yeoman farmers and a struggling working class in the Progressive Era.

What can the original Progressives teach us about how to tame predatory lenders and promote savings among Americans of modest means? A lot, as we'll be examining in greater detail in the next two chapters. But for now remember that their efforts in these realms were but part of a much larger vision of thrift that has clear application to many other crises and challenges that have now cycled back from the Progressive Era.

What would the original Progressive say about the obesity epidemic, for example, or about global warming, energy shortages, mindless chat on the blogosphere, the rising price of food, the mounting cost of health care, unfunded pensions, the shrinking middle class? They would say, and say rightly, that all are matters of thrift—or the lack thereof.

The Body Whole

Like today's Progressives, their counterparts of one hundred years ago believed strongly in environmental influences on human development and in the improvability of human nature through what we would today call "consciousness-raising." Yet the original Progressives were far more likely to act strongly and consistently on these convictions. For example, few doubted for a moment that strong government action was needed to stamp out youthful exposure to pornography and gratuitous violence when a new medium arrived that, like the Internet and video

games, made such exposure a pandemic phenomenon. If we are all creatures of our environment, then it matters a lot what images we see and
what habits we form, particularly in youth. With similar reasoning, and
in a way totally neglected today, the original Progressives strove to
inculcate financial literacy and the virtues of thrift, which they believed
should start at the earliest possible age and be strengthened by a wide
range of reinforcing institutions throughout life.

For the original Progressives, there was quite literally no realm of
life or field of study in which the need for thrift education did not
urgently apply. "We are living in a progressive age," read the report of
the National Conference of Thrift Education, held in Washington, DC,
in 1924 at the very end of the era.

> With a school curriculum already over full, it is clear that to be
> effective, thrift must be taught not so much as a subject in itself as
> in its application in other subjects. Our courses of study in elemen-
> tary and secondary schools can profitably be given a thrift setting.
> Arithmetic, geography, literature, the sciences, industrial arts,
> home economics—all may be enriched and vitalized if they be
> taught in the light of the principles of thrift.[15]

Instruction in thrift started with financial education, which, with
the spread of salary lenders, installment plans, and increasingly sophisticated mass media advertising, became essential as never before to prevent the mass of Americans from slipping into penury. Under the
auspices and tutelage of one thrift promotion group, the Educational
Thrift Service, 1.6 million American children set up bank accounts in
their schools, where (in today's money) they did $4.5 million in busi-
ness every Tuesday morning and held deposits totaling $14 million by
1924.[16] The total number of school banks in operation that year was
seven thousand, with total deposits of $39 million, adjusted for infla-
tion.[17] Today, the first experience most younger Americans have with
a bank comes during freshman orientation at college, when they come
across a table laden with giveaways and credit card applications.

Progressives understood, both instinctually and through the findings of their newly created social sciences, the importance of behavioral

conditioning, and they weren't at all shy about putting those findings into practice. Today, there are new efforts to set up what are called conditional cash transfer programs. Under New York mayor Michael Bloomberg's Opportunity NYC program, for example, the city offers payments to participants who engage in desired behavior, such as completing a job training program or sending one's children to school regularly. The policy strikes many people as revolutionary—either revolutionarily wrong or revolutionarily smart. But long before the recent findings of behavioral economics brought conditional cash transfer programs into vogue, Progressives pioneered the idea and put it into far more sophisticated practice by combining it with incentives to save.

In the early twentieth century, for example, a long-forgotten man named Samuel Saucerman was running so-called Trimmer Clubs throughout Iowa. These offered a penny a day to any Iowa boy who refrained from tobacco, liquor, gambling, and swearing. After earning their first dollar, the boys were required to deposit at least 50 cents in a savings account, which with matching contributions would grow to $12 in three years—on the condition of continued clean living. Enthused one account of the Trimmer Clubs published in 1909, "The object is to establish habits of savings, which will enable every boy at twenty-one to have saved sufficient to start him in life or go to college."[18]

The Camp Fire Girls, a prototypical Progressive Era institution established in 1910 by Luther Gulick, MD, and his wife, Charlotte, inculcated not just home economics but thrift in health. Each member received a "thrift chart," in which she marked each day for three months the various "health habits" she observed. These included "sleeping with the windows open, brushing your teeth after every meal and before going to bed; drinking a glass of water on going to bed and on arising; sleeping at least nine hours at night; airing your clothing; washing your hair at certain periods, preferably twice a month or once a month; and walking at least one hundred miles during a month."[19]

After three months, Camp Fire Girls sent their thrift cards to the national headquarters for review and, if met with approval, received a coveted honor card. Typical of the Progressives' belief in the moldability of human character, one of the program's administrators explained, "The program of the Camp Fire Girls is a habit-forming program. . . .

After having kept the chart for three months it will not be very easy for her to break the habits which she has formed and practiced conscientiously during that period."[20]

The concept of thrift in health also added straightforwardly to the growing support—among secular forces and the religious alike—for the increasingly rigid regulation of beverage alcohol that marked the Progressive Era. *American Issue*, a publication of the powerful Anti-Saloon League, tied the two subjects together nicely when it observed that "seventy per cent of the drink bill of the United States is contributed by the American laboring man. . . . [L]iquor money is usually bread money, meat money, shoe money and money that ought to go for clothing."[21]

Temperance had been building as a religious cause for decades before the Progressive Era. But Progressives, using the ideal of thrift, joined religious objections to ardent spirits with secular ones, and to tremendous effect. By 1910, state and local option dry laws had already made recreational use of alcohol illegal in all but 5 percent of the American landmass, including Alaska, Puerto Rico, and the District of Columbia, leaving two-thirds of the population wholly or partly deprived of legal liquor. In 1917, responding to another argument for prohibition based on thrift, Congress prohibited the "waste" of corn, barley, sugar, and other potential foodstuffs in the production of spirits, and it gave President Wilson the option to shut down beer and wine production as well should wartime shortages require further "food conservation."

This Wilson did at least in part. Two years later, ratification of the Eighteenth Amendment to the Constitution, with only Connecticut and Rhode Island holding out, rendered the entire county bone dry, in law if not in practice. The Progressive Era's embrace of thrift had finally put the century-long temperance movement over the top.

The Progressives' use of thrift as an argument against liquor production may not have much resonance today. Yet more and more voices are now stressing the connection between the rising use of ethanol gas to support America's wasteful driving habits and the rising price of food. Faced with the same trade-off—between using potential foodstuff to distill gasoline and using it to feed the hungry—Progressives would have strenuously waved the banner of thrift, calling for and building a more efficient transportation system based on the latest available technology, while also crusading against overconsumption of all sorts.

This is one of the few legacies of the original Progressives one finds clearly reflected in their modern counterparts: a shared concern with wasteful consumption and its environmental consequences. The thrift gene became recessive during the New Deal and long afterward, when liberals rejected thrift and embraced instead a Keynesian view that redefined waste as economic stimulus. But with the rebirth of the environmental movement in the 1970s, the Progressive Era's preoccupation with thrift found a new, if mutated, expression, which is building again today as concerns mount over global warming, energy, and food shortages.

Yet today we still lack the robust, organic concept of thrift the Progressives developed, particularly in relationship to the wise use of money but also in other realms. Few make any connection between personal finance and environmental stewardship, for example, because they lack the Progressives' integrating concept of thrift. Yet what should be clearer than that maxing out credit cards to buy knickknacks from China contributes mightily to one's carbon footprint? Or that saving money by deferring consumption benefits the environment?

Today, the loss of the Progressive Era's rich concept of thrift makes effective environmental advocacy far more difficult than it should be. "Human happiness, and certainly human fecundity, are not as important as a wild and healthy planet," the prominent biologist David M. Graber once wrote in the *Los Angeles Times*. "I know social scientists who remind me that people are part of nature, but it isn't true. Somewhere along the line—at about a billion years ago, maybe half that—we quit the contract and became a cancer."[22] Such antihuman sentiments are expressed frequently by leading members of the modern environmental movement, from Paul Ehrlich to the Prince of Wales. The original Progressives, by contrast, while they might irritate profligates with their calls to thrift, still offered a far more positive and "progressive" view of why conservation was necessary. They could argue for stewardship on behalf of future generations of human beings, for example, because they viewed manmade waste, not humanity itself, as an affront to thrift. They could also champion the environment without any hint of opposing civilization, because they understood clearly the relationship between increasing industrial efficiency and the conservation of resources, whether energy, clean air and water, human health, or manpower.

This is a big difference. How much sacrifice in consumption will people make on behalf of "the planet," compared to how much will they sacrifice on behalf of themselves, their children, and the ideal of human progress? The question answers itself.

Rediscovering the original Progressives' concept of thrift is essential to fostering the changes in mass behavior needed to confront many of major issues of our times, from global warming, obesity, and the crushing cost of poorly managed chronic disease, to energy independence and the widespread loss of financial security due to credit card debt, subprime mortgages, and the spread of other antithrift institutions such as casinos and state-sponsored lotteries. All are clearly related, but only if viewed through the prism of the Progressive Era's ethos of thrift.

True, that ethos did not survive the powerful ideological and commercial interests that built up against it throughout the twentieth century. America in the 1920s and especially after World War II became a mass consumption society addicted to debt and rapid depletion of natural resources. Fittingly, it was auto companies that first got the mass of Americans in the habit of borrowing to finance a rapidly depreciating asset. Two out of every three cars sold by 1926 were bought on the installment plan. Financial historian Leonal Calder notes, "Installment credit generated a psychology of affluence that contributed immensely to the spirit of the Roaring Twenties. It financed a middle-class consumer society."[23]

Even during the Great Depression, while the unemployed lost access to credit and overall debt levels declined, those who could afford it happily took on more installment debt, encouraged by retailers like Montgomery Ward and Sears. The one holdout, Macy's ("No one is in debt to Macy's!"), began installment lending in the 1930s.

In the postwar period, it became official that thrift was not just obsolete but a threat to the nation. During the recession of 1958, President Dwight D. Eisenhower would twice go before the American electorate and tell them that it was their patriotic duty to BUY NOW, just as George W. Bush did after 9/11. The last Thrift Week was celebrated in 1963 and barely made the papers. The last school banks shut their books in the 1970s without public discussion, as inflation pushed sponsoring thrift institutions closer to insolvency while also punishing their depositors. Meanwhile, economic policy advisers, from Kennedy's "growth men" to Reagan's "supply siders," habituated Americans to chronic government deficits to stimulate higher consumption.

The burial of thrift ethos was so deep that when Americans involved in the counterculture of the 1960s and 1970s began to reinvent some of its precepts on their own, most lacked any knowledge of the Progressives' rich tradition of thrift—a tradition that, had it transmitted clearly across the generations, might have given the counterculture's critique of mass consumption a seriousness and potential for mass appeal that it sadly lacked. As Jean Bethke Elshtain of the University of Chicago Divinity School has observed, "Curiously enough, the hippie culture promoted its own form of anti-consumerism, but this didn't flow from a moral economy of thrift. Rather, it derived from a vague animus against 'capitalism' and 'the system.' Acquiring got a bad odor but consuming triumphed."[24] Still, it is not too late to become acquainted with the true history of the Progressive Era and to adopt its lessons, however musty its ideals of thrift and yeomanry may seem at first hearing.

CHAPTER 4

Debt's New Rules

D URING THE long American high that began after World War II, thrift was hardly the way to get ahead. Instead, getting a good education, a good job, and the most house you could possibly afford were the three key ingredients to upward mobility, and the more you could leverage their cost, the better.

Think of a bright young soldier returning from World War II, like the young Tony Bennett, or Daniel Patrick Moynihan, or William Rehnquist. What if a penny-pinching father, or some other remnant of the Progressive Era's thrift movement, had persuaded them to take a factory job and save up their paychecks rather than going to college under the GI Bill? Or think of a World War II vet whose instinctive fear of debt persuaded him to decline the government's offer of a zero-down, 3 percent, 30-year VA mortgage and put his savings into Treasury bonds or a thrift institution instead. We imagine him forty years later still renting his garden apartment and wondering why his inflation-eroded savings won't even pay for a condo in central Florida.

And what of that man's children? Many, if not most, baby boomers have not yet paid a price for their extraordinarily low savings rate. Baby boomers in midlife saved at only half the rate their parents did at a similar time of life; the youngest boomers saved the least of all.[1] Yet for many, the growing returns to higher education, combined with increasingly easy access to cheap credit, guaranteed a rising standard of living without recourse to thrift. The stock market boom of the 1990s and later the housing boom made it possible to build up very high levels of equity while saving very little. For younger boomers, fully half of the increase in their net wealth between 1995 and 2005 came from asset appreciation.[2]

During this long era, taking on debt was a positive experience for most people, especially if they used their debt to finance a college education or a home. In the Progressive Era, reformers would often say that the poor were poor because they wouldn't save, and they pushed for the creation of savings and loans, credit unions, and other institutions to foster working-class thrift. But by the 1960s and 1970s, reformers would often say that the poor were poor because they couldn't borrow, and to a large extent they were right. "Access to credit and capital is a basic civil right" became the rallying cry of the movement to overcome redlining and other forms of racial discrimination in lending. The refusal of banks to lend in neighborhoods in which African-Americans lived fed a vicious cycle of underinvestment, declining property values, and urban decay, which led to the creation of the Community Reinvestment Act in 1977.

During the 1990s, the growing ability of low-income Americans to secure mortgages and credit cards was celebrated as the "democratization of credit." Speaking on Martin Luther King Jr. Day in 1996, President Clinton's comptroller of the currency, Eugene A. Ludwig, evoked the civil rights leader's memory in calling on "all of us to renew our commitment to get it done and discover new ways to extend credit to creditworthy borrowers and into neighborhoods of all types and income levels."

Over the years, there were those who warned that an emerging "buy now/pay later" mentality would ruin the nation's morality and work ethic, to say nothing of its finances. As the consumer credit revolution took off in the 1950s, Harvard economist John Kenneth Galbraith wondered in *The Affluent Society*, "Can the bill collector be the central figure in the good society?" Writing in the 1970s, Harvard sociologist Daniel Bell thundered, "The greatest single engine in the destruction of the Protestant ethic was the invention of the installment plan, or instant credit. Previously one had to save in order to buy. But with credit cards one could indulge in instant gratification."[3]

Yet easy credit didn't turn Americans into slouches. Indeed, a higher percentage of us, particularly women, went to work than ever before, working longer and longer, largely because we had to finance our ever-increasing debts. By 2002, the average middle-income, two-parent family was working 660 more hours per year, or 16 more weeks, than in 1979. America became the reigning workaholic nation; the average worker toiled 1,877 hours in 2000, more hours than even the Japanese.[4]

I Owe, I Owe, So Off to Work I Go

Charge cards didn't turn us into hedonistic grasshoppers, as Daniel Bell and others feared. Instead, meeting our mounting monthly installments turned us into harried, multitasking worker ants and thereby spurred the economy to new heights.

And for a long time, many of us were just fine with that. Common was the American woman who said she preferred to work outside the home, even if her family's growing burden of debt no longer gave her a choice. In recent decades, many young couples have said they didn't want to have children right away—or more than two, in any event— even if it was the dead weight of their student loans, credit card balances, and mortgage that made starting a family any time before age thirty-five unthinkable.

Eventually, there came to be 2.3 times more credit cards in the United States than there were people. Easy mortgage money inflated home prices, threatening to put homeownership out of reach for those not already in the game. Then the invention of exotic new debt instruments, such as the worst subprime mortgages, empowered even people with no savings to get in on the real estate bubble. Meanwhile, more and more payday lenders popped up in shopping malls, but they seemed as normal and unthreatening as the Applebee's next door.

It was how we lived; it's how our neighbors lived. Few people were all that extravagant, truth to tell. On a good day, we could look forward to a long overdue three-day vacation, groove to the digital radio while commuting, maybe savor a few kudos at work before falling contentedly asleep beneath the glow of a new hi-def, amazingly affordable flat-panel television made in China. Largely because so many jobs went overseas, wages stagnated, but the credit kept flowing. The price of energy and food crept up, while the cost of college education, health care, homeownership, and other staples of middle-class life exploded. Two-paycheck families needed daycare and at least two cars, and they paid 25 percent more in taxes than the typical single-paycheck family had thirty years before. But no matter—just tap into that inflating home equity and get the credit card bills back down under the limit. "My life, my card," as American Express used to advertise. "Visa: all you need."

In a Federal Reserve survey conducted in the early 2000s, 51 percent of people taking out home equity loans said they used them to cover living expenses and pay down credit cards, while another 25 percent used the funds to pay for a car, cover education expense, or pay for health care.[5] Despite all the talk about "luxury fever," "urge to splurge," and "affluenza," most people were increasing their debt just to cover the staples of middle-class life. But compound interest worked its way while a new a new kind of financial crack cocaine hit the streets and ended an era.

The Big Crack-up

Joyce Griffin was the first member of her family to break out of public housing and buy a home. She was making $12 an hour as a certified nursing assistant, and she saved for the down payment for two decades, stuffing dimes, dollar bills, and whatever loose change she had into a plastic jar in her bedroom closet. When the water jug was full, she had $5,000. She pooled that with $5,000 from her then-fiancé, Herberto Tubaya, and they bought a duplex just north of Annapolis, Maryland, for $123,000 in May 2001. They planted a garden and added a small screened-in porch. She taped a photo of her new home to her kitchen window, and every time she looked at it, she thought, with a yeoman's pride, "You've accomplished something."

Then, unexpectedly, while sitting at the dining room table Christmas morning 2004, Herberto had a massive heart attack and died. That loss was hard enough, but in her grief Griffin realized her monthly mortgage payments were too much to handle alone. A few weeks later, she called Ameriquest Mortgage, with whom she had refinanced to pay for the porch. She asked for a deferral and to have Tubaya's name removed from the deed.

An Ameriquest agent came to her home about midnight, she said, and had her sign a sheaf of papers. Griffin said she thought she was signing to remove Tubaya's name from the deed. Instead, she later learned, she had refinanced into an expensive $153,000 subprime loan with an adjustable interest rate that was set to rise to as much as 14 percent in coming years. Unable to make the payments, Griffin filed for reorganization under Chapter 13 of the federal bankruptcy code—but she was too late, for Ameriquest had already decided to foreclose on her. Griffin was stunned. "They shouldn't be able to take our homes from us out of the blue like this," she said. If she loses in court, she will have nothing.[6]

Joyce Griffin is among the more than two million—and growing—hardworking Americans duped by predatory lenders into losing their homes. She started off with "good" debt—a mortgage on reasonable terms, financing a house she could afford that was gaining in value. But Ameriquest exploited the tragedy of Tubaya's death and used it as an opportunity to get her into "bad" debt. We're all now paying that debt one way or another, as evidenced by falling home prices and the burgeoning cost to taxpayers of trying to keep a poisoned global financial system from killing the economy as a whole.

Dante's Seventh Circle

What is "bad" debt? Let's be clear: debt in itself is not evil. Nor is it inconsistent with thrift and the yeoman ideal. Without debt or credit, many people couldn't afford to buy homes, especially while still young enough to have children. Many more couldn't afford to get a college education or start their own businesses. Credit also allows us to weather financial shocks, as well as smooth out our consumption over a lifetime, borrowing when our incomes are lower, repaying it when our incomes are higher. Within limits, even credit card debt can be a spur to industry. Without credit, few Americans could accumulate real wealth, and the modern economy could not function.

But for as long as there has been credit flowing in human history, going back at least as far as the code of Hammurabi, circa 1750 BC, there has also been usury—meaning abusive or predatory lending—and laws to prevent it. The Old Testament tells of the prophet Ezekiel, who included usury in a list of "abominable things," along with rape, murder, robbery, and idolatry (Ezekiel 18:10–13). Roman law capped interest rates at between 8.3 and 12 percent. According to the Qur'an, "Those who charge usury are in the same position as those controlled by the devil's influence" (Al-Baqarah 2:275). Dante condemned usurers to the seventh circle of hell, along with blasphemers and sodomites. Martin Luther argued that any interest rate above 8 percent was immoral, and the Puritans who settled the Massachusetts Bay colony agreed, adopting America's first usury law 150 years before the Constitution.

Most of America's Founding Fathers thought them right to do so. Notes credit law historian Christopher L. Peterson, "Throughout the history of the American Republic, all but a small minority of states have capped interest rates on loans to consumers with usury law."[7] In the Progressive Era, reformers pushed a Uniform Small Loan Law that capped interest rates at 36 percent, and they limited the rates to specially licensed lenders adhering to strict standards of lending. As late as 1979, all states had laws of some sort that capped interest rates.

This short history of usury laws puts into perspective just how bizarre the credit markets of the United States became over the last forty years. Usury law is, in the words of one financial historian, "the oldest continuous form of commercial regulation," dating back to the earliest-recorded civilizations.[8] Yet starting in the late 1970s, some powerful people decided we could live without it.

First to go were state usury laws governing credit cards. Before 1978, 37 states had usury laws that capped fees and interest rates on credit cards, usually at less than 18 percent. But in 1978, the Supreme Court, in the fateful *Marquette v. First Omaha Service Corp.* decision, ruled that usury caps applied only in the state where the banks have their corporate headquarters, instead of in the states where their customers actually live. Banks quickly set up their corporate headquarters in states, especially South Dakota and Delaware, that have no usury laws and thus were completely free to charge whatever interest rates and fees they wanted. Meanwhile, states eager to hold onto those banks headquartered in their own states promptly eliminated their usury laws.[9]

In 1996, the Supreme Court handed usurers another stunning upset. In *Smiley v. Citibank*, it ruled that credit card fees, too, would be regulated by the banks' home states. You might think that market forces would set some limits to how high credit card fees and interest can go. After all, there are only so many creditworthy borrowers, and competition for their business is stiff. But with shrewd use of a new financial instrument, banks and other lenders found they could make more money from those who could *not* afford credit cards and other forms of credit than from those who could.

How did they pull that off? Beginning in the 1980s and especially in the 1990s, Wall Street learned how to bundle thousands of individual auto and student loans, as well as credit card receivables, into new investment vehicles known as asset-backed securities. Investors in these securities knew nothing of the character of the millions of ordinary people whose debts they were buying. But because of the large number of debtors involved, investors supposed that the percentage who would default would be as predictable as the life tables used by insurance companies. Large computers using complex algorithms produced seemingly precise estimates of the risks involved, and the market priced these instruments accordingly.

For a long while, the system appeared to work, even though the asset-backed securities were ultimately financing depreciating cars, students who didn't finish college, and credit card bills that never got paid. Because these securities could seemingly spread risk widely and adjust price to risk, they appeared to offer a way to extend credit to people who otherwise could not, or should not, get it, while paying investors handsomely.

Securitizing consumer debt raised a lot of capital from around the world at a time when the U.S. savings rate was verging on zero. But it also set the stage for the stunningly abusive lending practices to come. Lenders no longer had to worry (or at least thought they didn't) if individual borrowers could afford to carry their debts. The price of asset-based securities already had a certain default rate built into them. And in any event, the most lucrative customers were those who slowly sank deeper and deeper into debt before finally refinancing to avoid bankruptcy.

So began lending practices such as "universal defaults," whereby one missed payment on just one credit card triggers an interest rate increase on all the holder's credit cards; "double cycle billing" (interest charges on already-paid balances); triple or quadruple interest rates for one late payment; and constant due date changes and payment center moves, increasing the likelihood of missed payment deadlines. Another insidious practice was requiring cardholders to understand terms incomprehensible to Harvard Law School students, while reserving the right to "change the terms of the agreement at any time for any reason."

Because of the money to be made from these and other abusive practices, banks began targeting the working poor, African-Americans, single moms, and eventually students ("Get a credit card, get a free T-shirt!"). At one point, six billion such solicitations were going into the mail each year—twenty for every man, woman, and child in America.

Banks no longer cared if you had a checking or savings account with them or any relationship with them. What mattered was that your debt slowly brought you down as you continued to pay out all those fees and interest charges. By the time you finally approached bankruptcy, you'd probably refinance your debt and leave some other lender stuck.

Meanwhile, the last major holdouts, supermarkets and fast-food chains, broke down and started accepting credit cards, thereby fueling more demand. Boshara's family, who owns a restaurant in Barberton, Ohio, used to have a sign above the cash register that said, "In God We Trust, All Others Pay Cash." Now credit cards are accepted.

The result: three of every four households in America now have at least one credit card. Roughly half of them carry no monthly debt, but those who do have an average balance of $8,467. Overall credit card debt has tripled from $238 billion in 1989 to $1 trillion today. In 2006, credit cards generated $115 billion in revenues and over $18 billion in profits; credit card operations are often banks' most profitable operation.

The Subprime of Your Life

New dragons emerged. The elimination of usury laws, combined with the invention of asset-based securities, paved the way for subprime mortgages like the kind that cost Joyce Griffin her home.

To understand what happened to her and so many others like her, think of the movie *It's a Wonderful Life*. Made in 1946, it stars Jimmy Stewart as a small-town building and loan executive named George Bailey. As the run on deposits depicted in the movie suggests, all was not so wonderful in the world of banking those many years ago. But here is what was profoundly different and better: George Bailey knew his customers, and they knew him, and both could judge each other's character.

True, even in George Bailey's day, thrifts and banks didn't always hold on to mortgages they lent out. They sometimes sold them to institutions like Fannie Mae, which financed them by issuing corporate bonds—with an implicit Treasury guarantee—in the capital markets. This practice deepened the liquidity of mortgage markets, which meant that small banks could lend out more money than they otherwise could. Although this secondary mortgage market involved strangers holding each other's money, the system was ultimately based on real human relationships of the kind Bailey had with his customers, and they with him.

Bailey made loans only to people with good credit histories, who'd made down payments, and who had the income to make regular payments. He didn't sell mortgages with hidden explosive devices inside, for three reasons: it was illegal; nobody, including Fannie Mae, would buy such paper; and the good people he lent to were also his neighbors.

And as it turns out, replacing George Bailey is not so easy. Little remembered is Wall Street's attempt to do that coming into the Progressive Era. By the 1880s, private mortgage companies were making loans around the country, including to cash-strapped homesteaders out west, through local agents. These mortgages were then "securitized" into so-called mortgage-backed bonds that got peddled on European markets. Foreshadowing the problems in today's market, the results were unfortunate. "The system proved extremely unstable," writes credit law historian Christopher L. Peterson:

> Because distant and uninformed investors bore the ultimate risk on individual home mortgages, lenders and their local agents had an incentive to use inflated appraisals and fraudulent origination practices to generate upfront profits. When recessions in the 1890s

produced widespread consumer defaults, all of these mortgage companies folded, and their investors took horrendous losses.[10]

Forgetful of this history, Wall Street tried again a hundred years later. It started offering mortgage-backed securities, which included now-infamous subprime mortgages that contained even more abusive terms than those hidden in credit card contracts. For a while, the subprime market made some investors very rich, while also turning many people into homeowners who otherwise wouldn't have been. Then it blew up.

The major problem was lack of accountability. By the time Joyce Griffin refinanced her mortgage, most people no longer had a personal relationship with a bank officer. Most mortgages were originated by free-floating brokers, like the one who showed up at Griffin's door at midnight. According to a *Miami Herald* investigation, in Florida alone between 2000 and 2007, 5,306 people with criminal histories became loan originators—a rate of nearly two a day. Among them were 2,201 who had committed such crimes as fraud, money laundering, bank robbery, racketeering, mortgage fraud and even murder.[11]

The banks and finance companies these brokers worked with didn't care that many of the folks they were lending money to wouldn't be able to pay it back; in theory, large numbers of defaults were built into the pricing of the securities into which these mortgages would be folded. And even if there were more defaults than expected, who cared? Each buyer up the chain no longer bore responsibility for the performance of that loan.

For borrowers as well, George Bailey's absence from these transactions lessened accountability. Once housing prices started to fall, and many people found themselves owing more for their house that it was worth, the decision to default no longer meant having to face Bailey in church or neighbors whose savings depended on their repaying the loan. Instead, underwater homeowners could tell themselves that default would harm only distant and often greedy investors. That perception was not far from true, at least in the short term. Those who might have wanted to work out their loans had no one with whom they could talk; anonymous investors around the world owned different slices and dices of their debt. George Bailey could sit down and work out a plan with a borrower like Joyce Griffin who got in trouble. The Central Bank of China and other large holders of mortgage-backed securities could not.

These were the sorts of imponderables the wizards on Wall Street could not capture with their fancy algorithms. As expert Ellen S. Seidman, a former head of the Office of Thrift Supervision, remarks, "The slicing and dicing has created securities with risks virtually impossible to evaluate, let alone price, which in turn has led to too much money chasing too few good loans."

Meanwhile, that investor in China—or England or Norway—really had no idea what risk he was sitting on and no way to find out. The big economic story of 2006 and 2007 concerned the little guy—record numbers facing maxed-out credit cards, exploding mortgage loans, and personal bankruptcy. By the end of 2008, the big economic story had moved to the top of the food chain, shaking the mightiest titans of finance, even with massive federal bailouts of Wall Street firms like Bear Stearns. The contagion has even spilled over to mortgage giants Fannie Mae and Freddie Mac, taken down the august House of Lehman, and caused the takeover of Merrill Lynch, Washington Mutual, and Wachovia. It has engendered the effective nationalization of the country's largest insurance company, AIG, and of the country's nine largest banks. By fall, there was open talk of another Great Depression. We hope that by the time you read this, the worst of the storm is over, but one thing is certain: the long era of cheap, easy, globally supplied credit is over.

Prohibiting Financial Crack

So what's to be done? Foremost, we must realize the interconnectedness of the debt crisis with other issues. Obviously, correcting abusive lending practices is a high priority. But remember that neither predatory lending nor consumer extravagance is the root cause of the debt crisis. The inflating cost of living a basic middle-class life is the primary driver of the crisis. Thus, helping Americans meet their health care, education, child care, transportation, and housing costs is, by far, the best thing government can do to reduce our reliance on debt—an agenda we lay out in subsequent chapters.

Also important is recognizing what every past generation of Americans, especially the Progressives, knew: usury emerges in any credit market and must be checked.

Let's begin with mortgages. Homeownership remains the most important form of wealth for the vast majority of Americans, including especially low- and moderate-income Americans. It's also at the heart of the country's yeoman ideal. Yet underwriting homeownership with financial crack is, by now, obviously self-defeating.

What's needed, we think, is a Basic American Mortgage.[12] This is a low-cost, fixed-rate, thirty-year instrument that lenders would be required to provide to Americans with decent credit standing, a 10 percent down payment in hand, and a proven ability to make regular loan payments. More favorable terms would be available to people buying homes in neighborhoods served by mass transit, because of the lower share of household income consumed by auto-related expenditures in such areas. If mortgage lenders didn't offer the Basic American Mortgage, they wouldn't be allowed to offer any other mortgage product; that is, they'd be shut down.

Mortgages on other terms would still be available to creditworthy borrowers. Yet to offer, say, an adjustable rate mortgage, lenders would have to meet much tougher underwriting and disclosure requirements, and they could only issue paper that earned the equivalent of the government's Energy Star rating for appliances. This rating would give prospective homeowners, including the vast majority of us who lack the ability to discern improvised explosive devices in the fine print, assurance that we were buying a sound product. Finally, the Basic American Mortgage and any other government-approved mortgage would build in an automatic savings feature so that when you made your mortgage payment, some portion of it would be "escrowed" or set aside every month in a savings account. That way, if you lost your job, couldn't work because of illness, or the roof needed a major repair, you'd have a savings account to draw upon.

Does this mean that borrowing to buy a house would be more difficult than it was during the housing bubble? Yes, it does. Giving people loans they cannot repay is no favor. In the end, there is no substitute for thrift.

We also propose a Basic American Student Loan that would work much the same way. Private—that is, nongovernment-guaranteed—student loans, now account for 20 percent of the student loan total, up from 5 percent just ten years ago. According to the Project on Student Debt, "Borrowers who accept these loans subject themselves to interest rates and fees that can be as variable and onerous as those on credit cards." Interest rates on private student loans reach as high as 16 percent a year on top of upfront fees of up to 10 percent of principal borrowed. Worse, unlike credit card and other debt, these loans cannot be discharged through bankruptcy—a detail student borrowers should know.

The Project on Student Debt also warns, "Borrowers can . . . be confused by aid packages that include private loans branded with the college's name (such as an Acme College Gate Loan), which leads students and parents to assume that they are special and safer than loans from other sources."[13] No more. If student loan lenders wanted to stay in the business, they would be required to offer a government-certified Basic American Student Loan that students and parents could trust. Just as Congress had to step in and regulate the Medigap insurance market to protect seniors from abuses, it needs to offer equivalent protection for students, as well as home buyers.

Credit cards are also long overdue for more effective regulation. It's simply stunning that many abusive, predatory practices—universal defaults, double-cycle billing, redundant late fees, utterly incomprehensible "agreements" and terms, and contracts that can change "at any time and for any reason"—are still legal. A recent crackdown by the Federal Reserve does not go far enough.

It's also appalling to learn how many institutions of higher learning and alumni associations have been secretly taking huge payments from credit card companies in return for students' personal information and for sponsoring credit cards with deceitful terms. In exchange for $1 million, for example, the University of Iowa's alumni association sent a credit card mailer to students that announced in large bold letters, "outstanding financial benefits for students," including a 4.9 percent interest rate. "Don't miss this unique opportunity to show your University of Iowa pride, while you enjoy truly outstanding credit card benefits and services." According to an investigation by *Business Week*, "Iowa students who scrutinized the accompanying paperwork found that the 4.9 percent rate lasted only six months before leaping to 18.2 percent."[14] We agree with the many who argue that colleges and alumni associations should be prohibited from all sponsorship agreements with credit card companies that involve any type of mailing list sharing/bag stuffing/solicitation (on or off campus).

Also, all payday lenders, check cashers, and other antithrift institutions should be subject to reasonable usury laws, including restrictions not only on rates but also on fees. Both the Center for Responsible Lending and the Commission on Thrift (on which we both serve) have concluded that a maximum rate of 36 percent is more than enough to keep small-dollar, short-term credit availability for those who need it in emergencies. That is the rate Congress has imposed on payday lenders who do business with Americans serving in the military. Moreover, it's demonstrable that a fair profit can be made at this interest rate, particularly if the lending is done by institutions that have strong personal relationships with and knowledge of their customers, such as small-scale credit unions. But why protect just military families and leave firefighters, teachers, janitors, health care workers, and other hardworking Americans unprotected? We need national usury laws that cover all citizens.

As with any regulation of financial markets, the danger of going too far and creating a black market of loan sharks exists. But the effective rate many payday lenders charge—upward of 300 percent—is higher, we're told by a learned source, than that charged by the New York Mafia at the peak of its powers in the 1960s. We are very far from being in danger of overhigh usury caps.

We should also encourage more responsible players to join the business of providing small-dollar, short-term credit, for which some legitimate need will always exist. This service was the original mission of the credit unions that spread across America in the Progressive Era, and many are still doing good work. North Side Community Federal Credit Union of Chicago, for example, has developed alternative payday loans that allow people to borrow for immediate needs on nonusurious terms. Another example is the Faith Community United Credit Union in

Cleveland, Ohio. So is the North Carolina State Employees Credit Union, which makes payday advances at 12 percent APR with no extra fees, while also adding an innovative savings feature similar to one we recommend for the Basic American Mortgage: borrowers must put 5 percent of the loan amount into a savings account to cover shortfalls and emergencies. The FDIC's Small Dollar Loan Pilot also includes an automatic savings feature, which we hope will eventually reach all banks.

These reforms, though helpful, don't get to the heart of the financial crisis that began spreading around the world in late 2008. To deal with that crisis, we have to restore the mutuality of interest between borrowers and lenders pioneered by small-scale, Progressive Era bankers.

CHAPTER 5

Mutuality

WHEN PAUL HUDSON, the chairman and CEO of Broadway Federal Bank in Los Angeles, spoke of the financial crisis engulfing the world in late 2008, he sounded altogether placid. "It's going to be difficult, because everybody participated in this low-cost-credit, high-value-asset scenario," he said. "But I'm not overly stressed."

While giant banks tumble, his own bank is doing fine, and there's a lesson in that. Broadway Federal, founded in 1946 to provide loans to the growing African-American community of Los Angeles, is a small institution with five branches located in middle-class, largely black neighborhoods of the city. It has eighty-four employees, assets of $390 million, and a loan portfolio divided more or less equally among single-family homes, apartment buildings, churches, commercial real estate, and small businesses. Hudson, sixty, is the grandson of one of Broadway Federal's founders. The bank knows its borrowers, and its borrowers know their bank. "Our loan portfolio is still performing well compared to the industry," he said.

Aesthetically, Broadway Federal's branches are less evocative of 1946 than of 1972—copious concrete, cheap terrazzo, fluorescent lights, clunky logo. But in 2008, an old-fashioned look can be an advantage, for it suggests old-fashioned banking. While Broadway Federal may have been less adventurous or profitable than some of its competitors over the past few years, today it enjoys the traditionalist's compensation of being both sane and solvent. In fact, according to data from the Federal Deposit Insurance Corporation (FDIC), Broadway at the end of 2008 enjoyed a substantially higher return on equity and assets than JPMorgan Chase did. (It also has a lower proportion of nonperforming loans.)

Broadway Federal's story isn't exceptional. Easily overlooked amid the crisis of big banks today, small-scale financial institutions are, for the most part, holding steady—and sometimes even better than steady. According to FDIC data, the failure rate among big banks (those with assets of $1 billion or more) is more than seven times greater than among small banks. Moreover, banks with less than $1 billion in assets—what are typically called community banks—are outperforming larger banks on most key measures, such as return on assets, charge-offs for bad loans, and net profit margin.

One reason community banks have held up so well through the financial crisis is that they never became too clever for their own good. When other lenders, including underregulated giants like Ameriquest and Countrywide, started peddling ugly subprime mortgages, community banks stayed away. Banking regulations prevented them from taking on the kind of debt ratios assumed by their competitors, and ties to their customers and community ensured that predatory loans were out of the question. Broadway Federal, for its part, got out of single-family mortgages when they stopped making sense. "A borrower comes and asks, 'Do you do interest-only, no-down-payment-option ARMs?'" recalls Hudson, with a chuckle. "No!" The bank focused instead on expanding its reach to niche borrowers, such as local churches.

Today, however, even as many financial institutions are refusing credit, Broadway Federal quietly continues to extend it. One recent recipient was a nonprofit called the Domestic Violence Center of Santa Clarita Valley, which needed $40,000 as a bridge loan in the midst of state budget holdups. Nicole Shellcroft, the executive director of the center, says that no large bank was willing to lend the money. Under the terms worked out with Broadway Federal, though, the domestic violence center was given a three-month loan for a fee of $900 in interest. "Our board was really happy with the terms," says Shellcroft. "It was actually better than a line of credit." Beyond offering special loans, Broadway has been attracting customers simply by being accommodating and personalized. "I can proudly take in my money daily, deposit it, and get access to my money directly," notes Angela Dean, founder of DeanZign, a local fashion company. After giant Washington Mutual seized up and had to be rescued, Dean switched her business over to Broadway Federal for her business checking. She's not alone. In 2007, before the crisis had properly struck, Broadway Federal experienced $7 million in net deposit growth. As of June 30, 2008, net deposit growth was at $25 million.

Community banks come in different forms. Some are "country club" banks for the wealthy. Others are "community development banks," such as Chicago's ShoreBank, formed as part of an idealistic effort to serve the "unbanked" in blighted neighborhoods. Others, like Broadway Federal, are small-scale banks, credit unions, and thrift institutions, many of which trace their origins back to the Progressive Era and earlier, when working-class men and women began pooling their savings and making loans to one another in order to overcome the discrimination they faced from established banks. What all of these varieties have in common are a connection to a small geographic area and a personalized approach to customers based on mutual interest. Whereas large banks rely on "transactional banking"—in which formulas and set calculations govern lending decisions—community banks rely on "relationship banking," in which all sorts of personalized considerations enter into the picture. This allows people like Nicole Shellcroft to secure prudent loans that might otherwise be out of reach. "That's what a community bank does," Hudson says. "It sits down with you and works it out."

Today, with the world's system of anonymous high finance in crisis, small-scale community banks, thrifts, and credit unions—all regarded until recently as vestigial players in a new world of global consumer finance—are setting an important example. If federal policies were in place to provide proper support to small-scale financial institutions, Washington could do a lot to alleviate the country's most serious economic problems: its lack of savings, its runaway consumer debt, its dwindling supplies of social capital, and its vulnerability to financial contagion brought on by Wall Street excess. By encouraging thrift, responsibility, and a sense of community, small-scale financial institutions could play a leading role in helping us dig out of this financial meltdown—and in helping fend off the next one.

Big Banks, Big Bust

For decades now, most experts have argued that bigger is better in finance. With their economies of scale, larger institutions are more efficient, goes the reasoning. They can match up lenders and borrowers on a global scale. In places where money is piling up (like China or the United Arab Emirates), banks with worldwide reach can tap into these savings and direct them to borrowers in places where money is scarce (like Stockton, California, or East Cleveland, Ohio).

Such reasoning has held sway for a generation. The Monetary Act of 1980 made it easier for banks to merge, while also embracing a world in which middle-class Americans would put more and more of their savings into mutual funds and money market accounts. Another major change occurred in 1994, when large bank holding companies secured the freedom to set up branch networks outside their home states. Perhaps the biggest shift came in 1999, when (at the urging of Federal Reserve chairman Alan Greenspan) Congress and the Clinton administration repealed the Depression-era Glass-Steagall Act, which had placed barriers between different kinds of financial institutions. After this repeal, commercial banks, investment houses, and insurance companies began to merge into complex, hybrid institutions that put ever-greater distance between borrowers and lenders.

With the shift in rules, transactional banking started to replace relationship banking. Big institutions bought up many community banks and set up new branches and ATM networks across state lines. Consumers responded favorably to the convenience of having access to everything in one place—brokerage accounts as well as traditional savings vehicles—and to being able to bank wherever they traveled.

Many small financial institutions tried desperately to compete by getting bigger themselves, and more than a few succeeded. Meanwhile, those that stayed small faced increasing challenges. Enormous, largely unregulated institutions like Countrywide and Ameriquest—"nonbank" banks—were competing very effectively for customers. These behemoths raised their funds not from depositors but from global capital markets, and, since they did most of their business over the Internet or through freelance mortgage brokers, they had minimal overhead. Exempt from the legal requirements to invest in the local communities that normal banks must honor, these institutions could easily have been seen as predatory. Instead, however, many people applauded how entities like Countrywide were "democratizing credit"—long a goal of liberal public policy.

At the same time, social attitudes subtly changed, thanks in no small measure to shrewd advertising. Mortgage originators like Lending Tree ran TV commercials mocking the idea that a consumer would show personal loyalty to any one bank or banker. "When banks compete, you win" is the Lending Tree slogan.

As transactional banking expanded, the market share of small-scale financial institutions shrank dramatically. In 1985, there were fourteen thousand community banks with inflation-adjusted assets of less than $1 billion. Today, their number is smaller by half. Many communities, especially those in urban America, have lost most or all of their local banks. This situation has not only left people in many communities with no place to open a savings accounts or take out a small loan (aside from payday lenders). It has also dried up a critical source of lending to small businesses (community banks make nearly three times as many small business loans on a dollar-for-dollar basis as do large banks, according to the Federal Reserve).[1]

Until the current crisis, many ascribed such outcomes simply to the logic of the market. Looking back, however, we can see that global-scale finance wasn't really so efficient after all, except in the sense of being very efficient at wasting the world's capital. Throughout this decade, the world, if not the United States, became awash with savings. Rising energy prices created trillions of petrodollars that had to be invested somewhere. America's continuing trade deficits left our trading partners with massive surplus funds that needed to be put to work somewhere. That somewhere turned out to be in complex and often nonsensical financial concoctions—most of them based on empires of McMansions and tract houses in remote, jobless suburbs. The easy money fueled more demand for imports, thereby keeping the global financial system in balance—until, that is, it imploded.

Today we can see that the world's surplus of capital could have been more profitably invested in just about anything else. (How much better to have borrowed money to repair our infrastructure, retool our industry, or promote sustainable energy.) When the going still seemed good, though, big banks borrowed more and more to stay competitive. By the end, Lehman Brothers was borrowing $45 for every dollar of its own that it was lending. Like a shark, it had evolved into a highly efficient predator that had to keep moving or perish.

Small financial institutions, by contrast, had neither the opportunity nor the incentive to imitate the large ones. Cushioned by their deposits, they could hunker down while the mortgage markets went crazy. This also meant they could get by if credit markets froze—as they eventually did. In community banks, both borrower and lender maintained a serious stake in the long-term outcomes of their transactions. For deposits, the banks kept relying on the same people to whom they made loans. Because the banks held on to their loans instead of selling them to distant investors, they took care to avoid granting loans to customers who couldn't repay them. Social pressure also helped stave off predatory lending. When savers, borrowers, and lenders all live in the same a community, lenders don't write loans that amount to financial crack. They know their business depends on their good reputation. Similarly, borrowers, who prize the good opinion of their neighbors, don't easily walk away from their loans.

In small-scale banking, then, borrowers and lenders can effectively see one other. They're rich with what Federal Reserve chairman Ben S. Bernanke calls "informational capital," which, as he explains, they develop through "gathering relevant information, as well as by maintaining ongoing relationships with customers."[2]

Or as the Federal Reserve Bank of Dallas put it with more prescience than it probably realized in a 2004 report: "While lending decisions have increasingly relied on data-rich statistical analyses, in many cases the most relevant indicators regarding the creditworthiness of individual small businesses still take the form of firsthand information gained through close lender–borrower relationships."[3]

George Bailey put it better in his clinching argument to his panicked depositors in the 1946 film *It's a Wonderful Life*. The residents of Bedford Falls could rest assured that their money was safe because they knew each other: "Well, your money's in Joe's house. That's right next to yours. And in the Kennedy house, and Mrs. Macklin's house, and a hundred others. Why, you're lending them the money to build, and then, they're going to pay it back to you as best they can."

Having an abundance of informational capital not only helps prevent bank runs; it also keeps default rates low (which is why, for example, faith-based credit unions can afford to offer payday loans at nonusurious rates). Lending based on character also becomes possible. The bright young man or woman with a strong business plan doesn't get turned down just for missing some lending formula ratio concocted in a faraway bank holding company headquarters by bureaucrats who know nothing of local conditions or the character of local customers. As one Federal Reserve report notes, "Locally focused community banks have a clear advantage at assessing the creditworthiness, and monitoring the ongoing condition, of small and medium-sized businesses. These loans are customized to reflect the idiosyncrasies of these borrowers and cannot be 'put in a box' for credit-scoring and securitization."[4]

A healthy relationship between borrowers and lenders can have another important effect: promoting greater savings. Without easy access to global financial markets, small banks are heavily dependent on their depositors for capital. This means they have a financial incentive to inculcate thrift, as all banks once did before America began importing so much foreign capital. Older readers will remember Thrift Week (discussed in chapter 3), an institution sponsored by the banking industry, among others, that used to start each year on Benjamin Franklin's birthday until it petered out in the 1960s.

They'll also remember how major banks used to offer customers promotional items like toasters for opening savings accounts and tried to inculcate thrift in youngsters through school banking programs. Before we began importing most of our savings, all banks needed customers who saved sufficiently and were not ruined by debt.

Naturally, being so closely tied to the fortunes of the community makes small banks more vulnerable to local downturns than large banks. But this isn't all bad, since it gives local bankers an interest in bringing their town's business community and civic groups together to solve common problems and find new ways to prosper. For community banks, community involvement is central. In a Grant Thornton survey of community bank chief executive officers conducted in 2001, almost all reported participating in civic groups (94 percent) or their local Chamber of Commerce (92 percent). More than half reported that their banks supported local relief efforts and special help to low-income segments of the community. Today, many parts of the country have lost their civically engaged local bankers, and their absence is strongly felt.

None of this is to say that small-scale banking is virtuous in every respect. In the past, if you couldn't form a good relationship with your community's bankers—perhaps because you were from the wrong ethnic group or just unpopular—you were often out of luck. Community banks have frequently been clannish in choosing their customers. They have also been known to take in deposits from customers in poorer neighborhoods while reserving their loans for customers in richer neighborhoods.

But public policy can do (and already has done) a lot to ensure that community banks are investing in their own communities. For three decades before the current financial crisis, for example, the Community Reinvestment Act nudged banks large and small into lending in areas that were previously "redlined"—that is, avoided by banks. (Although conservatives have recently been eager to tar the Community Reinvestment Act as responsible for the current crisis, the contention is ludicrous. Numerous studies have shown that the overwhelming number of bad subprime loans were made by financial institutions not covered by the act.)

Moreover, even without federal regulation, small-scale banking has always offered an opportunity for excluded groups to help themselves in the face of discrimination. In 1913, for example, there were more than two hundred so-called immigrant banks—fifty-five for Italians, twenty-two for Germans, sixteen for Poles, and six for Jews—in Chicago alone.[5] Many such immigrant banks survive today and have since shed their exclusivity. Suburban Baltimore's Madison Bohemian Savings Bank no longer limits its loans to the Bohemian farmers of Hereford County—or even to Bohemians. Broadway Federal Bank, was founded by African-Americans for African-Americans in redlined areas of Los Angeles so they would finally have access to home loans, and one day it, too, let's hope, will also outgrow its original purpose.

Taming Goliath

Perversely, even as Washington distributes rescue dollars, it is once again the big banks that stand to come out ahead. When the latest crisis shakes out, the United States may well be left with just three or four titanic institutions that will be not only "too big to fail" but also excessively powerful, even if heavily regulated. Already, just three institutions— Citigroup, Bank of America, and JPMorgan Chase—hold more than 30 percent of the nation's deposits and 40 percent of bank loans to corporations. Half of all Americans do business with Bank of America. Now, some of the big banks receiving "rescue money" from the Treasury report that they intend to use it to acquire smaller banks. Only if community banks are given a fair chance in this environment will Americans have proper, sober alternatives to being banked by Goliath. Otherwise, the distance between lender and borrower will only grow, creating even more problems in the future.

Under the Treasury's rescue plan, some healthy small banks have the chance to apply for infusions of publicly funded equity capital. But this is a temporary, emergency measure. For the longer term, we need to ensure that the small aren't devoured by the large and that the system as a whole remains balanced.

Community banks and credit unions don't need a bailout, but they could use support to deal with a few serious major challenges. First, predatory lenders—the worst of the mortgage brokers, pawnshops, payday lenders, and the like—must be shut down, so that space will be cleared for traditional financial institutions dedicated to thrift and long-term relationships. (When Washington, DC, finally shut down payday lending, local credit unions saw an upsurge in business.)

Second, and more urgent, small-scale financial institutions must have readier access to capital. That means having enough funds on hand to make loans that generate a modest but reasonable rate of return. Currently, community banks are experiencing an upsurge in deposits from Americans burned by losses elsewhere, but a robust community banking sector requires long-term funding, and deposit levels, by nature, fluctuate as individual customers move their money in and out of their accounts. The best source of the funding community banks need to make long-term loans is equity capital from investors. But most small banks are privately held, and lately, convincing investors to buy bank stocks is difficult.

That's where Washington could come in. A "Community Bank Trust Fund" could be established to provide small-scale financial institutions that met certain federal standards—in terms of size and of level of investment in the local community—with equity capital. The trust fund could purchase preferred stock in institutions that were looking for capital to grow, just as the Treasury's rescue plan is now doing for mostly large banks on a temporary, emergency basis. Instead of merely borrowing the money—as we are currently doing with the Treasury's rescue plan—we could do something more fiscally responsible and impose a tax on transactional banking. Specifically, we could impose a fee on the securitized loan transactions that are at the heart of the current crisis—and use the money to invest in the Community Bank Trust Fund. In other words, every time JPMorgan Chase wants to bundle up a bunch of mortgages, credit card debts, and student loans, slice-and-dice them into impossibly complex derivatives, and sell the paper to unsuspecting investors around the world, it should pay a tax on the transaction, with the money going to support small-scale, relationship banking.

Certainly, no one wants special coddling or protection of small-scale bankers, eroding their competitiveness and spirit of enterprise. And, to be sure, there is a useful role to be played by properly regulated global financial institutions. But friendly policies aimed specifically at community banks would be a helpful counter to several decades of bias toward large institutions. As Paul Hudson of Broadway Federal says, "The point is, people should have a choice." They should also have a financial system that is more resistant to contagion of the sort now afflicting large banks.[6]

Since the Progressive Era and earlier, community banks, thrifts, and credit unions have served customers in a manner that promoted community building and mutuality while also serving as a check against monopoly finance. Before the recent meltdown of the global financial system, singing the virtues of such small-scale banks might have seemed nostalgic and romantic. After the painful bursting of three financial bubbles in a decade, however, paying attention to those virtues is both essential and hard-headed. It's an essential first step as we attempt to recover from years of financial abuse and excessive faith in all things large.

CHAPTER 6

Financial Independence

LENIN BRITO of Los Gatos, California, sorts mail for the U.S. Postal Service. It's a job he likes but one that doesn't seem to get him and his family ahead. So Brito, also a musician, began working overtime to save enough to realize his dream of owning his own music business. That, too, might have been futile, except that a local nonprofit, the Assets for All Alliance, matched his savings, which eventually reached $6,000—enough to get the business license, recording gear, software, keyboard, microphone, and computer necessary to launch One Way Productions in 2007. Brito hopes One Way Productions, through packaging songs, videos, and T-shirts together, will eventually grow large enough that he can quit his job at the post office. But he's equally excited about using the business to teach his four children how to budget and manage money, and he dreams of passing One Way Productions on to his children someday so it can support his family, as Brito says, "now and forever."[1]

Brito hasn't seen all the Labor Department reports showing declining real wages over the last generation, but he just knows firsthand that, these days, it's hard to get ahead with any blue-collar, and even many white-collar, jobs. He hasn't read all the books put out by academics in the last decade saying that to really have economic security, to really get ahead and reach the America Dream, and to really pass on opportunities to his kids, he needs to save and build wealth. But this, too, he just knows in his heart. And Brito hasn't heard about all those studies showing that, when people own things, it instills a sense of pride, a feeling of control, and, especially, a future orientation, but he intuits that as well. In fact, if you sat him down and explained all these findings and fancy new ideas, he would be pleased to hear that theory has caught up to reality and common sense.

Yet "asset building," as Michael Sherraden describes it in his 1991 seminal book, *Assets and the Poor*, is a concept that only in recent years has begun to catch on among policymakers, foundations, and others concerned with crafting America's social welfare and savings policy.[2] If it sounds obvious to you that accumulating assets is important to escaping poverty and dependency, it has been anything but to those who wrote the laws governing asset accumulation for the better part of the last century. Instead, the general thinking has been that poor people can't save; that if they do they should lose their benefits; and that any policies to promote savings should take the form of tax subsidies, such as tax-favored Individual Retirement Accounts (IRAs) and 401(k)s, that disproportionately benefit high-income individuals. These are the terms our current social contract when it comes to savings, and they are just nuts.

Let's start with the way we subsidize asset accumulation. You might think that the people who have the least trouble saving are wealthy and that those who have the most trouble are poor. And you would be right. You might further think that the federal government offers few if any subsidies to savers who are rich and instead favors those of who actually need to accumulate more. And you would be wrong.

Robin Hood in Reverse

Overwhelmingly, most federal subsidies supporting asset accumulation flow to high-income individuals through the tax code. These tax breaks total $408 billion per year, including $160 billion for homeownership, $111 billion for investments, $112 billion for retirement, and the rest—about $8 billion—for education. Poor and working-class people typically don't see any of this money, while the bulk of it goes to those who earn the most.[3]

According to a study commissioned by the Federal Reserve, the three largest asset-building policies—the mortgage interest deduction, property tax deduction, and preferential rates on capital gains and dividends—deliver 45 percent of their benefits to households whose average income exceeds $1 million. "Put another way," the report continues, "the poorest fifth of Americans get, on average, $3 in benefits from these policies, while the wealthiest one percent enjoy, on average, $57,673. Households with incomes of $1 million or more receive an average benefit of $169,150. The benefits to upper-income households also far outstrip their share of federal tax liability."[4]

Some people have trouble seeing how a tax break, like, say the mortgage interest deduction, is a subsidy. "Aren't we just getting are own money back," goes a common refrain. But a benefit delivered through the tax code costs the government and taxpayers every bit as much as a benefit delivered in the form of a check. Indeed, "tax expenditures," as the policy wonks call them, are akin Social Security and other entitlements in more ways than that.

As Howard E. Shuman once noted:

> Tax expenditures and spending entitlements are a common breed. They are like the animals in Noah's Ark which marched aboard side by side. Both are automatic and paid out by law and formula. Neither is regularly reviewed. Both are uncontrollable without a change in the law. Once legislated, they create powerful interest groups that are dependent on their benefits, deeply entrenched and difficult, if not impossible, to oppose. Tax expenditures and spending entitlements are entered on opposite sides of the budget ledger. While they may not be of the same gender they are of the same species.[5]

Tax expenditures began innocently enough. Back in 1918, when patriotic fervor for U.S. troops in Europe was running high, political leaders in Washington felt they should do something dramatic to reward the doughboys. Facing a tight budget, though, Congress hesitated to raise veterans' benefits directly. Instead, some forgotten Progressive took a look at the five-year-old federal income tax system and came up with a nifty idea: why not "raise" veterans' benefits simply by exempting such benefits from the tax?

Over the years, many more tax expenditures followed, nearly all of them created entirely off-budget, with no estimation of eventual cost and far from the scrutiny that normally accompanies direct appropriations. Several, including the exclusion of employer-paid health care, which is at the heart of our broken health care system, were created by offhand IRS rulings in the 1930s and 1940s. At the time, no one paid them much notice, because tax rates were low, benefits were modest, and company health plans were rare.

By the 1970s, however, rising federal tax rates caused the value tax expenditures to soar or, it's equally true to say, vice versa. At the same time, the ever-rising disparity in wealth and income in the United States meant that tax subsidies, particularly for asset accumulation, became wildly regressive without the mass of Americans ever realizing it. In 1997, one of us (Longman) published a book calling for a global means test on tax subsidies, but the idea did not catch on.[6] Instead, politicians of both parties, including Bill Clinton, continued to add new tax subsidies for retirement, college savings, and the like. That way they could be claim to be "cutting taxes" while also trumpeting that they were helping ordinary folks realize the American Dream. These programs do help some ordinary folks, but in an extraordinarily wasteful way, because most of the benefits flow to people who would save anyway and are too rich to be in any need of subsidy.

There is another feature of many tax expenditures that politicians cannot resist. Much of their cost falls beyond the ten-year budget window that the Congressional Budget Office uses to estimate how much a program contributes to the deficit. So even as they ran up the country's unfunded liabilities by creating tax shelters, politicians of all stripes could say they were cutting taxes without increasing the deficit to help folks save.

Adding to the con on ordinary Americans is the fact that, due in part to the mounting cost of these tax subsidies, tax rates will likely be higher in the future than they are today. This means that when today's working-aged people retire and start drawing their IRAs and 401(k)s, they will pay taxes on their withdrawal at rates that are likely to decrease the value of their savings significantly—unless, that is, we rethink the whole system.

American Stakeholder Accounts, for Kids

What if we if recrafted America's wealth accumulation policies so that they primarily helped people with no or modest assets to build a stake hold?

Nothing could be more American. That's what the Homestead Act did. It's what the GI Bill did. And it is what no less of a patriot than Thomas Paine argued was essential to preserving American liberty.

Paine once proposed endowing every citizen at age twenty-one with a seed fund, explaining the idea's advantages to both individuals and society:

> When a young couple begin the world, the difference is exceed-ingly great whether they begin with nothing or with fifteen pounds apiece. With this aid they could buy a cow, and implements to cul-tivate a few acres of land; and instead of becoming burdens upon society, which is always the case where children are produced faster than they can be fed, would be put in the way of becoming useful and profitable citizens.[7]

The difference is indeed exceedingly great whether a couple starts out in life with nothing (or, worse yet, already in debt) or has enough savings to capitalize on whatever their best opportunities in early adult-hood may prove to be. African-Americans whose ancestors never got their "forty acres and a mule" are today particularly likely to lack the stake hold necessary to take entrepreneurial risks, as are tens of millions of other Americans who are descended from families that have always lived hand to mouth.

This is why we propose, as a first "baby step" in righting America's Robin-Hood-in-reverse asset policies, that a child born in America, once he or she receives a Social Security number, be endowed with an American Stakeholder Account, or ASA, containing $500. Children, their parents and grandparents, and anyone else who cared to, including philanthro-pies, could contribute additional funds to these accounts. ASAs would be automatically created and endowed as well for every child under age eighteen, provided they are citizens or permanent legal residents.

When an account holder reached eighteen, he or she could begin withdrawing, but only for purposes of pursuing postsecondary education and training, with payments going directly from the account to the education provider. At age twenty-five, funds could be used for education, put toward buying a first home, or earmarked for retirement. Later in life, everyone would be required to return their original $500 stake hold, so that future generations might benefit from it as well. All funds would be managed by a special entity within the Treasury Department modeled after the wildly successful Thrift Savings Plan, which oversees the retirement accounts of over three million federal workers.

The ASPIRE Act, backed by conservative Republicans and liberal Democrats in the U.S. Congress, would make savings accounts at birth for all newborns a reality. Outside the United States, it already is a reality. The Child Trust Fund has been up and running in the United Kingdom for the last several years, creating seven hundred thousand savers and stakeholders at birth every year. And Canada, South Korea, and Singapore also offer at-birth accounts to promote education and opportunity, especially for kids from lower-income households.[8]

Why do we emphasize turning children into savers so early? One reason is a feature of human nature that Progressive Era reformers understood when they put so much effort into school banks. Having a nest egg at a young age, no matter how modest, and watching it grow has very positive psychological effects. It gives a sense of ownership and fuels aspiration. It sets a fifteen-year-old living in poverty to thinking, "Now that I have $10,000 in my account, how much more would I need to go to college, and how can I change my behavior to get it?" It teaches thrift, in other words, which most of us are not born knowing. There is now an emerging social science literature on these so-called asset effects on children, as well as on adult psychology.[9]

School banking is long gone. But at least one of us is old enough to know the experience of having had a children's passbook account at a small savings and loan. Longman's initial deposit, as he recalls, was a $10 Christmas check from his grandparents. This seed money got him to thinking about the possibility of building an HO-scale model railroad. Out of a 25 cents allowance, 10 cents went to the church (by parental mandate) and 15 cents to a savings deposit. Ten weeks of savings produced enough to buy a box car or gondola for his "pike." Six months generated enough to buy a diesel engine, somewhat more for a steam engine. It was a life lesson in how to make future/present trade-offs, which is the essence of thrift. Yet today, with most banks no longer interested in small accounts, even parents who wanted to replicate this experience for their children would have trouble doing so, especially if they themselves have no relationship with financial institutions besides payday lenders.

American Stakeholder Accounts, established at birth for every new-born as well as for all existing kids, would help rebuild a savings culture and also teach financial skills to children. Their existence would, for example, give schools the opportunity to organize their financial education and math curricula around them—exactly the plan in the U.K. with the Child Trust Fund. Imagine how much more interesting it is for an eighth grader to learn how to calculate compound interest when the question at hand is how much more his account will be worth at age eighteen if he stops spending $10 a week on candy and deposits the money instead. Imagine how much more interesting it would be for a high school student to learn about how the U.S. economy works when the question at hand is "Should I direct the money in my account to stocks, bonds, or certificates of deposit?"

There is also the matter of how compound interest can particularly advantage the young because they are still young. Five hundred dollars is not much of an endowment. But if is matched by additional annual contributions of just $500 earning 5 percent above inflation, it turns into nearly $16,000 at age eighteen (in today's money) and more than $37,000 at age thirty. That's enough for a 10 percent down payment on a $370,000 house. (As we write this, Wall Street is burning, banks are failing, and earning 5 percent over the rate of inflation sounds like a lot, but historically this hasn't been hard to do. If our plan had been in place during the last Great Depression, participants would have seen the value of the Dow Jones Industrial Average increase from 41 in 1932 to 280 in 1952. Depressions are actually great times to get kids investing.)

We envision that children whose families qualify for the federal child tax credit would have up to $500 added to their accounts each year by government. Ideally, more would be added by grandparents, churches, local charities, states, and others. Contributions from all sources would be capped at $2,000 per year. The existence of these ASAs would also make it easy for school districts and philanthropies to graft on conditional cash transfer programs, which offer cash payments to the poor in exchange for getting immunization shots, good school attendance, and so forth. A school district might, for example, offer students a $500 deposit into their accounts if they achieved perfect attendance or remained drug-free for a year.

Another virtue of these accounts is that they help overcome a perennial dilemma of American life. We honor the principle of equal opportunity, but children are manifestly not born equal when it comes to financial inheritance. At the same time, we tend not to believe in equality of result and therefore are more adverse than most other modern nations to redistributing income. The progressive, more politically appealing solution, as the late, great American philosopher John Rawls once observed, is to predistribute property, so that all children start out with a stake hold. Some children will use their accounts in ways that help them amass great fortunes later in life; others, to be sure, will squander their savings. But any resulting inequality of income will be easier for both winners and losers to live with if every child starts life with at least some seed money—a stake that, if well managed and combined with hard work and some luck, can put them far ahead of each new generation's "trust fund" babies.

Generational equity is also a consideration. Americans not yet born are already deeply in debt because we have borrowed against their future earnings in myriad of ways. The national debt as of this writing is $9,542,621,896,854, up some $5 million since we first checked the U.S. National Debt Clock sixty seconds ago.[10] Writing months before the big bank bailouts of late 2008, the head of the Congressional Budget Office, Peter R. Orszag, observed: "Under any plausible scenario, the federal budget is on an unsustainable path—that is, federal debt will grow much faster than the economy over the long run."[11]

Then there's the cost of benefits promised but not funded under Social Security, Medicare, and other entitlements. According to Boston University economist Laurence J. Kotlikoff, the fiscal gap caused by the structural federal budget deficit and the obligations to our seniors through entitlement programs is so big that it would take a 70 percent increase in personal and corporate income taxes to close, assuming, heroically, that such a tax increase didn't tank the economy.[12]

Most of the projected fiscal gap is caused by the soaring cost of health care, and, as we'll see in next chapter, there is much we can do to control health costs that will also improve its quality. Still, by any accounting, the next generation of Americans is going to be stuck with huge liabilities from the past, ranging from underfunded state and local pension systems to depleted natural resources, neglected infrastructure, and environmental degradation. Endowing each member of that generation with $500 in seed money would seem the least we could do, particularly if the cost is financed not by taking on more debt but by allocating our nation's wealth-building subsidies more equally to all Americans when major tax reform is on the table in the next year or two.

American Stakeholder Accounts, for Adults

What about grown-ups? Savings behavior, like most behaviors, can't be changed by just telling people what they should do; indeed, more than half of all Americans already know they should be saving more, according to the Consumer Federation of America, but for one reason or another they don't.[13] Here we need to take advantage of both the wisdom of Progressive Era reformers and the more recent findings of behavior economics. Both emphasize the all-importance of institutions and their design in fostering thrift.

Start with a truth of the human condition. During our entire lives, we all live in a permanent "now," and it can be no other way. In this permanent now, there are always temptations and distractions. Even when we think of the future, we can only imagine what will make us happy or sad. And as we grow older, we learn that even when dreams come true, they often disappoint. No wonder, then, that humans all have a built-in tendency to discount, if not ignore, the future and to cling to the status quo.

This is one reason why conventional economics, which assumes we are fully rational creatures bent on maximizing our utility curves and smoothing our consumption over our lifetimes, so poorly explains how people actually behave when it comes to saving. If conventional economics were right, the national savings rate would have soared as the huge baby boom generation passed through middle age. Instead, it fell to zero.

Far more than rationality, what most explains people's savings behavior is inertia, it turns out. This is not surprising, if you think about it. It's true in all realms of life involving trade-offs between the present and the future. Whatever the default settings are in our individual lives—the credit cards we use, the job we hold, how we use our evenings—we're strongly biased toward sticking with them even if we know we can and should be making changes. This does not mean that we are all just stuck in a rut. But what it does mean, as Progressive Era reformers understood and behavioral economists now reaffirm, is that how the ruts run in our lives makes a big difference in the courses of action we take, including when it comes to the use of money.

A prime example comes from the experience of employers who offer defined contribution plans, such as 401(k)s. The "take-up" rate on these plans—that is, the percentage of employees who sign up to participate in them—is surprisingly low and definitely irrational. Generally, about 30 percent of workers eligible for these plans don't join, even though it usually means forfeiting employer matching grants. The United Kingdom has plans in which employers pay 100 percent of the contributions, and still scarcely half of workers choose to participate. In their important book on behavioral economics called *Nudge*, Richard H. Thaler and Cass R. Sunstein note, "This is equivalent to not bothering to cash your paycheck."[14]

Yet it turns out that making one very small difference in the design of these plans enormously changes how many workers wind up participating in them. If workers are automatically signed up for the plans but also allowed to opt out, participation rates skyrocket. In one instance, they shot up 90 percent immediately and to more than 98 percent within thirty-six months. Why? Many of the same folks who never get around to doing the paperwork to opt in to a plan will also never get around to doing the paperwork to opt out. Such is the power of inertia, and an example of how it can be used to nudge people into beneficial behaviors while preserving their freedom of choice.

Another example of putting inertia to work, along with other constants of human psychology, comes from so-called Save More Tomorrow plans. These are plans under which employees have the option of having a portion of any future wage increases automatically added to their plan contributions, unless they go to the trouble of changing the arrangement. This taps into not just inertia but also loss aversion (workers never see their paychecks go down) and the psychology of resolution (people are often willing to make very hard choices for themselves so long as the pain comes later). Plans with these features, which are now available from Vanguard and other providers, have proven highly successful in getting more people to join plans and increase their contribution rates.[15]

How do these principles apply to public policy? For one, they show the power of what some now call "soft paternalism." Individual freedom, including the freedom to make bad choices, is preserved. But institutions are structured with default settings and incentives that nudge people into courses of action they often want for themselves but lack the initiative, willpower, or clear-mindedness to take on their own.

This is hardly a new idea. Progressive Era reformers, while not shrinking from mandates and prohibitions, also made much greater use of soft paternalism than we do today. They did so by creating institutions, like school banking, that structured and conditioned choices, thereby inculcating appropriate habits of life.

The school bank, as an institution, created what today's behavioral economists call a "choice architecture" with a specific default. The default was that all children had an account, and one day a week was school banking day. The choice for the students was how much to put into or take out of their accounts, a choice conditioned by the fact that school banking was what the whole class did on, say, Tuesday mornings.

The Trimmer Clubs described in chapter 2, which paid a penny a day to any Iowa boy who refrained from tobacco, liquor, gambling, and swearing (on condition that he save most of the money), are another example of Progressive Era soft paternalism. They were voluntary but provided incentives that structured choices. As nearly as we can tell, they were also highly successful, which bodes well for the conditional cash transfer programs being experimented with today.

This brings us to the question of how to apply these insights, old and new, to the urgent task of getting more Americans to do the savings they know they need to do but don't. We suggest the simplest, most effective reform would be for Congress to do for the American people as a whole what it has done for itself and all federal workers: get every American into an automatic savings plan with a good choice architecture.

The plan we have in mind would be patterned on the Federal Thrift Savings Plan (TSP), mentioned earlier, an enormously successful savings program that is essentially a 401(k) plan for federal workers, including members of Congress. Under the TSP, participants receive matching contributions, including an automatic contribution equaling 1 percent of pay even for employees who elect to make no contributions of their own. Participants have their choice of six different investment vehicles (bond funds, stock funds, mixed "life cycle" funds) provided by carefully regulated private sector investment firms. Because of the size of the TSP and its ability to have some of the administrative functions performed by government agencies, it is able to negotiate substantial discounts on the fees charged by investment companies, adding to the returns that participants get. The American Stakeholder Savings plan we have in mind would enjoy even larger economies of scale, since every American—again, all citizens and permanent legal residents, including children—would have an account opened in his or her name.

We wouldn't disturb the millions of Americans who are happy with their current company plan. But all new workers—those starting work once ASAs are established for all kids—would automatically be enrolled in an American Stakeholder Account and endowed with a $500 starter deposit. Employers would be relieved of the burden of administering a retirement plan since that would now be done by the TSP-like entity within Treasury. Employers would, however, be responsible for enrolling their employees in the plan. Moreover, both employers and employees would be required to contribute 2 percent of wages to the accounts, with these contributions restricted for retirement. Americans not generating earned income—whether unable to do so or preferring not to do so to raise children, for example—would also have an ASA in their name.

Like ASAs established at birth, contributions from all sources would be capped at $2,000 per year, with certain low- and middle-income households eligible for up to $500 per year in matching funds. With-drawals would be limited to pursuing postsecondary education and life-long learning, buying a first home, and saving for retirement. Account holders would have several options as to how their money was invested, just as participants in the Federal Thrift Savings Plan do. The only major difference would be the choice architecture for retirement savings. There would be a range of choices but also a default vehicle into which all retire-ment savings would flow unless an account holder specified otherwise. This vehicle would be an index fund that offered a ratio of stocks and bonds that adjusted automatically according to the account holder's age.

The establishment of universal ASAs gives governments at all lev-els an easy-to-use vehicle for helping the working poor build assets. A portion of the Earned Income Tax Credit, for example, could be auto-matically diverted into these accounts, using the new IRS form num-ber 8888, which lets you send your refund directly to up to three different accounts. More boldly—and building on the conditional cash transfer concept mentioned earlier—they could be used by both pub-lic and private programs to reward people who quit smoking, managed their diabetes, volunteered in nursing homes, taught in inner-city schools, or engaged in any other behavior that might benefit society—just think of your favorite cause.

American Stakeholder Accounts would, as we've already discussed, be restricted to savings that lead to longer-term, productive assets—higher education, a first home, and a nest egg for retirement. But Amer-icans also need unrestricted savings: to fix or replace the car they need to get to work, repair the washing machine, replace the roof, buy some time off between jobs, pay medical bills, reduce the credit card bill, and, for some, start a small business. That's why we also encourage govern-ment and the private sector to do more to help Americans build up flex-ible savings. For example, what if, at tax time, your refund was electronically deposited into a souped-up debit card that could also pay bills, receive paychecks and government payments, and hold your sav-ings? What if your employer set up an automatic payroll deposit into a regular, unrestricted savings account? And what if we made it easier at tax time, indeed, at all times, to buy good old, easy-to-use Savings Bonds, which deserve a renaissance?

We also like the idea of using these ASAs to ameliorate the terrible damage done to the thrift ethic and to the finances of the poor by state lotteries. Today, forty-two states and the District of Columbia run lotteries, raking in $57 billion a year, with the lowest-income Americans losing the greatest percentage of their incomes to lotteries. Arguably, lotteries should be illegal, as they were for most of American history before 1964. Yet with universal accounts and a change in design, they could actually foster thrift. For example, what if when you bought a lottery ticket, some portion of the sale was automatically credited to your Stakeholder account? That way when you didn't win the big prize (and what are the chances you will?), you'd end up with more savings, not less. Such a lottery is up and running in Britain, called Premium Bonds.

We should also think about turning casinos into savings institutions. Again, all it would take is a provision that diverted some share of each bet to a gambler's Stakeholder account. In countries such as South Africa, Mexico, Japan, and Colombia, financial institutions routinely offer "prize-linked saving products" that generate new customers, regular deposits, and profits—proving that with the right choice architecture, the pleasures of gambling can serve to increase savings. The only reason financial institutions in the United States don't offer prizes to savers is because of the ban on "private lotteries"—a law that should be rethought.

Annuitize This

Stakeholder accounts could become the vehicle for all sorts of additional policy innovation. But we'll close this chapter by pointing out that with just two additional features, these accounts can overcome a problem that bedevils planning for retirement. It's the question of whether you will outlive your savings. If you're a thirty- or forty-year-old prudently trying to figure out how much you should be saving for retirement, you can plug your numbers into all kinds of fancy and sophisticated retirement calculators like FinancialEngines and get some very precise-sounding estimates. But those calculators can't reckon with the possibility that you might drop dead on the first day you retire or live forty or more years longer. How can you plan for that?

For populations as a whole, it is not difficult to calculate average life expectancy at any given age. Sometimes the actuaries get it wrong, but at most by only a few years. But for individuals, excepting those who know they are terminally ill, it's very difficult to know how long you will live, especially while you are still young.

One of the virtues of Social Security and traditional defined-benefit pension plans is that they ameliorate this "longevity risk" by offering regular monthly annuity payments that continue until death, however late it is in coming. They can do this with more efficiency than individuals can do for themselves in large part because they only have to worry about financing average life expectancy. This is much shorter and more predictable than maximum life expectancy, which is what individuals insuring themselves have to worry about.

But traditional, defined-benefit pensions have many other problems, including a tendency for companies to underfund or raid their reserves, and are rapidly vanishing. In their place have come defined-contribution plans like 401(k)s. Today, people participating in these plans can mitigate the risk of their outliving their savings by purchasing annuities when they retire. But there is a big problem with the private annuity market. Annuities cannot be bought at an actuarially fair price.

The reason is what actuaries call "adverse selection." The older people get, the easier it becomes for them to make at least a reasonable guess about how many years they have remaining. And for this reason, those who find they are healthy at, say, age sixty-five, tend to buy annuities more than those who do not. This selection bias means insurance companies can only make money on annuities if they price them high, which is why most people, when they look into converting their life savings into annuities, are shocked to see how small their monthly check will be.

Here's where universal American Stakeholder Accounts fit in. They can offer reasonably priced annuity benefits if we add just two, admittedly "hard" paternalistic features. First, as already suggested, all Americans entering the workforce and their employers would each be compelled—with no opting out—to contribute 2 percent of earnings to the stakeholder accounts, with these contributions restricted for retirement. Second, these savings would be automatically converted into annuities upon retirement.

This would greatly reduce adverse selection in the annuities market. Also, because of the very large numbers of people involved, longevity risk would be spread very widely, thereby further reducing the cost of annuities below what they otherwise would be. As economist James M. Poterba has written: "Requiring all persons to annuitize their retirement account balances at a specified age is one way to substantially reduce the degree of adverse selection in the annuity market. More generally, however, any policy that encourages a large fraction of the population to participate in the annuity market is likely to have a similar effect."[16]

Studies have shown that for people whose wealth consists largely of defined-benefit pensions, annuitizing their remaining assets in retirement does not necessarily maximize their welfare. But for the vast majority of Americans whose retirement savings are or will be held in defined-contribution plans, the chance to annuitize their savings, particularly at rates that do not reflect adverse selection (or gouging management fees) will leave them much better off.

When one of us sketched out this plan to John Rother, policy director for the AARP, he joked, "You've just reinvented Social Security." But there is a fundamental difference. Yes, like Social Security, Stakeholder accounts would use coercion to offer actuarially fair annuity benefits. But unlike Social Security, they wouldn't rely on intergenerational transfers or contain huge unfunded liabilities. Instead, all accounts would be fully funded from day one and would always remain so.

The Big Picture

Some might choose to think of Stakeholder Accounts as an "add-on" to Social Security. The two systems operating together would indeed offer participants a nice hedge against the market risk of investing in the real economy through Stakeholder Accounts and the very low return available from Social Security in an aging society.

Why is this "add-on" needed? Let's pan back a bit and look at the big picture. We don't think Social Security will "go broke." But it will either be trimmed or become much more expensive. Social Security uses current taxes to finance current benefits. This means its finances are extremely sensitive to the ratio of workers to retirees, and with the baby boomers smashing into old age, there will soon be substantially fewer workers to support each retiree. Thus, without benefit cuts, Social Security will grow more and more costly, consuming resources America badly needs for other purposes. By 2035, according the latest Trustee's Report, Social Security left on current course will consume 40 percent more of the economy than it does today.

If you don't think that is a lot, consider that Social Security already consumes one of every seven dollars most Americans earn. Yes, more money can be gotten from high-income individuals to finance Social Security, but doing so in any substantive amount will erode Social Security's image of being "social insurance," thereby eroding its political support as well. There's a reason the architects of Social Security capped payroll taxes above a certain threshold, and this is it.[17]

Adding to the strain, the real cost of keeping Social Security on its current course will be much higher if economic growth is sluggish, and there are good reasons to believe it will be. Here's just one reason why. Over the next twenty years, the American population will become as old as the populations now found in slow-growing European countries. A lot more than population growth determines the course of an economy, of course. But growth in gross domestic product is by definition a combination of growth in the labor force and productivity growth, and our labor force has little growth left in it. Between 2010 and 2030, according to the Census Bureau, the working-age population of the United States will increase by a mere 3.6 percent, even assuming continued high rates of immigration.

When you hear that America is still a rapidly growing country, remember that, starting in the near future, most of that growth will coming from the soaring ranks of the elderly. While the working-age population will remain essentially stagnant between 2010 and 2030, the population over sixty-five will increase by 77 percent. These numbers are quite certain, because every person they count is already alive. Where are the extra new workers needed to build economic growth the way the baby boomers did when they were young? They were never born.[18] This doesn't have to mean recession, but it is worth noting that John Maynard Keynes, and many other economists of his time, pointed to falling birthrates as a major cause of the Great Depression.[19]

Meanwhile, and on point, the cost of health care continues to soar. According to the Congressional Budget Office, health care is on course to consume a third of the economy within twenty years.[20] There's lots we can do about that, as we'll see in the next chapter. Yet it is utopian to believe that health care won't continue to consume an increasing share of the nation's income, putting pressure on all other forms of spending and investment, both public and private, including Social Security. It's also utopian to the think that America can or will escape many other costly debts coming due from the past: the deferred maintenance on our crumbling infrastructure, for example, or the massive cost of, at long last, breaking our dependence on oil and converting to cleaner, more secure, but probably more expensive forms of energy.

So there is little prospect that Social Security benefits can prudently be made more generous and a good chance they'll need to be cut, say, by raising the retirement age (again). Yet we know that most Americans are woefully unprepared for retirement even if they wind up receiving all their currently promised benefits. Some will make due by working longer, but the obesity epidemic and the increasing prevalence of chronic illness, to say nothing of the rapid obsolescence of job skills in today's economy, means that option won't be available to many.

So what to do? Sadly, it's too late for the miracle of compound interest to be of much use in meeting the challenge of the baby boom generation's retirement. We should have created something like Stakeholder accounts three decades ago, when it was perfectly clear that this crisis was coming and time to advert it with much less pain.

Baby boomers who want something else to grumble about in old age can reflect on how they actually did "set aside" 2.1 percent of their income every year after 1983 through what was in effect a forced savings plan. That's the amount by which their payroll taxes and everyone else's went up in 1983. The plan was that the money raised by this tax hike (which more than eliminated the benefits of the Reagan tax cuts for most Americans) would be kept safe in a "lockbox"—remember? That way, come today, it would be available to meet the predicable cost of financing the baby boomers' and succeeding generations' old age benefits. But Congress and successive presidents raided the money in the "lockbox," using the "surpluses" in the Social Security trust fund to finance the federal budget deficits year after year. Now the money's spent and can't be spent again. Woulda, coulda, shoulda paid attention.

Let's not make that mistake again. A forced saving plan channeled through Stakeholders accounts invested in private equities could not be raided by politicians the way Social Security was. Nor could it become a mechanism for back-door borrowing from the young. Instead, it would add to capital formation, making us less vulnerable to foreign creditors and helping fund the investment America needs to preserve the American Dream.

We should have also adopted many other measures to build a sustainable, progressive thrift culture over the last thirty years. But we didn't. Instead, we failed to protect Americans of all ages from the spread of predatory lending; allowed new antithrift institutions like casinos and lotteries to flourish; gambled on worthless Internet stock; overinvested in flimsy real estate and gas-guzzling SUVs; lost control of health care spending; lost control of immigration; helped the rich get richer with costly tax cuts, subsidies, and deregulation; and charged into Iraq and Afghanistan, all the while transferring more and more of our wealth to oil-producing countries sponsoring terrorists. No wonder most Americans are tapped out.

This is the legacy of a second Gilded Age that is now ending. And so we are left with challenges as large, and in many ways the same, as those faced by Progressives trying to undue the excesses of the first Gilded Age: building up institutions at all levels of society that will instill the value of thrift and small-scale ownership to craft a sustainable world.

CHAPTER 7

Progressive Health Care

H ARVARD BIOCHEMIST Lawrence J. Henderson was one of the Progressive Era's most renowned men of science. He was also keenly aware of the limits of medical science in his time. He once observed that it wasn't until somewhere around 1911 that the progress of medicine at last made it possible to say that "a random patient with a random disease consulting a physician at random stood better than a 50-50 chance of benefiting from the encounter."[1]

We've come a long way since the Progressive Era in our scientific understanding of how the human body works, thanks in no small measure to the work of Professor Henderson, who died in 1942. Yet how shocked would Henderson be today to learn that when Americans consult with their physicians, according to a groundbreaking RAND study, their chances of receiving appropriate, evidence-based care is still only about 50-50, despite the fantastic sums we have spent and continue to spend on medical education, research, and health care.[2]

The staggering inefficiency, ineffectiveness, and cost of America's health care system is the single largest threat to a renewal of progressivism in the United States. Left unreformed, the cost of health care will rise from consuming 16 percent of the nation's economic output in 2007 to 25 percent in 2025, according to the Congressional Budget Office. Put another way, by 2025, Americans will be working through the end of April before they have paid off the country's health care bill, with no end in sight. If you just make a straight-line projection from historical and current trends, health care will consume more than 50 percent of the country's gross domestic product within the lifetime of today's children.[3]

Traveling along that trajectory means what? It means that every year, the cost of health care consumes more and more resources that otherwise could and should go to other pressing social needs, from education and infrastructure, to investments in alternative energy sources and increased energy efficiency. Already we see once-proud corporations like General Motors made insolvent and forced to downsize in large part because of their ruinous liabilities for employee and retiree health care benefits. We see state and local governments raising taxes and the federal government going deeper and deeper in debt as they try to cover the exploding cost of publicly financed health care programs. We see the federal government standing by as the exploding cost of Medicare and Medicaid squeezes out spending in other vital areas.

Medicare's share of the federal budget has more than doubled since 1983, to about 13 percent today. Medicaid, which provides health care primarily for indigent nursing home patients and poor children, has tripled its budget share since 1983, to 7 percent. By contrast, a mere 1 percent of the budget now goes to energy research and alternative fuels, environmental protection and natural resources, child nutrition programs, and research in the physical sciences.

We also see millions of Americans trapped in place—unable to start a new business, go back to school, or even take time off to care for a loved one—because changing jobs would mean losing their employer-provided health care. We see the ranks of the uninsured swelling year after year and the crush of medical expenses emerging as the number one source of personal bankruptcy. Because of its soaring price, we see millions of workers forced to forgo raises and to assume more and more of the cost of their health care, even if they are still lucky enough to have group insurance.

If all this spending on health care brought significant improvement to the health of the American people, it would arguably be worth making large sacrifices in other areas to pay for it. But as we'll see, at least a third of U.S. health spending is pure, avoidable waste or, worse, harmful.

Americans spend more per person on health care than residents of any other country, yet they have very little to show for it except more medical bills and too many ineffective and even harmful treatments. Per capita spending on health care is only $684 in Costa Rica, for example, or less than one-tenth the level of U.S. expenditures, yet life expectancy there and here is virtually the same.[4]

This is very good news, if you think about it. Solutions to America's health care crisis exist that don't involve rationing effective care, leaving impossible debts behind for our children to pay, or forgoing vital investments in other areas. Indeed, it's demonstrable that higher-quality health care and lower cost can go hand in hand, if only we open our eyes to the true nature of the crisis before us. And once again, the example of the original Progressives can help us see the way to effective reform.

Women, Plumbers, and Doctors

During the Progressive Era, life expectancy improved at twice the rate we are witnessing today. Yet medicine was primitive by today's standards and often harmful. How did they do it?

A hallmark of Progressive Era health care was its emphasis on prevention. A child born today can expect to live a full thirty years longer than a child born in 1900. But what role did improvements in medicine play in this stunning achievement? Surprisingly little. Experts in public health widely agree that medical care contributed no more than five of those thirty extra years of life achieved during the twentieth century.[5] The rest is attributable to public health efforts that reached their apogee during the Progressive Era, most notably, securing pure food and water supplies, improving living and working conditions, encouraging personal hygiene and exercise, while discouraging substance abuse.

Progressive Era reformers had their work cut out for them, to say the least. In cities across America at the turn of the last century, the air stank of coal dust, manure, sewer gas, and rotting garbage. Lacking indoor plumbing, most people still used latrines and outhouses. "There were boxes and barrels of kitchen offal on all the sidewalks," noted a repulsed character in William Dean Howell's 1890 novel *A Hazard of New Fortunes*. Set in New York, the novel goes on to describe "frozen refuse melting in heaps, and particularly the loathsome edges of the rotting ice near the gutters, with the strata of wastepaper and straw litter, and egg-shells and orange peel, potato-skins and cigar-stumps."[6]

The only available milk or meat was often spoiled; the water supply, untreated. Fully 16 percent of the population was infected by trichinosis, a dangerous parasite found in meat, while food-borne bacteria such as salmonella, clostridium, and staphylococcus killed millions—especially children, 10 percent of whom died before their first birthday.[7] Tuberculosis, "the White Plague," particularly ravaged the poor and working classes, taking more victims than cancer now does. Among a study of five thousand adults living in Framingham, Massachusetts, conducted by the Metropolitan Life Insurance Company, 77 percent were recorded as ill with some disease.[8]

Into this world charged Progressive Era reformers with myriad measures to improve public health through nonmedical means. Harriette M. Plunkett, with her book *Women, Plumbers, and Doctors*, inspired many middle-class women to become "municipal housewives" who took charge of efforts to crack down on spitting, improve garbage collection, and eliminate dreaded sewer gas. At Jane Addams' Hull House in Chicago and settlement houses like it, workers distributed fresh "certified" milk and taught maternal and infant hygiene. By 1915, there were also at least 538 baby clinics in America, most of them run by city health departments.[9] Revealingly, reformers referred to these facilities as "clinics" rather than "dispensaries," which were previously found in poor neighborhoods. As sociologist Paul Starr observes, the use of the term *clinic* "reflected the increased use of diagnostic techniques and a reorientation from the mere giving of drugs to the more complex task of promoting changes in child care, diet, and living patterns."[10]

Armed with new knowledge of how disease spread through bacteria, reformers targeted children's habits of living as well. In 1915, under the aegis of the National Tuberculosis Association, the "Modern Health Crusaders" program began. Youthful participants would progress up a scale of honors, becoming "pages," "squires," and "knights," as they performed various "hygienic chores" such as washing hands before meals and brushing teeth twice a day. By 1919, more than three million schoolchildren around the country were enrolled in the program, besides those participating in many others like it, such as the Camp Fire Girls' hygiene program described in chapter 3. Americans, who were once stereotyped by Europeans as odiferous and unkempt, came to be known instead around the world for their obsession with germs and personal hygiene, and they began making fun of the French for not bathing enough.[11]

Medical science during this era did begin to come up with some remedies that were more than randomly effective, such as an antitoxin useful in the treatment of diphtheria. An arsenic-based compound, salvarsan, came on the market in 1910 and was used in effect as chemotherapy to treat syphilis, with modest success (it helped if it didn't kill you). Medical education became more rigorous and scientific; and effective surgery, more common. But overwhelmingly, most of the large improvements in health and life expectancy that came about during the Progressive Era were the result of improvements to the environment in which most Americans lived, along with improved habits of living. Death rates from tuberculosis, for example, fell from 200.7 per 100,000 in 1895, to 150 in 1910 and 120 in 1920, even though it would be until the 1940s before any effective medical treatment for TB came to exist.

Not only did cities become much cleaner and less crowded, but massive investments in streetcars and interurban trolleys, as well as improved roads, made it possible for more and more Americans to escape overcrowded cities and raise their children in more wholesome, suburban environments. Passage, in 1906, of the Pure Food and Drug Act and the Meat Inspection Act also typified the Progressive Era's focus on prevention, while crusades against spitting, cigarette smoking, alcohol, and narcotics further improved public health.

Whether passage of the Eighteenth Amendment in 1919 subsequently reduced alcohol consumption is hotly debated. But there is no doubt that per capita alcohol consumption fell sharply during the years leading up to Prohibition, due to some combination of rising taxation, local option bans, spreading opprobrium attached to drunkenness, and increased public concern with personal health. Between 1911 and 1919, deaths per one hundred thousand caused by cirrhosis of the liver, which is a reliable proxy for heavy alcohol consumption, dropped by 44 percent, while death attributed to alcoholism dropped by 59 percent—this all before Prohibition went into effect![12]

A 1904 editorial in the *Saturday Evening Post* noted, "This new excitement and enthusiasm over health is often spoken of as a fad— like angel sleeves and roller-skating and pigs-in-clover—something that is sweeping through the country to blow out to oblivion and be heard of no more. But was it?" No, answered the editors in typical Progressive fashion. "The craze for betterment is one that will die only with the race."[13]

The Limits of Medicine

What can we learn from the Progressive Era's stunning success in improving public health? Respect for the limits of medicine, to begin with, and a much greater appreciation for the value of prevention.

In the second half of the twentieth century, medical care became enormously more sophisticated and effective, particularly in managing pain and preventing sudden death from traumatic injury, infection, and heart attacks. Yet the resulting overall improvements to longevity were still modest. The greatest gains came from strategic vaccination campaigns, which virtually eliminated diseases that previously were common in the United States, including diphtheria, tetanus, poliomyelitis, smallpox, measles, mumps, rubella, meningitis, and polio. The discovery of vitamins, starting with vitamin A in 1913, also helped. But even these triumphs involve treating people before they were sick. If one looks at the ability of modern medicine to cure people, the results are discouraging. The consensus estimate, accepted by the Centers for Disease Control (CDC), is that medicine has contributed only two of the seven years in added life expectancy achieved been the 1950s and the 1990s.[14]

In the future, medicine's role in extending the average American's life span is likely to be even more modest. One reason is straightforward. If you spend the first sixty days of your life in an intensive care unit, medical intervention may extend your life span ninety years or more—but much less so if you're already fifty, and still less so if you're already ninety. With great reductions in infant and child mortality already achieved, the potential for large gains in life expectancy from any source is much diminished.

Also, there's the factor of "competing risk," as it's known to epidemiologists. When medicine helps us dodge one life-threatening condition, this increases our risk of contracting another. Chemotherapy, for example, may put a man's skin cancer into remission. But having escaped death from that cause for now, he lives on to face the risks of dying from heart disease or other chronic diseases, including the insults done to his body by the chemotherapy itself. Even if the man had managed to avoid getting skin cancer in the first place, this health experience would have raised his odds of contracting Alzheimer's and other chronic diseases of old age. This is not an argument against medical intervention but a demonstration of its limits and diminishing returns. As Willard Gaylin, MD, notes, "It is often difficult to appreciate that good medicine does not reduce the percentage of people with illnesses in our population. It increases that percentage."[15]

Then there is the question of what ultimately determines how long we will live and how healthy we will be. In an important study published in the peer-reviewed journal *Health Affairs*, three researchers from the Robert Wood Johnson Foundation surveyed scores of studies going back to the 1970s on the various factors that cause people to die before their time in the United States. The consensus of this literature is that genetic predispositions account for 30 percent of premature deaths; social circumstances, 15 percent; environmental exposures, 5 percent; behavioral patterns, 40 percent; and shortfalls in medical care, 10 percent.

As these researchers are quick to point out, these proportions are easily misinterpreted. Ultimately, everyone's health is determined by a combination of factors. So, for example, while only about 2 percent of human diseases are caused by inherited genetic mutations alone, nearly all of us carry various genetic dispositions that, when combined with a hazardous environment or unhealthy lifestyle, can contribute to ill health. But this nuance only reinforces the overwhelming importance of behavioral and environmental factors, and the relatively weak role medical intervention plays (even when it is practiced with utmost safety and effectiveness, which it very often isn't) in preventing premature death.

Fortunately, and thanks in large part to their efforts, we today live in a far cleaner environment than Progressive Era reformers encountered, at least when it comes to air pollution, sewage treatment, water quality, and sanitation in urban areas. Also, a much smaller share of the population lives in abject poverty or is worn down by around-the-clock manual labor starting in childhood. Yet it remains as true today as it was then that medicine is but a weak force in determining our health compared to how well we eat, how much we drink and smoke, how often we exercise, our working conditions, our socioeconomic status, and how well we avoid the multiple vectors of infectious disease, from dirty hands and needles to unprotected sex and vermin.

This was much harder to see forty years ago, when modern medicine was seemingly wracking up triumph after triumph, from penicillin and the polio vaccines, to heart transplants and nuclear medicine. In 1966, *Time* magazine surveyed medical leaders to get their predictions for what the health of the American people would be like by the year 2000. "Nearly all experts agree," the magazine reported, "that bacterial and viral diseases will have been virtually wiped out. Probably atherosclerotic heart disease will also have been eliminated. Cells have only a few secrets still hidden from probers, who are confident that before the year 2000, they will have found the secret that causes cancer."[16]

Since then, however, thinking people, at least, have been sobered by the diminished achievements of modern medicine, even as we must pay more and more for it. Indeed, the more people know about health care, the less faith they have in doctors and their remedies. While fully half the public now says it lacks trust in "scientific solutions" for health care, nearly 80 percent of health care policy professionals share this doubt. Indeed, according to a study published in the *Milbank Quarterly*, the largest single factor driving down trust in doctors—among the general public, but especially among health care policy professionals—is mounting concerns about the ineffectiveness of modern medicine.[17]

What bothers health care policy professionals the most about the course of modern medicine? To begin with, infectious diseases have come roaring back. In the last thirty years, at least twenty infectious diseases that were once thought conquered, ranging from tuberculosis to malaria and cholera, have reemerged, often in more virulent form. Meanwhile, today's humans are afflicted by at least thirty new infectious diseases, including HIV/AIDS, Lyme disease, H5N1 avian influenza (bird flu), hepatitis C, and infections caused by the hantavirus, Ebola virus, and the SARS corona virus. Many scientists now warn that global warming, another purely environmental factor, will vastly extend the reach of deadly tropical diseases, such as malaria.[18] Increases in global trade and travel, rising urbanization in the developing world, and other factors now cause many experts to fear that the world is now poised for a pandemic of contagious disease on a scale not seen since the Progressive Era.

Perversely, the very antibiotics that gave medicine so much prestige forty years ago have, through misuse, spawned superbugs against which we have a diminishing arsenal of weapons except changes in behavior or the environment that might reduce their transmission. The perfect symbol of today's medicine is the patient who undergoes a complex operation, involving lasers, advanced imaging, and masterfully controlled anesthesia, only to go home with a multidrug-resistant infection against which antibiotics developed two generations ago are now useless.

About ninety thousand people die each year from bacterial infections acquired in U.S. hospitals, with 70 percent of those infections now being resistant to at least one drug, according to the CDC. Methicillin-resistant infections, once primarily affecting hospital patients, now have spread into the community. Children scream with ear infections for which there are fewer and fewer effective cures, and many now die from untreatable infections. Strapping professional athletes, such as the Toronto Blue Jays' Alex Rios and Ty Taubenheim, are laid low, as were two Miami Dolphin football players who had to be hospitalized after small cuts became infected with superbugs. More recently, even more lethal "gram-negative" bugs, such as klebsiella, have evolved and begun migrating out of hospitals and into the community, raising the specter of a return to a preantibiotic era in which the only recourse to sever infection is amputation. These are clear-cut examples of how the practice of medicine itself has created a more deadly, infectious environment.[19]

At the same time, the spread of obesity, sedentary lifestyle, and poor diet are combining to cause an epidemic of chronic disease such as diabetes. These chronic diseases can at best be "managed" by modern medicine, and usually even at that most health providers fail. In Boston, which arguably has the most highly credentialed and prestigious medical community in America, diabetics patients receive appropriate care from their doctors only 45 percent of the time, according to a careful review of medical records by the RAND Corporation.[20]

Similarly, despite increased screening and earlier detection, the five-year survival rates for most cancers remains barely changed. What declines we have seen in cancer rates are found mostly only among the well educated, who are more likely to engage in healthy lifestyles. Between 1983 and 1999, men's life expectancy decreased in more than fifty-nine U.S. counties, and for women it was worse. In one-quarter of all counties in the United States, female life expectancy is on the decline.[21]

These are familiar truths to many, yet how absent they are from our health care policy debates. Today, those debates are primarily about access to the existing health care system—that is, the problem of the uninsured—and to a much lesser extent about cost containment, with hardly any regard at all to the ineffectiveness of current patterns of health care spending. The overwhelming share of our medical research dollars, for example, goes to investigation of molecular-level reality—splicing genes, harvesting stem cells—while it is body-scale reality and larger social realities that most determine human health. The strongest correlation to be found anywhere in medical science isn't between genetic or biochemical phenomena: it the iron law that correlates low socioeconomic status and poor health.[22]

This the Progressives instinctively understood, even if some became distracted from it by the increasing scientific pretensions of medical professionals in their era. They understood that improving public health involved medical intervention but also, and much more so, reducing poverty, cleaning up the environment, eliminating contaminants from food and water, reducing accidents, and promoting healthy habits of living.

What if we were to take a page from Progressive Era health care and update it to modern conditions? What would American health care look like? In the next chapter, we will look at how the Progressives' emphasis on efficiency, scientific management, and institution building could improve the quality and safety of our currently highly fragmented and highly chaotic health care delivery "system" or the lack thereof. But here we want to dwell on progressive approaches to health care that involve social interventions, or what many of the Progressives called "thrift in health."

Death by Sprawl

Persuading Americans to take better care of themselves is not at all easy. As Prohibition and the War on Drugs prove, simply criminalizing unhealthy behavior doesn't work. Similarly, imposing sin taxes on undesirable behavior, while effective, can only go so far without creating black markets. And anyway, most Americans are appropriately resentful of government efforts to penalize them for their chosen lifestyles. But what if, instead of trying to punish or castigate citizens for unhealthy behavior, we took the same soft paternalism approach we applied to savings? That would start with making changes in the built environment, including residential development and transportation, to encourage healthier and less risky patterns of behavior.

Start with sprawl. On a purely statistical basis, what's more likely to get you killed over the course of a year: (A) living in Israel, in the midst of the Intifada; (B) living in a crime-ridden inner city like Baltimore or Houston; or (C) living in the outer suburbs of those cities?

The answer overwhelmingly is (C). The great migration of Americans out of crowded, crime-ridden cities may have improved public health a hundred years ago. But the expansion of new development over the last generation into sprawling, auto-dependent, outer suburbs has become a huge cause of premature death. Yes, in sprawlville you're less likely to be killed by a knife- or gun-wielding stranger. But you are far more likely to be killed by a stranger driving an automobile—so much so that the mortality risk of living in the suburbs is actually higher than in cities. To cite just one example, residents of inner-city Houston face about a 1.5 in 10,000 chance of dying during the coming year either at the hands of a murderous stranger or as the victim of an automobile accident. But in Montgomery County, a sprawling suburb of Houston, residents are 50 percent more likely to die from one of those two causes, because of the much higher rate of automobile accidents.[23]

Sprawling, auto-dependent suburbs are unhealthy in other ways as well. In such an environment, for example, almost no one walks—and for good reason. Every year in the United States, about 4,800 pedestrians are struck and killed by automobiles, and another 70,000 are injured. Walking is by far the most dangerous mode of travel per mile— roughly twenty times more likely to get you killed than driving. For children, being hit by a car is the third-leading cause of accidental injury, even though these days, children hardly walk anymore. Only about 14 percent of children's trips to school are made on foot, down from 50 percent in 1969.[24]

Not surprisingly, metro areas marked by sprawling development and a high degree of auto dependency—most notably Orlando; Tampa; West Palm Beach; Miami–Fort Lauderdale; Memphis; Atlanta; Greensboro, North Carolina; Houston; Jacksonville, Florida; and Phoenix— are the most dangerous regions to walk today. (The high concentration of Florida cities on that list, by the way, is not due to the high proportion of elders in that state, who are not overrepresented among those who get run over. Instead, the explanation is the hideous sprawl and traffic that mars so much of Florida's landscape.)[25]

But, of course, rarely walking is also deadly. The risk of a sedentary lifestyle is comparable to, and in some studies greater than, the risk of hypertension, high cholesterol, diabetes, and even smoking.[26] According to the Surgeon General, the direct and indirect economic costs of obesity come to about 9.4 percent of all health care spending.[27] Americans who never exercise cost the health care system some $76.6 billion a year.[28] Sprawl does not fully account for Americans' increasingly sedentary lives, but, it is nonetheless a major factor, and that makes it a leading cause of premature death.

Howard Frumkin, a professor of public health at Emory University, shows the logic: "Sprawl is associated with decreased physical activity as driving replaces walking and bicycling. Decreased physical activity leads to overweight. Both decreased physical activity and overweight are risk factors for a wide range of health problems, including cardiovascular disease and cancer."[29]

One must add that sprawl, besides all the auto-related pollution it creates, is also associated with high levels of social isolation (people lacking casual, day-to-day contact with neighbors or networks of acquaintances) and with low involvement in community affairs. Indeed, as Robert Putnam, a professor of public policy at Harvard University, has shown in his well-known book *Bowling Alone*, for every ten minutes spent driving to work, involvement in community affairs drops by 10 percent. What's the public health implication? A large amount of literature shows that the health risks of being socially isolated are comparable to the risks associated with cigarette smoking, high blood pressure, and obesity.[30] Indeed, Putnam finds that an isolated individual's chances of dying over the next twelve months is cut in half by joining one group and cut by two-thirds by joining two groups.[31]

So it turns out that among the biggest policy levers available for improving public health involve reducing subsidies to sprawl. These include gas taxes that are nowhere near high enough to cover the cost of maintaining roads and highways, let alone the environmental cost of driving or the direct and indirect toll in injury and premature death. They also include directing more investment to mass transit, bike trails, and safer sidewalks. And they involve reengineering suburbs to be more like they were in the Progressive Era: shady and pastoral, but with shops and homes closer together and connected to each other by safe sidewalks and efficient transit systems.

Obviously, such changes involve huge structural adjustments, many of which we need to do for reasons unrelated to health, such as energy independence, transportation efficiency, and the need to preserve home values in outer-ring suburbs where the foreclosure crisis is most concentrated. We'll be taking up the needed reforms and how to pay for them in greater detail in chapters 9 and 10. But for now, we'll share a few small ideas for promoting health through individual incentives.

The Americans Without Disabilities Act

Regardless of how you feel about the Americans with Disabilities Act, you have to admit that the legislation is invasive. It mandates everything from how parking lots and public bathrooms are arranged to how employers organize work. Yet it does nothing to prevent disability. Why not adapt parallel legislation that would attack the problem of how to keep Americans from getting disabled in the first place—and do so in a way that is not so invasive? Here are a few "soft paternalistic" examples:

- **Offer free vegetables.** Expand Food Stamp eligibility, and entitle recipients to a generous, free weekly allowance of fruits and vegetables. The National Cancer Institute recommends a minimum of five servings of fruits and vegetables a day. However, fruits and vegetables have gone up in price more than any other food category in recent years. Meanwhile, overhaul that broken legacy of the last Progressive Era, the Food and Drug Administration, so that it can effectively prevent food-borne illness.
- **Slim down and save.** Offer any overweight American who participates in a certified and regulated diet and exercise program, and who slims down to an appropriate body mass index, a $200 credit in his or her American Stakeholder Account, as described in chapter 5. If subsequent annual checkups show maintenance of proper weight, then more credits are available. Participants should have the option of pledging to return any credit should they lose control of their weight. Similar conditional cash transfer programs could be offered, at any level of government as well as by philanthropies, to problem drinkers, drug abusers, and smokers.
- **Tread to save.** Offer vouchers for gym memberships as a right of citizenship. (The German welfare state offers an entitlement to spas.) To make sure people actually go to the gym, use currently available information technology to direct credits into their savings accounts according to how many hours they spend on a treadmill or other exercise machine, with a daily maximum set to discourage overexercise. A sliding scale could be created so that low-income individuals received more pennies per step. Using wireless technology and pedometers, it also is possible to compensate pedestrians according to the lengths of their walks or jogs.
- **Ride to save.** Walking to the local train or trolley stop is good for you, but using mass transit is also good for the planet and your fel-

low citizens: You deserve compensation. Instead of transit users having to feed a fare box, they should receive a dollar credit on their swipe cards for up to three rides a day, financed by drivers, who will enjoy less traffic, cleaner air, and a lesser burden on the health care system. (If we want to promote financial thrift at the same time, the credits could be automatically deposited into the American Stakeholder Accounts.)

- **Reverse tolls for cyclists.** Using abandoned railroad right-of-way where available, create an Interstate Bicycle Highway System. Instead of charging tolls, install machines that pay cyclists according to the number of miles they've pedaled. A similar system could be used to pay people for taking the stairs in public buildings.

- **Tax junk food.** Require a reformed Food and Drug Administration to develop an operational definition of "junk food," based on fat, salt, and sugar content. Require health warnings on junk food, and make it subject to sales taxes commensurate with those imposed on cigarettes and alcohol. Ban sales of junk food in school cafeterias. Ban junk food advertising on children's television. Ban the use of "Joe Camel" equivalents, such as Ronald McDonald, in all junk food advertising.

- **Zone out fast-food vendors.** Just as most jurisdictions hold down concentrations of liquor stores through licensing and zoning, do the same for fast-food joints. Restaurants serving items meeting the FDA's definition of "junk" would require a special license to operate, with the supply of new Burger Kings and McDonald's strictly limited by regional quotas. Meanwhile, the Small Business Administration could offer low-cost loans to farmers markets, food co-ops, and small groceries that sell wholesome food in low-income neighborhoods.

- **Mandate no "free" parking."** Just as the ADA mandates that a set number of parking spaces be set aside for people with disabilities, let the Americans Without Disabilities Act mandate that all new planned urban developments contain a set length of sidewalks and trails per resident, while limiting the construction of parking lots to a minimum.

- **Set kids in motion.** Limit the size of school districts so that most students can reasonably walk or bike to school. Redesignate more parking spaces at high schools as handicapped only. Make physical fitness one of the metrics for No Child Left Behind.
- **Distribute free nicotine patches.** The cost of these patches currently exceeds that of a one-pack-a-day habit. Give them away to any smoker who wants them. This should be far less controversial than handing out free condoms and hypodermic needles and, given the annual four hundred thousand premature deaths related to smoking, will save far more lives.
- **Offer smoke-free health care premiums.** Following the example of private life insurance, entitle Medicare beneficiaries to reduced premiums if they test negative for nicotine. Further reductions in premiums and copayment could be achieved by those who had certified attendance in exercise programs.
- **Legalize a THC patch.** Make the use of a marijuana patch legal for persons over twenty-one. The dramatic drop in tobacco smoking over the last generation demonstrates that legalization of addictive substances does not necessarily induce increased demand. Meanwhile, the War on Drugs creates incentives for dealers to peddle ever more potent drugs, such as crack or meth, because they are easier to smuggle than bulky marijuana. To solve these problems and make marijuana use safer, encourage manufacturers to produce patches that deliver a moderate dose of trahydrocannabinol (THC, the psychoactive substance found in cannabis), and tax them heavily. Use the resulting revenue, plus the massive savings to the criminal justice system, to develop safe, effective, and nonaddictive recreational drugs that will reduce the demand for alcohol and other dangerous, mind-altering substances.
- **Target medical research dollars on changing behavior.** The National Institutes of Health (NIH) should put much greater resources into discovering the biological causes of addiction, depression, and obesity. Canada's equivalent of the NIH now directs research dollars away from high-tech research that, while possibly very beneficial to a small number of individuals, does little or nothing to improve public health.

Many of these proposals may lack political viability for now. But, frankly, so flabby and unfit has the American population become that without serious health promotion efforts, there can be no cure for America's worsening health care crisis even if we get everything else right.

Some believe that health promotion will not save money but merely extend lives. The argument is that we all must die of something, and it is usually during the months leading up to our deaths that we consume the most amount of health care dollars. But should you be attracted to such an argument, remember that the more we can reduce the incidence of long-term, chronic disease related to behavior and the environment, the less money society has to spend managing those diseases right until the time death, and the more money people will be able to earn (and pay in taxes) with their extra years of productive life.

Because we recognize the libertarian streak in American life, we call for no new bans and mandates on individuals to promote public health. Rather, we take the "soft paternalism" approach most often favored by the original Progressives, who restructured their cities and infrastructure to make them less polluted and infectious, while also putting heavy emphasis on settlement houses, baby clinics, "health crusader" clubs, and other institutions to nudge children and adults into developing healthier habits of living. Progressivism preserves, within wide limits, our all-American right to make bad decisions about health and much else, but it also strives to create an environment in which making the right decision is far easier than it otherwise would be.

CHAPTER 8

Yeoman Doctors and Scientific Management

A new scientific truth does not triumph by convincing its opponents and making them see the light, but rather because its opponents eventually die, and a new generation grows up that is familiar with it.

—Max Planck, Nobel Prize winner for physics, 1918

I N HIS GROUNDBREAKING book, *The Structure of Scientific Revolutions* (1962), Thomas Kuhn focused on a peculiar pattern running throughout the history of science, from the beginning through modern times. Each generation inherits fixed ideas about how the world works, such as the Earth is flat or the center of the solar system. But over time we notice anomalies that seem to contradict the reigning paradigm. Columbus observed, for example, that the masts of ships appear on the horizon before their hulls.

Typically, the first reaction to such observations is that the graybeards either deny their existence or try to fit the new observations into prevailing notions with ever more elaborate theories, such as the multiplying cycles within cycles astronomers before Copernicus used to try to explain the motions of the newly observed planets. But eventually, the contradictions just keep building, often threatening power elites (just ask Galileo or Max Planck) until at last a new generation comes along that commits to a "paradigm shift"—a phrase originally coined by Kuhn.

Cognitive Dissonance

Today, three well-documented anomalies exist that would seem to contradict almost everything most people think they know about the practice of medicine in the United States. First, when uninsured Americans receive treatment for their acute conditions—in emergency rooms, free clinics, community hospitals, and the like—they receive care that is as high or higher quality than that received by insured patients.

Yes, you read that right. According to a study published in the *New England Journal of Medicine*, uninsured patients receive only 53.7 percent of the care experts believe they should get—that is, appropriate, evidence-based treatment. That's a depressing number and about what you might expect of an often-callous health care system. But according to the same study, patients with private, fee-for-service insurance are even less likely to receive proper care. Indeed, among Americans receiving acute care, those who lack insurance stand a slightly better chance of receiving proper treatment than patients covered by Medicaid, Medicare, or any form of private insurance.[1]

It gets stranger. You might suppose that the practice of medicine in the United States is primarily driven by scientifically established protocols of care. Don't medical researchers conduct all sorts of experiments, trials, and studies to determine the safest, most effective way for treating different conditions? They do. Yet there's a big anomaly. It turns out that how patients with the same condition are treated varies enormously from doctor to doctor and from city to city. For instance, if you were living in Elyria, Ohio, in 2004 and had a heart condition, your doctor was three times more likely to tell you that you needed an angioplasty operation than if you lived in Cleveland just thirty miles away. Why would that be?[2]

Or why is it that even among elite medical centers, the amount spent per Medicare patient in the last six months of life varies tremendously—from $26,330 at the Mayo Clinic to $40,181 at Massachusetts General Hospital to $50,522 at UCLA Medical Center? As renowned

Princeton economist Uwe Reinhardt has asked, "How can it be that 'the best medical care in the world' costs twice as much as the best medical care in the world?"[3]

The third great anomaly creates even more cognitive dissonance. Beginning in the 1990s, researchers for the first time began defining metrics of quality in health care and measuring them systematically. These metrics include how well providers manage high blood pressure or adhere to such protocols of evidence-based medicine as prescribing beta-blockers for patients recovering from a heart attack. They also include measures like the number of medical errors committed, patient satisfaction, properly adjusted mortality rates, the percentage of patients receiving screening for chronic conditions, and spending per patient in the last six months of life. And when the answers started coming back, they were completely counterintuitive.

Generally, the new findings show that the higher the reputation of hospitals and doctors and the more they spend per patient, the poorer the quality of care they provide. At the same time, the one health care provider in the United States that consistently ranks at or near the top on all different measures of quality, including adoption of cutting-edge health information technology and the evidence-based medicine it makes possible, is a large, unionized government bureaucracy with a long history of scandal: the Veterans Health Administration, which runs the nation's VA hospitals and clinics.[4]

If this information makes your head smoke, it should. More insurance should buy you better acute care than no insurance; medical practice should not vary widely if it's based on science; America's best hospitals should not turn out to be its worst, and vice versa. One's first inclination might be simply to dismiss these findings as false. But that's not easy to do, as more and more supporting evidence piles up year after year. The more useful response is to ask, What does it mean, and what are the implications for solving the health care crisis?

Overtreated/Undertreated/Mistreated

How can it possibly be that uninsured patients receive better acute care than those blessed with full coverage? To solve this riddle, you have to bear in mind two underappreciated facts about the American health care system. First, contact with it puts you at enormous risk of being damaged by medical errors. Second, that contact also puts you at tremendous risk of being damaged by unnecessary surgery and other forms of overtreatment—unless, that is, you lack insurance.

Start with medical errors. The numbers are simply staggering. According to landmark study by the Institute of Medicine, up to ninety-eight thousand Americans are killed every year in hospitals as a result of medical errors—a toll that exceeds that of AIDS, breast cancer, or even motor vehicle accidents. If, year after year, three jumbo jets crashed every other day killing all on board, you can bet we'd be working on a total overhaul of our aviation system. But that death toll still would not match the number of people killed by medical errors in American hospitals.[5]

According to another Institute of Medicine study, Americans experience on average one dispensing error (wrong medicine, wrong dose, wrong time, wrong patient) every day they are in the hospital. Other common preventable errors include sponges and surgical instruments left in patients after surgery, administration of incompatible blood products, dropping patients, and losing track of patients. In exasperation, Medicare and Medicaid announced in 2008 that they would no longer compensate providers for the cost of treating all the complications resulting from the most common medical errors.

Let's not forget, either, the ninety thousand hospital patients who die each year from increasingly lethal hospital infections. This death toll is not the result of medical errors as usually defined. But most infections are nonetheless preventable by simple measures like doctors and nurses washing their hands, properly sterilizing their equipment, and having patients on ventilators sit up. Many other Americans no doubt acquire infections at doctors' offices, but the U.S. health system is so fragmented and its record keeping so scattered that it is impossible for researchers to produce a firm estimate.

Now we can see one big reason uninsured patients receive better acute care than those with coverage. To be sure, the uninsured generally lack access to routine preventive care or help in managing their chronic conditions, and for that reason, some twenty thousand die each year for lack of affordable care, according to the Institute of Medicine. But hospitals have a duty to treat and stabilize those facing acute conditions, and they also want them out the door as soon as possible. This means that uninsured patients being treated for acute conditions have shorter contact with the health care system and therefore less risk of being damaged by medical errors and hospital-acquired infection. It's one good thing about having no insurance, not that we recommend it.

Hospitals and doctors also, of course, have no incentives to subject uninsured patients to unnecessary surgeries, redundant tests, or other forms of overtreatment. There's no money in it. This is another good thing about being uninsured. About one-third of all health care spending in the United States goes for treatments that are not medically appropriate and often harmful.

How do we know this? It's revealed by the tremendous variation in practice patterns across the United States. In some regions, the intensity of care patients receive (number of specialists involved in their care, number of tests and procedures, etc.) is one-third higher than in other regions, yet there is no significant difference in outcomes.

The first hint of this variation came in the 1970s, when researchers John E. Wennberg and Alan Gittelsohn noticed strange patterns across regions in how doctors treated patients. By combing through old medical records, Wennberg and Gittelsohn discovered wide and seemingly inexplicable differences in how often doctors diagnosed people with peptic ulcers, for example, or in how often people received such operations as tonsillectomies. In the town where Wennberg's kids went to school, Waterbury, Vermont, 20 percent of the children had their tonsils out by age fifteen; but in next-door Stowe, 70 percent of the children got tonsillectomies.[6]

Differences in socioeconomic status could not explain the contrast. Nor was it plausible to believe that the kids in Stowe were far more in need of tonsillectomies than were kids in Waterbury. The wide variation in practice patterns suggested that something beside scientific rationality was at work in deciding which patients received what care— an idea that at the time was as radical as it was novel. Doctors, after all, were supposed to be professionals who put their patients' interests before their own and who administered care according to the dictates of science.

Gradually, Wennberg and other researchers, most of them on the faculty of the Dartmouth Medical School, found clever ways to tease out what was going on, and the emerging truth was grim. For most Americans, the two biggest factors determining what kinds of treatments they receive are how many doctors and specialists hang a shingle in their community and which one of them they happen to see. The more doctors and specialists around, the more tests and procedures performed. And the results of all these extra tests and procedures? Lots more medical bills, exposure to medical errors, and a loss of life expectancy.

It was this last conclusion that was truly shocking, but it became unavoidable when Wennberg and others broadened their studies. They found that it's not just that renowned hospitals and their specialists tend to engage in massive overtreatment. They also tend to be poor at providing critical but routine care. For example, Dartmouth researcher Elliot S. Fisher has found that among Medicare patients who share the same age, socioeconomic, and health status, their chance of dying in the next five years is greater if they go to a high-spending hospital than to a low-spending hospital. One reason is that patients in high-spending hospitals with lots of specialists and high technology are also less likely to receive many proven routine treatments.

For example, standard evidence-based medicine has identified aspirin as a highly effective treatment for heart attack victims. Yet in the highest-spending hospitals, only 74.8 percent of heart attack victims receive aspirin upon discharge from the hospital, as opposed to 83.5 percent in the lowest-spending hospitals. This may be one reason survival rates for heart attack victims are higher in low-spending hospitals than in high-spending hospitals.

Patients in high-spending hospitals are also far less like to receive flu vaccines (48.1 percent vs. 60.3 percent) as well as such routine preventive measures as pneumonia vaccines, Pap smears, and mammograms. This general lack of attention to prevention and follow-up care in high-spending hospitals helps explain why not only heart attack victims but also patients suffering from colon cancer and hip fractures stand a better chance of living another five years if they stay away from "elite" hospitals and choose a lower-cost competitor. By doing so, they not only gain a better chance of receiving effective preventive and follow-up care, but they also gain a better chance of avoiding unnecessary and often dangerous surgery. Given this unexpected reality, it is perhaps not surprising that patient satisfaction also declines as a hospital's spending per patient rises.[7]

From evidence like this, Fisher estimates that if medical practice in the highest-spending hospitals could only be brought in line with medical practice in the lowest-spending hospitals, financial savings of up to 30 percent could be achieved in Medicare, thereby preserving the solvency of its trust fund indefinitely. And, not only would we have that happy result, but Medicare patients would receive less dangerous and higher-quality care as well.

Results like these have been repeatedly confirmed by a cascade of similar studies. Tellingly, doctors themselves seem to know instinctively the truth behind them. In 2006, when *Time* magazine had the brilliant idea of asking doctors what scared them most about being a patient, three frequent answers were fear of medical errors, fear of unnecessary surgery, and fear of contracting a staph infection in teaching hospitals.[8]

Best Care Anywhere

This brings us to the third great anomaly in American health care. How is it that the VA keeps emerging as the highest-quality provider in the United States? There's a funny thing about the VA. Among most Americans, it still has a reputation for mediocrity at best and abysmal care at worst. In the spring of 2007, when the *Washington Post* reported on scandalous conditions at Walter Reed Army Medical Center, many observers mistakenly saw the news as another black eye for the VA— not realizing that Walter Reed is in fact run by the Defense Department, a separate cabinet agency.

Due to restrictions on eligibility imposed by the Bush administration in 2003, there have also been lots of headlines about veterans who have had trouble gaining access to VA health care. For those who do manage to get in, however, it's a different story.

For years, the VA has received the highest consumer satisfaction ratings of any public or private sector health care system, according to surveys done by the National Quality Research Center at the University of Michigan. It is a world leader in integrating information technology to practice of medicine, with its open-source VistA software, written by VA doctors for VA doctors. As Harvard's John F. Kennedy School of Government gushed when awarding the VA a top prize in 2006 for innovation in government: "While the costs of health care continue to soar for most Americans, the VA is reducing costs, reducing errors, and becoming the model for what modern health care management and delivery should look like." In studies of health care quality, few private systems even come close to the VA.[9]

Nor can they beat the VA on efficiency. At a time when health care inflation has been galloping along in double digits, the VA's cost per patient is the same as it was in 1995. The VA now treats 104 percent more patients than it did in 1995, using ten thousand fewer employees.[10]

One of us (Longman) has written extensively on the VA's transformation and its implications for reform of the U.S. health system as a whole.[11] The burden of writing on this subject is to explain how a rule-bound government agency with 198,000 employees from five separate unions could possibly outperform the best the private market had to offer. The ultimate answer is the near-lifetime relationship the VA has with its patients and the strong incentive this gives the VA to keep its patients well—incentives that are weak or absent elsewhere in the health care system.

Unique among health care providers, the VA's relationship with its patients typically lasts for decades. It starts when they leave the service and lasts until the end of life, including, for many, long-term nursing home care.

This means the VA as an institution has strong incentives for investing in prevention, evidence-based medicine, and effective disease management. If it doesn't learn how to manage the care of its diabetic patients, for example, those patients go on to present the VA with expensive liabilities for dialysis or amputations. If it doesn't have effective smoking cessation programs, it incurs huge expenses for treating patients with cancer and heart disease. If its formulary doesn't contain the safest and most effective drugs, it is on the hook for any long-term complications. If it subjects patients to unnecessary or unproven surgery, or to ineffective drugs, which is a huge problem elsewhere in American medicine, it doesn't make money; it loses money.

These incentives for quality care are lacking elsewhere in the health care system. There, patients churn from one insurance company to the next and from one provider network to the next. This means the patient alone has a financial interest in his or her long-term well-being. The benefits of investing in electronic medical records or in preventive medicine, for example, wind up going not to the health care system that makes the investment but to a competitor. The same is true of any money invested in discovering which drugs and treatments have the best long-term outcomes. By the time the benefits are realized, the patient has moved on to another plan.

In short, from the provider's point of view, there is little or no business case for quality. This, more than any other factor, explains why market forces don't perform the magic in health care that they do elsewhere in the economy. And it explains why—against all expectation—a sprawling, unionized federal bureaucracy turns out to have highest-quality metrics of any U.S. health care system.

Historically, to be sure, the VA has faced many challenges and still does. Unlike Medicare and Social Security, it has no trust fund to assure adequate and predictable funding. In building or closing hospitals, it faces micromanagement from Congress. In recent years, it has also come under intense pressure from the Bush administration to outsource health IT and other functions to politically favored vendors.[12] Its patients are older, poorer, and far more prone to addiction, traumatic injury, and chronic illness than the population as a whole. It is subject to intense, and not always helpful, scrutiny from the press, veterans services organizations, and other special interest groups. It has to plan against imponderables other health care providers can safely ignore, such as when and for how long America will go to war and what the casualty rates will be— including both physical and mental. And while the VA is not a monopoly, many of its patients are too poor to switch to competing providers.

Yet all these factors have not been enough to prevent the VA from emerging as the bright star of the American health care system, which ought to tell you something big. Particularly these days, when long-term chronic illness is the dominant threat to the health of the American population, a system of care under which the provider has a stake in the patient's long-term interest more than overcomes any other structural features that might cause problems, even including being a rule-bound, unionized, government bureaucracy.

Paradigm Shift

What would the original Progressives make of these three big anomalies of twenty-first-century American health care, and what would be their counsel? To answer that, you have to remember what the Progressives set out to do in constructing the foundations of the health care system we have today.

When it came to reforming the practice of medicine, most Progressives had two main instincts. The first was to inject much more science into medical practice to improve its efficiency and effectiveness. The second instinct, consistent with the yeoman ideal, was to carve a safe place for small-scale producers in medicine—that is, individual doctors in business for themselves.

The imperfect solution for obtaining both goals, worked out contentiously over decades, was to secure much tougher and scientifically rigorous standards in medical education, and then to bar graduates of diploma mills and self-taught doctors from practicing medicine. This, it was hoped, would turn doctors into scientifically knowledgeable, sovereign professionals while also largely sheltering them from both corporate competition and competition from quacks.

It is not well remembered today that at the turn of the last century, many large-scale industrial concerns, particularly railroads, were running their own hospitals and clinics for their workers, using physicians on salary or paid a fixed sum per patient. Railroads alone employed six thousand surgeons by 1900, who had their own associations and journals specializing in railroad surgery. Other corporations, though tripped up by hostile Progressive Era judges, were also moving to create what were called "corporate practices," or what we would today call health maintenance organizations (HMOs), in which it was necessary, for example, that doctors get second opinions before engaging in surgery.

"The members of the profession," fumed an Ohio doctor in the journal of the newly revamped American Medical Association in 1902, "are constantly humiliated and insulted by wealthy corporations, state county and city officials."[13] A local steel magnate, he went on to complain, was refusing to pay more than 60 percent of his bill for emergency services.

> As it is, if I do not accept the fees the company offers, the work will go to another physician and the company knows it can get plenty of doctors to do their work for whatever they are willing to pay. What the medical profession needs is a leader, to take it out the of the valley of poverty and humiliation, a Mitchell, as the miners have, or a Morgan, as the trusts have.[14]

Like small farmers and artisans, independent doctors, too, saw their income and autonomy threatened by the forces of industrialization, and they fought back—with far more success, it turned out, than yeomen in any other walk of American life. What doctors wound up doing, however, was far more effective than building a union or a trust. Acting primarily at the state and local levels, they organized to pressure licensing boards to deny licenses to all but the graduates of rigorous and certified medical universities, such as the newly established Johns Hopkins Medical School.

Opened in 1893, Hopkins had an unprecedented requirement that all entering students arrive with college degrees. It also set the precedent of requiring not just four years of formal training but round-the-clock hospital residencies in which doctors in training lived as monks for as long as seven years. Complained one house officer in 1899, who could barely stay on his feet, "Gentlemen, we cannot all live in the Johns Hopkins Hospital forever." The resident immediately "gained the approbation of his fellows."[15]

In effect, what the rapidly organizing medical profession was offering the rest of Progressive Era America was a deal: we will kick the quacks out the profession and dedicate ourselves to scientific progress in medicine, if you will allow us to preserve our autonomy and control entry into the field.

It was a grand bargain that appealed to Americans at all walks of life. Labor unions were suspicious of the trend toward company doctors and corporate medicine, as were most ordinary Americans. Then as now, Americans placed great value in having an individual relationship with their doctors. And in those days they placed even higher faith in both the promise of science and in the value of checking corporate expansion in all realms of life.

To be sure, some Progressive reformers were frustrated that newly empowered doctors pushed back against not just corporate control but against early efforts to enact universal health insurance, which doctors feared would bring government control over how they practiced medicine and how much they were paid. But in the end, the cause of universal health insurance was not dear enough to most Progressive Era reformers to make them stand in the way of a self-regulated medical profession, free of corporate control and committed to scientific advance.

People could sense the profession's rising self-confidence and were impressed by its proclamations. "To have lived through a revolution," wrote Sir William Osler, widely considered the father of modern medicine and the founder of the Hopkins Medical School, "to have seen a new birth of science, a new dispensation of health, reorganized medical schools, remodeled hospitals, a new outlook for humanity, is not given to every generation."[16]

Indeed. So how would the original Progressives compare their medical accomplishments with our own? One imagines that if Dr. Osler were with us today, he would be duly impressed by our theoretical understanding of biochemistry, genetics, and the workings of the human body generally, but he would also be appalled by the actual practice of medicine in the United States.

Above all, when Osler was pioneering modern medical education at the turn of the last century, he believed he was engaged in a great struggle to bring professionalism and scientific rigor to the practice of medicine. Yet today he would be confronted by the wide variations in practice patterns in the United States, and he would have to conclude that what twenty-first-century health care providers actually do is barely informed by scientific research into which drugs and procedures work better than others.

Worse, he would have to confront the reality that mere contact with the medical profession has become a leading cause of death in the United States, due to egregious overtreatment, harmful surgeries, medical errors, the breeding of microbial-resistant superbugs through the misuse of antibiotics, and the widespread prescribing of dangerous drugs like Vioxx, which by itself killed more Americans than die every year in automobile accidents.

Osler would also be shocked to learn that, even as personal computers and the Internet transformed one industry after another, American health care providers (outside of the VA) have barely begun to use electronic medical records (EMRs). As the VA has demonstrated, digitalizing medical information not only dramatically improves diagnosis and patient safety but also provides a powerful, easily searchable database that researchers can use to study the outcomes of different treatments. We have every reason to believe that Osler would have jumped at the potential of EMRs, because he couldn't emphasize enough to his students the importance of sound record keeping to the progress of medicine. As recounted by one of his disciples, his counsel to young doctors was as follows:

> Observe, record, tabulate, communicate. . . . Record that which you have seen; make a note at the time; do not wait. . . . Memory plays strange pranks with facts. . . . Viewed through the perspectives of memory, an unrecorded observation, the vital details long since lost, easily changes its countenance and sinks obediently into the frame fashioned by the fancy of the moment.

Or, again: "Always note and record the unusual. Keep and compare your observations. Communicate or publish short notes on anything that is striking or new. Do not waste your time in compilations, but when your observations are sufficient, do not let them die with you."[17]

Osler was stuck with nineteenth-century information technology (pen and pad), which made outcomes research extremely difficult and time-consuming compared to what researchers can do today with digital information retrieval. Yet he did the best he could to discover how patients actually fared from different treatments. Under his administration, for example, Hopkins sent a form letter to patients about six months after their release from the hospital. It began by noting the dates of the patient's hospitalization and offered an expression of the superintendent's best wishes. It then read, "Kindly write us on the other side of this sheet and, if possible, come to the hospital to see us. The best hours are _____. If this is not possible, then please answer and inform the hospital of your present condition."[18]

That approach might seem primitive by today's standards, except that today, most health care providers outside of the VA are still using nineteenth-century information technology, and population-level outcomes research is accordingly stymied. At a time when patients are typically treated by many different specialists, the lack of comprehensive electronic medical records not only deeply compromises patient safety but also makes it possible for high levels of overtreatment, mistreatment, and undertreatment to go undetected year after year.

What would Osler do with the fact that overtreatment, according to estimates by Dr. Elliott Fisher, kills as many as thirty thousand Medicare recipients annually? How would he process the notion that American cardiologists perform about four hundred thousand heart bypass surgeries and one million angioplasties, even while research suggests few patients who receive such operations benefit from them?[19]

What would he make of treatment fads in the highest orders of established medicine? In the 1990s, tens of thousands of breast cancer patients endured bone marrow transplants and high-dose chemotherapy before "modern" medicine eventually got around to doing clinical trials to see if this painful and expensive treatment works. Turns out it doesn't. What would he make of the fact that one in three women has had a hysterectomy by age sixty and one in two by age sixty-five, even while research indicates that 70 percent of these invasive operations are not needed?[20]

Finally, what would Osler and other Progressive Era reformers make of the fact that affordable health insurance can now only be bought through employers? Through creating high barriers to entry into the medical field, Progressives managed to preserve the financial independence and autonomy of doctors for decades to come, but at great and growing threat to the independent yeomanry they so cherished, whose remaining members now find that their access to health care depends on their taking salaried jobs.

We think it fair to speculate that Osler and other reformers of the Progressive Era would not sit still were they transported to our time and confronted with the actual practices of twenty-first-century American health care. Muckraking journalists and Progressive politicians would be concentrating not on how to provide more Americans with cheaper access to a broken system; they'd be concentrating on the broken system itself; documenting its lack of evidence-based protocols, its inefficiency, its annual death toll in the hundreds of thousands; and campaigning for a thorough reengineering. And Progressive men of science would be throwing themselves into the question of what happened to their vision of a health care system driven by science.

Chronically Ill Yeomen

That's a long, sad story, of course. In short compass, Progressive Era reformers, despite their enthusiasm for rationalization and systematic solutions in other realms, could not bring themselves to apply scientific management to the practice of medicine.

One reason, already discussed, was deference to the yeoman ideal. It was tempting to believe that modern medicine could at once be informed by advancing new fields like biochemistry and remain ultimately in the control of certified, independent, sole practitioners. But another, ultimately more important reason was that Progressive Era reformers could not see clearly enough how the combination of rising rates of chronic disease, increased specialization, high population mobility, and third-party payer systems would conspire to undo the model of health care they worked so hard to build.

The rising prevalence of chronic illness in the population perhaps should have been anticipated by Progressive Era physicians and reformers, but it wasn't, primarily because chronic disease was then so uncommon in comparison to today. In his classic 1901 textbook, *The Principles and Practice of Medicine*, Osler described diabetes as a "rare disease in America" affecting approximately one out of every 380,000 Americans. Today, more than one in twenty Americans is diagnosed with the disease. Osler did not anticipate how the long era to come of effective antibiotics and improved living standards would dramatically lower the mortality of infectious diseases like pneumonia, which Osler described as "The Captain of the Men of Death." Nor could he see how once the Captain of Death had been tamed by antibiotics, this would leave more and more people surviving long enough to develop complicated, chronic conditions like cancer.[21]

The model of medical practice pioneered by Osler and other Progressive Era reformers did not adapt well to the rising prevalence of chronic disease. By its nature, the course of chronic disease is determined overwhelmingly by environmental and lifestyle factors, yet medical practice in the twentieth century wasn't geared for prevention. Chronic disease also requires long-term, often complicated management. Osler described pneumonia as "the friend of the aged," because it quickly carried so many away and thereby relieved them of suffering from other diseases. "Taken off by it in an acute short, not often painful illness, the old man escapes those 'cold gradations of decay' so distressing to himself and his friends."[22] But with the declining prevalence of diseases like pneumonia, doctors were left to treat primarily those "cold gradations of decay," and they were not well prepared to do it.

Independent doctors, in business for themselves, naturally gravitated toward specialization, because it offered the most money. Medicare and other third-party payers offered specialists the highest rates of compensation, in no small measure because different specialists lobbied to make this so. Though it may be hard for the layperson to believe, there are to this day vanishingly few scientific efforts made to evaluate the relative value of different specialties or to discover the effectiveness of the different treatments they provide.

So medical practice has evolved to the point that the typical patient suffering from chronic illness sees many different specialists, both at any given time and over time, with no one doctor having authority over the others or often even any awareness of what the other are doing or have done. "Forgetfulness is such a constant problem in the system," says Donald Berwick of the Institute for Health Care Improvement. "It doesn't remember you. Doesn't remember that you were here and here and then there. It doesn't remember your story."

Are all doctors involved in a patient's care working from the same medical record and making entries that are clearly legible? Do they have some sort of system to make sure they don't collectively wind up prescribing dangerous combinations of drugs? Are any of them prepared to challenge a specialist who tells the patient he needs an operation of dubious medical value? Is any one of them going to take responsibility for coordinating a patient's care so that, for example, he or she doesn't leave the hospital without appropriate follow-up medication and the knowledge of how and when to take it? Just about anyone who's had a serious illness or tried to be an advocate of a sick loved one knows that all too often the answer is no.

Chronic conditions, which are often accompanied by numerous comorbidities such as high blood pressure and cardiovascular disease, require constant monitoring and coordinated care involving dozens of people—specialists, nurses, radiologists, lab workers, physical therapists, counselors. The nature of these chronic diseases also demands that patients become vitally involved in their own care, such as in measuring their own blood sugar levels, and that a system be in place for keeping track of such measurements.

With specialization and the rise of chronic illness, quality in health care thus has become increasingly a question not just of individual doctors and their credentials, but also of systematic coordination among different people involved in a patient's care. Today, all these people are part of a system of care, and when the system lacks cohesion and quality control, as it most often does, many people will be injured, and many will die. Yet medical training since the Progressive Era, while emphasizing scientific understanding of the human body, has almost wholly neglected scientific management of health care.

By the 1980s, American health care had grown so fragmented, chaotic, dangerous, and expensive that many experts proposed "managed care" and the fostering of fully integrated HMOs. Unfortunately, many of the managed care providers that emerged were for-profit institutions that lacked any stake in their patient's long-term health. While they could effectively cut down on unnecessary surgeries and tests, market forces drove many to an opposite evil: undertreatment—or at least so has been the strong perception of most Americans since HMOs have become common.

Which brings us to today. If we are going to be empirical about health care, we have to look at best practices. And best practices today are found in a system that is not just government funded but government operated—specifically, the VA. We acknowledge that this assertion may cause cognitive dissonance for many Americans, but we suggest that, just as in the cusps of other scientific revolutions, such dissonance is evidence of a coming shift in paradigm.

The New Model of Health Care

In his book on the VA and in subsequent writing, Longman offers a blueprint for how the VA model can be made available to a larger share of the population. The potential benefits are enormous. For every American who can be lured from the Medicare Advantage program into the VA, for example, taxpayers will save about one-third while the patient will receive demonstrably higher-quality care.

In broad strokes, reform of the U.S. health care delivery system requires three major initiatives. First is the adoption of universal electronic medical records, which were pioneered by the VA. Fortunately, the information system used by the VA, known as VistA, is available for free to any provider who wants to use it. Written by doctors for doctors, it is a public domain, effectively open-source code. It is supported by a growing global network of idealistic health professionals and computer experts who volunteer their skills to continuously improve it, as well by as an established industry of installation consultants. VistA has been adapted by the public health systems of Norway, Egypt, Jordan, and many hospitals in Mexico.

That very few private U.S. providers have put VistA, or any other electronic medical system to work, is a travesty that can only be explained by the lack of a business case for quality under the current U.S. system. Using VistA, the VA has virtually eliminated dispensing errors, vastly improved diagnosis and disease management, gained tremendous labor efficiency, and improved the science behind clinical practice. The VA was the first to spot the dangers of Vioxx, for example, because the drug's correlation with heart attacks jumped out of its electronic records.

It is not uncommon these days to encounter doctors touting laptops. Unfortunately, they usually are not connected to much of anything. Some 15 to 20 percent of clinicians now use electronic medical records. But patient records are typically locked inside buggy, proprietary software that doesn't communicate to most of the people involved in a patient's care, such as specialists, pharmacists, and labs. By contrast, when a VA doctor opens a laptop, he or she has access to his patient's complete medical records going back to the mid-1980s as well as real-time vital signs that can travel over a modem from the patient's home.

If you visit a VA hospital, you'll see a ritual that demonstrates another virtue of truly integrated health information technology: patient safety. When VA doctors enter their orders into their laptops, the computer system immediately checks the patient's records. If the doctors working with a patient have prescribed an inappropriate combination of medicines or overlooked the patient's previous allergic reaction to a drug, the computer sends up a red flag and prevents the doctor from continuing until the concern is acknowledged. Later, when hospital pharmacists fill those prescriptions, the computer system generates a bar code that goes on the bottle or intravenous bag. This bar code registers what the medicine is, whom it is for, when it should be administered, in what dose, and by whom.

Meanwhile, each patient and nurse has an ID bracelet with a bar code. Before administering any drug, nurses must first scan the patient's ID bracelet, then their own, and then the bar code on the medicine. If the nurse has the wrong patient or the wrong medicine, the computer will provide a warning. The computer will also create a report if a nurse is late in administering a dose.

Outside the VA, such full integration of information technology into the practice of medicine is virtually unheard of, and the results are deadly. The federal government should adopt a policy that it will not make Medicare or other payments to providers who do not adopt VistA or install a fully compatible, open-source equivalent. Not until then will we begin to cut down the horrific rates of medical errors or begin building the population-level outcomes databases necessary to establish truly scientific, evidence-based protocols of care.

The Federal Reserve of Medicine

The second essential feature of any meaningful reform of our health care system is the creation of an independent body to study and pronounce upon the comparative effectiveness of different drugs, devices, and procedures. Today, the federal government spends some $29 billion a year on the National Institutes of Health. Virtually all of that money goes to study molecular-level aspects of human body; almost none goes to develop scientific evidence about which medical practices work better than others. Nor is that vital research being done by anyone else in the United States on the scale needed. The Food and Drug Administration generally requires only minimal testing of medical devices. In its testing of drugs, it relies on industry-funded clinical drug trials that generally compare new drugs to placebos, not to similar drugs to see which ones work better. The tiny Agency for Healthcare Research and Quality struggles on but is deeply vulnerable to political interference, as when it concluded that there was little evidence to support surgery as a first-line treatment for lower back pain. It was rewarded with a lobbying campaign by back surgeons that nearly zeroed out its budget.[23]

Before becoming Obama's pick to head the department of Health and Human Services, former Senate majority leader Tom Daschle joined the growing chorus calling for something like a Federal Reserve of Medicine, which would study the comparative effectiveness of different medical practices and be largely insulated from political manipulation. In his book, *Critical: What We Can Do about the Health-Care Crisis*, Daschle quotes a young surgeon, whose description of a medical "teaching conference" succinctly illustrates why such an institution is needed:

Ads for cool new things you had never heard of—a tissue-stapling device that staples without staples, a fiber-optic scope that lets you see in three dimensions—ran night and day on my hotel room television and even on the shuttle bus to and from the convention center. Drug and medical device companies offered invitations to

free dinners around town nightly. and there were over five thousand three hundred salespeople from some twelve hundred companies registered in attendance here—more than one for every two
surgeons.[24]

If medical practice in the United States is driven by science, what
is the need for giant contending forces of sales reps inserted into the
process? Why do drug companies find it worth their while to shower
doctors with free meals, paid speaking engagements, and visits by
comely pill "detailers"? Why can they boost profits through inventing
expensive drugs like Zantac to treat minor conditions like heartburn,
which most people can control perfectly well through the tried and true
"plop, plop, fizz, fizz" method?[25]

The corruption of medical science through sponsored research, lobbying, promotions, and advertising would most likely break the hearts
of the original Progressives. It would offend their faith in science and
deepen their distrust of corporate power. The waste in overtreatment
and mistreatment would offend their believe in thrift. And the resulting lack of affordable health care they would see as a deep and unacceptable threat to the yeoman ideal of financial independence. For all
these reasons, their most likely first response to America's current health
care mess wouldn't be to tinker with expanded or more deeply subsidized insurance coverage, but to create a new institution to set medical
standards that would be as powerful, independent, and effective as that
other great product of the Progressive Era: the Federal Reserve.

A Federal Reserve of Medicine could be funded by a dedicated tax
on pharmaceutical companies and medical device makers. It would
sponsor independent research into the effectiveness of different medical practices, using clinical trials but also, and probably more effectively, by surveying the population-level outcomes data created by
universal, privacy-protected electronic medical records. The creation
of truly evidence-driven protocols of care has the potential to cut American health care spending by a third while also improving its quality, just
by reducing overtreatment. Truly scientific standards in medicine could
also help reduce malpractice suits and the defensive, paranoid style of
medicine they create. They could also empower consumers to make

rational choices on the treatments they seek, as opposed to relying on Google searches, hearsay, and mere intuition about which doctors and medical institutions deserve their reputations.

Many other countries provide models for how a Federal Reserve of Medicine should work, such as Great Britain's National Institute for Health and Clinical Excellence, which provides guidance on the use of new and existing drugs, treatments, and devices. Of course, establishing such an institution means taking on the drug lobby, which spends more on lobbying than any other industry in America, but it must be done.

Health for Life

Our final suggestion for reforming the health care delivery system is one that the original Progressives would also probably like, because it involves a direct, hands-on engineering approach. In just about every major city in America, there are assorted St. Elsewheres—that is, big public hospitals, many of them built during the Progressive Era, that are going broke due to the cost of uncompensated care and other factors. Today, for example, Prince George's County outside Washington, DC, is in danger of losing its three hospitals due largely to their high volume of uninsured patients. Half of New Jersey's eighty-two hospitals run deficits, and the state is intent on closing most of them. For the past eight years, New York State's hospitals as a group have lost money, and under a terms of a special "hospital closure" commission, as many as a quarter will soon be gone.

Let's put ourselves in the shoes of people who work for or depend on one of these financially imperiled hospitals. Of course, everyone involved wants the highest quality. They'd like to install an electronic medical record system, improve prevention, and manage chronic illness effectively. It's what all the smart people in medicine say is the right thing to do these days—at least the ones without MBAs. The businesspeople point out that there is no way of recapturing the necessary investment because the hospital is paid (when it is paid) for treating patients rather than keeping or making them well. By the time any benefits from prevention show up, patients will have long since moved on to another health plan.

Meanwhile, suburban specialty hospitals are luring away many of public hospitals' most lucrative customers, such as cardiac or cancer patients. At the same time, there is ever more pressure from insurers, larger employers, and increasingly patients themselves to hold down prices. Many of the old-line manufacturing companies in the surrounding community will either have to get control of their health care spending or go out of business. Moreover, every year there are more uninsured patients, who may soon be joined by the hospital's own employees if they have to be laid off. Nobody involved—not local politicians, local businesses, or the folks in the neighborhood who depend on the hospital—wants that.

So here is our suggestion. Take these failing hospitals and make them the foundation for what would in effect be a civilian VA. For purposes of discussion, let's imagine that this new network takes the name VistA Health Care, because it has been inspired by VA's best-in-class VistA electronic medical record system and the high-quality model of care that it makes possible. The slogan for the VistA Heath Care Network could well be "Health for Life." That's because its prime, long-term objective would be to offer Americans who want it continuous and integrated lifetime care similar to that enjoyed by patients in the veterans health care system.

Governance of the VistA network would be in the form of a board appointed by the president, not subject to Senate confirmation, and serving staggered terms—in effect, a Federal Reserve of Medicine, as describe earlier. The board's first task would be to approach various public hospitals around the country that faced large loads of uninsured patients, and offer them a deal.

The board would ask various St. Elsewheres to install the VA's VistA health information management software and to agree to adhere to the performance measures and protocols of evidence-based medicine used by the VA itself (until we get the science to improve upon them). In exchange, the hospitals would get a contract to care for a guaranteed pool of people. Initially, this pool might be composed of people who have been mandated to buy health insurance, as has been done already in Massachusetts. It could also include the Medicaid population. Rates would include, in the jargon of today's health care policy debates, "pay for performance"; specifically, participating providers would be paid not according to individual treatments performed but according to how well they preserved and promoted the health of the people in their care.

Joining the VistA network would offer today's failing hospitals a lifeline. Yes, the hospitals that take VistA's offer would have to radically change the way they do business. They'd have to join the twenty-first century and learn to use electronic medical records, which the vast majority of providers currently do not rely on. They'd also have to shed acute care beds and specialists and invest in more outpatient clinics—in which, for example, diabetics could learn how to manage their disease, or people with high blood pressure could join smoking cessation programs. Doctors who work for these hospitals would no longer be constantly visited by pill salespersons, because decisions on what prescription drugs to use would be made on a scientific basis by the VistA board, and because the VistA network, like the VA, would negotiate as an institution to obtain the best prices from drug companies.

These and other changes would ruffle many feathers. But accepting the VistA deal means a failing hospital wouldn't have to close. Instead, the local community could take pride in having preserved an institution that not only serves the needy but offers them high-quality, high-value health care as well. As long as the hospital demonstrably adhered to the VA's model of care, local politicians could continue to use it as a source of patronage, while local restaurants, stores, and real estate agents could continue to live off the income its employees spread through the community.

Now, let's put ourselves in the shoes of those who would be the customers of the new VistA system. One segment would be lower-income people, who, for the most part, are already frequenting various St. Elsewheres for their health care needs. For them, the transition to the new system would be easy and, indeed, welcome. They'd be going mostly to the same hospitals and clinics they're used to. But they would be able to get preventive care, like regular doctor checkups, as well as acute care, and not be hit with impossible-to-pay bills that could force them into bankruptcy.

A second segment of VistA customers would be people—mostly young—who currently lack insurance because they're students or work for companies that don't offer it, or because they're healthy enough to feel that they don't need it. These people might not like being forced to buy insurance. But given that they'd have to under an individual mandate, they'd likely see the VistA network as an attractive option because of its low cost and its nationwide presence, which would mean they wouldn't have to change health care plans when they move. Younger people, too, are more likely than their parents and grandparents to recognize the benefits of electronic medical records and the evidence-based care they make possible. Moreover, if the "default" setting for people subject to an individual mandate to purchase health insurance is that they are automatically enrolled in VistA with the chance to opt out, that greatest force in the universe—inertia—will leave VistA not lacking for customers.

In the short term, this new VistA system would offer acceptable care to every American who currently lacks health insurance—a better deal than they're getting now. Over time, as the reforms imposed on the participating hospitals and clinics began to take effect, the quality of that health care would improve, and, as word spreads, VistA's popularity should increase even more. (Remember, the VA has the highest rate of patient satisfaction of any health care provider in the United States.)

For all this to work, VistA would need to have what the VA already enjoys: a lifetime relationship with the bulk of its patients, so that its financial incentives were in line with its patients' health needs. This could happen with a relatively modest legal fix: any person in the VistA system who gets a job with health insurance should be allowed to direct his or her company to pay premiums to the VistA system if that person wants to remain in the system. And, presuming the system worked well, most people would want to stay in it, given its national reach and the strong desire most of us have not to have to constantly change doctors and health plans.

Finally, let's put ourselves in the shoes of Beltway politicians. By the time you read this, they're probably going to have to decide which—if any—of the proposals for universal health care building momentum in the country they're willing to support. The VistA plan offers several politically comforting advantages.

First, unlike the 1993 Clinton health care plan, the VistA proposal does not directly take on the medical-industrial complex. It would not require any changes to the private insurance market, for instance, or place any costly mandates on employers. At least in the short term, VistA would be focused on customers who aren't now part of the private health insurance market.

Second, VistA should garner a wider array of political allies. Many private hospitals and doctors are likely to welcome the program, because it would relieve them of the burden of having to provide uncompensated care to the uninsured. Doctors working within the VistA system would also be free of the hassle of having to file claims to third-party payers and, as in the case of VA doctors, would not bear the burden of paying for medical malpractice insurance. Almost any universal health care proposal could hope to attract these kinds of allies—but VistA would rally an additional set. Every lawmaker who has a costly or failing public hospital in his or her district (and most do) will have a built-in constituency of local politicians, newspapers, medical professionals, and community activists who will see VistA as the best way to save their local institution.

The third political advantage is price. If VistA worked like the VA, it would almost certainly be the lowest-cost route to decent health care for all the uninsured. High-quality health care is also low-cost health care, especially over the long term, as the effects of prevention and evidence-based medicine pay off. Precise costs are difficult to calculate because of differences in the populations served, but remember, for every patient who transfers from Medicare Advantage to the VA, taxpayers save about one-third, while the patient, on average, gets much higher-quality care.

Besides employing the VA's cost control strategy, VistA would have other means of limiting its cost to taxpayers. Much of the money to pay for the VistA system would come from people who currently don't have insurance but who, because of the individual mandate, would have to pay at least something up front to defray the cost of their care. What subsidies the VistA system would require would also be largely offset by the forty-some billion dollars in federal, state, and local government spending that goes to treat the uninsured under the current highly inefficient, ad hoc system. Nor would creating a VistA Health Care Network require the government to incur huge capital costs or long-term debt. Though the network would have to build some of its own hospitals and clinics in certain underserved locations, most VistA-affiliated facilities would remain owned and operated by the private interests, charity organizations, and local governments that currently run them. VistA's role in these hospitals and clinics would be analogous to that of a franchiser: setting and enforcing standards, and achieving economies of scale in technology, purchasing, information management, and marketing.

By building on a system that already exists, then, the VistA plan would be the least costly and, initially, the least disruptive way to provide health care for the uninsured (and high-quality care, at that). But that doesn't mean conservatives and health care lobbyists won't go after VistA. They will. For while VistA would not, in the short run, pose a challenge to the private sector health care market, in the long run it's a different story.

Again, the VA experience is instructive. Thanks to quality improvements, many veterans not currently qualified for VA health care benefits are demanding access to VA hospitals. Among the American Legion's top legislative priorities is to allow veterans on Medicare to be able to receive their treatment at the VA.

Similarly, imagine that VistA is put into place and works as advertised. Over time, word gets out that the quality of treatment in VistA is pretty good—indeed, better than what most people with employer-provided health care receive. Pretty soon, persons who are not eligible for VistA start clamoring for the right to buy into the system. And employers, realizing that VistA is doing a better job of controlling costs than their own private sector health providers, start pressuring Washington for permission to contract with VistA to provide health care for their employees.

If this kind of competition were allowed to happen, private health care companies would either lose customers to VistA or be forced to find ways to curb overtreatment, reduce medical errors, and generally provide better, more cost-efficient care. Either way, the competition would lead to dramatic improvements in American health care. Just as the existence of state universities puts competitive pressure on private universities to pursue excellence, the existence of the VistA network would force the rest of the health care system to try matching it on quality and value.

Conservatives and health care lobbyists can be expected, of course, to denounce anyone who supports the VistA plan as advocates of "socialized medicine." They would do the same to any serious attempt to provide universal health care. The difference is that with VistA, it may be harder to make that case stick in the public mind.

After all, the model for VistA comes not from Canada or France, but from the U.S. military. Is the health care system we provide our troops really "socialism"? Also, the competition that the industry is worried about will happen—if it happens—down the road, only if VistA turns out to be a big success, and only if elected officials later decide to open up the system. The VistA program that today's politicians would be voting on would not alter the health care most Americans have—and this is a major political advantage.

In reality, "socialized medicine" is not the phrase to use when describing the VistA system. Nor is "single payer." The plan would expand the role of government in health care and achieve universal access, but no one would be compelled by law to join the VistA network, just as no one is compelled to receive treatment at the VA. In replicating the best features of the VA, VistA might offer the best care anywhere, but its existence would not erode our all-American right to make bad choices in health care.

Yes, there is a solution to the health care crisis. It starts with the comparatively limited step of creating a high-quality health care delivery system for the uninsured, as opposed to simply throwing more money in their direction or mounting an all-at-once overhaul of the entire health care sector. It ends with future generations of Americans wondering why we took so long to open our hearts and our minds and create the VistA "Health for Life" network.

CHAPTER 9

America in Motion

I T IS THE LEADING cause of accidental death in America and the most likely way to die young. It's also contributes mightily to America's epidemic of obesity and other chronic illness.

It's the major factor driving up the cost and depleting the supply of energy. It's also deeply implicated in climate change, the mortgage meltdown, and rising food prices.

It's a major reason why the poor cannot find jobs and why parents struggle to find time for their children and each other, except while driving. It's also the single biggest determinant of where we live, where we travel, go to school, and how much we must pay to do so.

It drives the course of economic development and has repeatedly redrawn the very landscape of American life, from cities to suburbia to exurbia. In all its different modes, it once provided Americans with so much mobility, both spatially and up the income chain, that people around the world strongly associated it with the promise of American life, but no longer. Instead, its crumbling infrastructure, strained capacity, inefficiency, and oversized carbon footprint have turned it into a global symbol of American profligacy and neglect of the future.

You might think that any "it" at the center of all this would be also be at the center of the nation's political and policy debates, but it isn't. To be sure, around kitchen tables, in boardrooms, barrooms, and waiting rooms, its day-to-day failures and imposed miseries are a constant subject of complaint, but rarely does it come up in national politics. In the last presidential campaign, neither Barack Obama nor John McCain even included a mention of it on their websites' lists of major issues facing the country. Every administration since Lyndon Johnson's has had a cabinet secretary who is supposed to be in charge of it, but most Americans would be hard-pressed to name a single person who has ever held the post.

In case you haven't guessed, we are referring to America's broken transportation system. As with health care, speaking of it as a "system" in some ways gives it more credit than it deserves, since it is in reality highly fragmented, poorly planned, and in many places literally falling apart. As with health care, too, its crisis has been long in the making and long denied. Yet a system in crisis it is, and one that causes or exacerbates nearly every other major challenge America faces, from the toll on family life created by long and stressful commutes, to the financing of terrorism by Middle Eastern petrodollars, to the meltdown of the financial sector caused by depreciating real estate in auto-dependent suburbs. Fortunately, at a time when consumer-driven growth in the economy has tapped out and unemployment is rising, fixing our broken transportation system offers many ways to put Americans back to work, save energy, increase logistical efficiency, and start building again for the future.

The Missing Issue

Conveying this truth is not easy because of ingrained habits of thought. The last presidential campaign, for example, featured an extended debate over whether offshore oil drilling is a better solution to the energy crisis than investment in alternative energy sources and higher auto fuel efficiency standards. There was also full recognition by both candidates of the need to reduce greenhouse gas emissions by some means or another. Yet absent throughout the campaign was any consideration of how the structure of the U.S. transportation system itself—its overreliance on energy-inefficient long-distance trucking, for example, or its failure to provide the majority of Americans with viable options to driving—is the single-greatest contributor to America's energy dependence and emission of greenhouse gasses.

According to the Environmental Protection Agency, transportation now produces nearly 30 percent of all greenhouse gas emissions in the

United States, and it is by far the fastest-growing source of the pollu-
tants implicated in global warming, surging at nearly double the rate of
all other sources.

Shortly before taking office, President-elect Obama pledged to
spend as much as $1 trillion on infrastructure to jump-start the econ-
omy and make up for past neglect, an outlay that Obama himself charac-
terizes as "the single largest new investment in our national infrastructure
since the creation of the federal highway system in the 1950s." We'll
soon be moving earth again like it's 1959. Yet almost all the talk out of
the Obama camp and Congress has been about spending for roads and
highway bridges, projects made necessary in large measure by America's
overreliance on pavement-smashing, traffic-snarling, fossil-fuel-guzzling
trucks for the bulk of its domestic freight transport.

This could be an epic mistake. Just as the Interstate Highway System changed, for better and for worse, the economy and the landscape
of America, so, too, will the investment decisions Washington is making now. The choice of infrastructure projects is *de facto* industrial policy; it's also *de facto* energy, land use, housing, and environmental
policy, with implications for nearly every aspect of American life going
far into the future. On the doorstep of an era of infrastructure spending unparalleled in the past half-century, we need to conceive of a transportation future in which each mode of transport is put to its most
sensible use, deployed collaboratively instead of competitively.

Thinking and writing clearly about transportation is difficult
because of rapid changes in how its different modes (walking, autos,
planes, trains, etc.) affect the lives of differently situated Americans. For
example, in the 1960s and early 1970s, inner-city residents revolted, in
some places violently, against the further bulldozing of their neighborhoods to make way for freeways. In the aftermath of the 1967 Newark
riots, LBJ adviser Daniel Patrick Moynihan received a letter from several of the city's residents that read, in part, "They are tearing down
our homes and building up medical colleges and motor clubs and parking lots and we need decent private homes to live in. They are tearing
down our best schools and churches to build a highway. We are over
here in provity [*sic*] and bondage. There are [*sic*] supposed to be justice for all. Where [*sic*] are that justice?"[2]

Urban highway building became for many a civil rights issue, and mass transit a liberal gesture toward Americans "trapped" in the cities and too poor to own cars. Highways, meanwhile, were seen by nearly all to be broad boulevards of upward mobility, allowing the middle class to grow and flourish across the expanding frontiers of suburbia. Yet today, many inner-city neighborhoods that weren't destroyed by freeways have become gentrified and graced by shiny new light rail systems that whisk upscale riders to work and play.

In metro areas served by well-functioning commuter rail lines, such as New York, Chicago, or Washington, DC, property values rise step by step as one walks nearer to a transit station, and they have held up quite well since the housing slump began. By contrast, it is in far flung, auto-dependent suburbs and edge cities where the pain of high gas prices, traffic congestion, falling home prices, and foreclosure are most felt. Except for some cities in deep industrial decline, such as East Cleveland or Detroit, the hardest-hit areas are sprawling places like Stockton, California, suburban Las Vegas, and central and south Florida, where traffic is hellish, mass transit is rare, and the price of gas is a major component of the cost of living.

In recent years, the combined cost of housing and transportation in outer-ring suburbs has become far higher as a percentage of family income than in denser areas. In transit-rich neighborhoods, families paid an average of 41 percent of their income for transportation and housing in 2007. In auto-dependent suburbs, the combined cost was 57 percent, due to the cost of energy.[3] If one counts the value of time stuck in traffic, the contrast in value is even more extreme, as is reflected in comparative property values.

For example, transit-rich Portland, Oregon, and sprawling Las Vegas started out this decade with nearly identical housing prices. Both experienced a bubble. But in the year ending June 2008, Las Vegas saw its home prices fall by 29 percent, while Portland suffered only a 6 percent decline, leaving home values substantially higher in Portland.[4] The sprawling, auto-dependent, outer reaches of suburbia now face a crisis that affects the whole country, including its financial system, and that can only be solved by the availability of better transportation choices.

Is it possible to look at America's transportation system with fresh eyes? That is the ambition of this chapter and the next two. We'll begin by going back to the first Progressive Era, when both "automobility," as it was then called, and aviation were brand new, and when all modes of transportation were undergoing extraordinary technological change. To take such as journey is to see how little is inevitable about current patterns of transportation and land use, and to realize how much they are the product of misguided regulation, interest group politics, hidden subsidy, and the law of unintended consequences. Surveying the current American landscape dominated by auto traffic and sprawling single-use development, libertarians pronounce that it is the preference of the American people as revealed by "the market." Knowing even a little of the history of American transportation since the Progressive Era reveals the absurdity of this claim.

The People's Lawyer

The lead story out of the nation's capital on November 25, 1910, would not come from President Taft or Congress but from a packed administrative courtroom. Today, the Interstate Commerce Commission is defunct, but at the time it was an institution with the unilateral power to enrich or ruin whole industries and to control the very course of the American economy. And on this day, its seven commissioners would hear what was arguably its most important and far-reaching case.

The atmosphere was solemn and judicious. "The Interstate Commerce Commission is surrounded by a reserve which is part of any court room," the *New York Post* reported. "Even the entry of the commissioners is impressive." The *Washington Post* supplied details for its inquiring readers even as to the order by which the commissions took their places at the bar. "Promptly at 10:00 o'clock," the paper noted,

> the door leading from an anteroom to the bench opened and the
> various members filed in. Harlan, whose seat was farthest from the
> door, came first, followed his associates in order named: Lane,
> Prouty, Knapp, Clements, Cockrell and Clark. As soon as Com-
> missioner Harlan appeared through the open door, everybody

down in the courtroom arose and remained standing until first Chairman Knapp and then the other commissioners were seated.[5]

Adding to the tension and drama in the courtroom that day was the presence of Louis D. Brandeis, the legendary "people's lawyer" of the era, whose future on the U.S. Supreme Court was secured in no small measure by the renown he would earn from his performance in this case. Today, the subject of Brandeis's inspired arguments might at first seem quotidian. Early in 1910, the eastern railroads of the United States had petitioned the ICC to grant them a 10 percent across-the-board increase in freight rates. Shipping interests had hired Brandeis to oppose the petition with whatever arguments his precocious, Harvard-trained mind could concoct. But far more was at stake in this dispute than just a tedious question of setting railroad tariffs.

Steel Wheel

It is impossible to comprehend how today's transportation system became so broken and out of balance without understanding the ruinous regulation railroads faced, beginning in the Progressive Era and especially afterward, from the ICC and other state-level regulatory bodies. The typical American today might believe that railroads declined simply because new modes of transportation made them obsolete. What this view misses is a world that might have been, and that many Progressives hoped would be, in which railways, trucks, and autos became part of an integrated, balanced system that took the best of what each had to offer in different applications and combined them into a true system of transport.

At the beginning of the twentieth century, a "Good Roads" movement emerged—initially led by bicyclists and later farmers—calling for more paved roadways. Railroads were strong supporters. The Pennsylvania Railroad, as well as the Southern and Illinois Central, for example, ran so-called object lesson trains into small towns along their routes. These carried the men and materials needed to pave a short stretch of local roadway just so the locals could see the possibilities. In 1901, the Southern railway sponsored such a cavalcade, emblazoning each car with large letters reading "Southern Railway Good Roads Train." U.S. senator J. W. Daniel, on hand to welcome the train's visit to Lynchburg, Virginia, described it enthusiastically as "an itinerant college on wheels."[6]

Railroads reasoned, logically enough, that with more paved roads, more people and goods could travel from greater distances to reach their lines. Farmers wouldn't get stuck in the mud trying to move their crops to market but could use newly available trucks traveling on all-weather macadam highways to reach rail heads. Since 1885, the railroads had been hauling farmers' wagons on flat cars. Why not trucks, too?

It's a vision of intermodel transport that makes perfect sense so long as one concentrates simply on the physics involved and not the politics. Railroads' essential technology, steel wheels rolling on steel rails, has one huge and enduring advantage over all other forms of land transportation. Steel wheels on steel rails meet with very little rolling resistance. If you have ever tried to push a car along a flat surface, you know what rolling resistance is and how much energy it takes to overcome it with a rubber-wheeled vehicle. By contrast, pushing a car equipped with steel wheels along a flat railroad track is a breeze, requiring about one-tenth the energy. The steel wheels don't compress and absorb energy from the surface the way a tire does, and the rail itself is much smoother than any road.

In addition, because of the way the rails absorb and spread the weight of a vehicle over long distances, railroads have another important energy advantage. When their loads increase in weight, so does their rolling resistance but by a much lower percentage than when the same weight is carried by a truck or car. The more you load up trains, the more efficient they become compared to other modes.

The Environmental Protection Agency calculates that for distances of more than one thousand miles, a system in which trucks haul containers only as far as the nearest railhead and then transfer them to a train produces a 65 percent reduction in both fuel use and greenhouse gas emissions. As the volume of freight is expected to increase by 57 percent between 2000 and 2020, the potential economic and environmental benefits of such an intermodal system will go higher and higher.[7] Railroads are also potentially very labor-efficient. Even in the days of the object lesson train, when brakes had to be set manually and firefighters were needed to stoke steam engines, a five-person crew could easily handle a fifty-car freight train, doing the work of ten times as many modern long-haul truckers.

So when the first automobiles and trucks came along at the dawn of the twentieth century, it made perfect sense that railroads wouldn't see them as a threat. Railroads faced many problems in their ownership, being frequently manipulated and mismanaged by Wall Street tycoons. They also had to contend with tough labor relations, and their inability to fend off the growing combination of interests that became the auto-highway complex would prove disastrous.

But as a matter of purely rational use of technology, the relationship between train, trucks, and autos should have been synergistic rather than competitive. Railroads couldn't go everywhere, so it made sense to use trucks and autos for short hauls or in areas where the density of population was very low. Even after cars and trucks themselves became far more powerful, reliable, and sophisticated, they could not begin to match the energy efficiency inherent in steel wheel technology, and they still can't today. In 2007, American railroads used only one gallon of fuel to move a ton of freight 436 miles.[8]

Because of their inherent efficiencies in energy and labor, it makes little sense for trucks to haul freight for distances of more than a few hundred miles, especially now that the use of containerized freight makes its easy and cheap to lift cargos from trucks to trains and vice versa. Yet you have only to get out on the interstate to know that they are crammed with trucks, many of them hauling clear across the country and returning empty. The only way to understand why this is so is to return to the Progressive Era and see how the unintended consequences of decisions made then led to extreme imbalances in transportation and, by extension, self-defeating patterns of land development.

Robbing the Future

During the early years of the twentieth century, the railroads' inability to price their products rationally led to a crisis from which the industry never fully recovered. If you want to know what will happen to our current transportation so long as users are shielded from the real cost of using it, and so long as it continues to receive insufficient capital to keep up with depreciation and increased demand, just examine the plight of the railroad industry one hundred years ago.

The proximate cause of what became known as the "railroad problem" was an economic phenomenon that had not been seen in living memory: inflation. Estimates by the U.S. Department of Labor showed a general rise in prices of 44 percent from 1897 to 1907.[9] In 1909, the New York Academy of Political Science asked C. C. McCain, a man with considerable experience as both a former ICC auditor and as a railroad association executive, to conduct a study of how inflation was affecting railroad finance. Published in *Political Science Quarterly*, McCain's research left little doubt that the carriers were headed for big trouble if the trend continued.

McCain found that over the decade ending in 1907, the cost of all major railroad industry inputs had risen sharply. The cost of coal for steam engines, for example, surged by as much as 66 percent as measured in tons used per mile. The cost of the industry's largest input, labor, also rose substantially. Meanwhile, as long-term interest rates rose in response to inflation, railroads—one of the world's most capital-intensive industries—were forced to pay more in interest charges as they rolled over their old debts and took on new ones.

Yet railroads, unlike their customers, had no means of passing on their increasing costs. Instead, the ICC, through its continuing findings in favor of plaintiffs in tariff disputes, forced a drop in average rates even as the dollar continued to depreciate. The result was that real railroad rates, after falling slowly since the 1870s, began a steep and dramatic decline after 1897. Within just ten years' time, real rates per passenger-mile fell by more than one-fifth, and the average price of moving a ton of freight one mile dropped in real terms by 24 percent.

The squeeze on railroad operating margins was made all the more ominous by the huge capital investment railroads were forced to make during this period to accommodate their surging traffic. Between 1894 and 1909, the number of ton-miles of freight carried by American railroads grew by an unprecedented 172 percent.[10] This growth in demand in no small measure reflected the artificially low cost of rail transport, just as low-cost oil in the 1990s caused staggering increases in auto, truck, and airline trips per person.

Railroads struggled mightily to meet the challenge. The number of miles of track added to existing routes increased by 95 percent over the period; the number of freight cars in operation, by 72 percent. Trains became dramatically heavier, longer, and more frequent on most lines. The number of ton-miles of freight moved per mile of line, for example, grew from 457,252 to 953,986, an increase of 109 percent.[11]

Exploiting the advantages of steel wheel technology, railroads also began to provide services we tend to think of as modern or in some cases even futuristic. The Pacific Fruit Growers Express delivered fresh California fruits and vegetables to the East Coast using far less energy and labor than today's truck fleets. The rhythmically named Chicago Milwaukee, St. Paul, and Pacific (aka Milwaukee Road) hauled hundred-car freight trains over the Cascade and Rockie mountains using electric engines drawing on the region's abundant hydropower. The Railway Express Agency (REA), which attached special cars to passenger trains, provided Americans with a level of express freight service that cannot be had for any price today, offering door-to-door delivery of everything from canoes to bowls of tropical fish to, in at least one instance, a giraffe. By the 1920s, it was not uncommon for a family to ship its refrigerator to and from a lakeside cabin for the summer via the REA; thanks to the physics of steel-on-steel conveyance, appliance-sized items could be moved for trivially larger amounts of money than smaller goods (think about that next time you shell out an extra $50 to check a suitcase of dirty clothes on a domestic flight).

High-speed Railway Post Office trains also offered efficient mail service to even the smallest towns that is not matched today. In his book *Train Time*, Harvard historian and rail expert John R. Stilgoe describes the Pennsylvania Railroad's Fast Mail train No. 11, which, because of its speed and on-board crew of fast-sorting mail clerks, ensured next-day delivery on a letter mailed with a standard two-cent stamp in New York to points as far west as Chicago. Today, that same letter is likely to travel by air first to FedEx's Memphis hub, then be unloaded, sorted, and reloaded onto another plane, a process that demands far greater expenditures of money, carbon, fuel, and, in many instances, even time than the one used eighty years ago.[12]

The glory days of American railroads are now beyond the memory of most Americans. Rail service was already in decline during the Depression, and the gas rationing and logistical strains of World War II made train travel a standing-room-only horror. In large part because of that generational experience, most Americans came to believe the decline of railroads was an inevitable part of the march of progress. But the reality is close to the opposite. Especially for long-haul freight, steel wheel on steel rail is a far superior technology, and its eclipse by rubber wheels is mostly the result of special interest politics, ill-considered public policies, and other factors that have nothing to do with efficiency.

The Masterstroke

Early on Monday morning, November 21, 1910, Brandeis introduced the nation to a phrase he had coined himself a few nights before: "scientific management."[13] What it meant, exactly, would never be defined, but the claims Brandeis made on its behalf were bold indeed. "Roads Could Save $1,000,000 a Day," exclaimed the headline in the next day's *New York Times*. "Brandeis Says Scientific Management Would Do It—Calls Rate Increases Unnecessary."

In his brief, Brandeis readily conceded that the railroads needed more money. But in a masterstroke, he insisted that the proper source was not higher rates from shippers but greater productivity from railroads. "As an alternative to the practice of combining to raise rates and hence to increase prices," Brandeis informed the commissioners, "we offer cooperation to reduce costs and hence lower prices. This can be done through the introduction of scientific management, resulting in greater efficiency and greater economy."[14]

The idea for this argument had come from one of Brandeis's previous clients, a shoe manufacturer who had achieved considerable increases in efficiency by adopting the ideas of a then-little-known industrial engineer named Frederick W. Taylor. Today, the extensive hagiography depicting Taylor as the "father of scientific management" is attributable largely to the national attention Brandeis brought to Taylor's ideas during the Advance Rate Case.

Taylor, along with other "efficiency experts" Brandeis assembled, enthralled the court with tales of how huge savings could be achieved through the application of "time and motion" studies and other trendy management techniques of the day. The court, for example, heard from Horace K. Hathaway, plant manager of Tabor Manufacturing Company, a Philadelphia maker of machinery, who told of being able to cut his labor force by 40 percent through studying the repetitive motion of men at their machines. Similar anecdotes were shared by representatives of the Link Belt Company, a manufacturer of industrial products, and Brighton Mills, a maker of cotton duck.

The only example of scientific management applied to the railroad industry came from Harrington Emerson, a consulting engineer who boasted of dramatically improved efficiency at a Santa Fe Railway locomotive shop under his supervision. Responding to Brandeis's questioning, Emerson observed that labor was always 5 percent inefficient under normal circumstances. Based on this assumption, Emerson went on to make the spectacular claim that railroads could save "a million dollars a day" through the application of "scientific management."[15] Curiously, it did not occur to any of the railroads' counsel to refute this sensational claim with the truth of arithmetic that a $1,000,000-a-day savings derived from a 5 percent gain in efficiency implies a total rail labor bill at the time of over $7.3 billion—a preposterous number.

The railroad men were taken completely by surprise. Soon shock turned to anger as they noted the keen interest by the commissioners and the country as a whole. The papers loved it. A typical reaction came from the *Philadelphia North American*, which not only embraced Brandeis's use of "scientific efficiency" to bash the hated railroads but applauded the publicity he gave to the idea.

> Without designing it, and against their wills, the railroads did a great public service when they combined to advance rates on merchandise. For they set the stage for the introduction of scientific efficiency to the public. Whether the railroads win, or whether the shippers succeed in defeating the combination to impose additional taxes on the business world, this rate case will be memorable for its vast educational value. Scientific efficiency has been thrust into national notice, tied to a subject of recognized national importance. It has within the space of a few weeks attained a publicity that might have taken years to achieve in the ordinary course of events.[16]

It would not take long for Brandeis's claims to be revealed as mostly pseudoscience. The most devastating critique came from Harvard economist William J. Cunningham, who in a study published in the *Quarterly Journal of Economics* demolished most of the testimony Brandeis had presented in court. Cunningham uncovered the fact, for example, that the efficiency gains Emerson claimed to have achieved in his Santa Fe locomotive shop were mostly attributable to the end of a long and bitter strike during which the shop had been run by inexperienced replacement workers. More fundamentally, Cunningham pointed out that most of the time and motion studies developed by Taylor and his followers, while perhaps useful in a manufacturing setting, had little application to the nature of most work on the railroads.

Given these obstacles, the steep efficiency gains the industry did achieve during the first decade of the twentieth century—mostly with improved locomotive technology—were truly remarkable. But such gains were not sustainable in the face of perpetual declines in real freight rates—a trend that accelerated after 1910 as the inflation rate mounted. Even Charles Adams, the intellectual father of the ICC, was appalled at the implications for the future: "The situation is unbusinesslike, illogical, and absurd as well as impossible," an elderly Adams warned in 1914. "The railroad candle has for some time been burned at both ends."[17]

By the middle teens, the financial condition of many major systems had become desperate. By 1916, more than thirty-seven thousand miles of line, nearly one-sixth of the national total, were being operated by receivers or trustees—this at a time when railroads still faced little or no competition from trucks and automobiles.[18] Railroad service deteriorated dramatically as cash-strapped railroads struggled to keep up with a continuing buildup in traffic volume. As former president Taft, in a Washington's Birthday address at Johns Hopkins University, at last confessed, "The inadequacy of our railroad system is startling. We have had many warnings from railroad men as to what would occur [and] . . . their warnings are now being vindicated.[19]

By 1917, the end was near. With America's entry into World War I, the railroad system was simply overwhelmed. Volume for the eastern railroads during the first nine months of the year shot up $123 million, but net profit declined $57 million.[20] Some of the country's oldest and proudest business institutions were headed for bankruptcy. At last, two days after Christmas, President Wilson signed a proclamation assuming control of the railroads on behalf of the people of the United States.

Perversely, and predictably, one of the first acts of the newly formed United States Railroad Administration was to enact a dramatic rate increase, which initially amounted to 28 percent followed later in the war by a 32 percent hike. But by then, the spirit of enterprise that had built the U.S. railroad system into the envy of the world had been extinguished—destroyed, in the phrase of economic historian Albro Martin, by "archaic progressivism."[21]

Though railroads would revert to private control after the war, the pattern of onerous rate regulation and stifled technology would continue for decades. When railroad began offering "piggyback" service, in which trucks rode on flatcars between making pickups and deliveries, thereby taking advantage of the inherent advantages of both modes, the ICC flat-out banned the practice in 1931.[22]

As we'll see, America also lost most of its passenger trains and became the only advanced country without high-speed passenger rail service because of misguided government policies that to this day distort transportation markets. Today, American freight railroads, having regained some of their pricing power through partial deregulation in 1980 and benefiting from the rising cost of energy, are making a comeback. But most still don't earn their cost of capital or are "revenue inadequate," in the phrase of the ICC successor agency.[23] We are still very far from correcting the excesses and follies of the twentieth-century transportation policy.

CHAPTER 10

Driven to Drive

OUR REASON for rehearsing the obscure history of Progressive Era transportation regulation is to underscore how little sense it makes to speak of markets and revealed consumer preference when it comes to movement of goods and people. Yes, plenty of competition goes on in this realm. But as with health care, government policy, most often driven by special interest group politics, overwhelmingly determines market outcomes and constrains the choices consumers have. This is not an argument for deregulation of transportation—far from it. Transportation is far too central to the economy and affects far too many other realms, from energy and land use, to property values and even public health, to let its structure be determined to market forces alone. But it is an argument for why we should not assume, as people frequently do, that the way we travel and ship today reflects the unconstrained "logic of the market," much less a rational use of transportation infrastructure. American transportation set off on a skewed course in the Progressive Era, becoming increasingly irrational, driven by subsidy and interest group politics, with results that are deeply unsatisfying to most Americans and now threaten their very livelihood.

Why did the Progressives, who excelled in so many policy realms, ultimately fail to apply true "scientific management" to transportation and suburban expansion? Many historians cite their lack of adequate administrative capacity. The ICC commissioners were overwhelmed by their case loads, and America, unlike Germany or France, lacked a large talented class of experts schooled in public policy and administration.

Progressives, by this view, simply could not grow the government fast enough to keep up with the rapid technological and economic changes of their era. But there is also no denying the stronghold of the yeoman ideal in the Progressives' thinking about transportation and related issues.

In its rate decisions, the ICC wound up serving above all the short-term interest of small-scale farmers, not understanding how the resulting undercapitalization of railroads would, as time went by, cause the liquidation of branch lines vital to the grange, drive up their shipping costs, and threaten their way of life. Similarly, the yeoman ideal no doubt influenced the Progressives' decision not to apply any rate regulation to the trucking industry. Early truckers, known as "gypsies," were often farmers themselves. These small-scale entrepreneurs and property holders helped other small-scale producers by undercutting "predatory" railroads.

Automobiles, too, once Henry Ford learned how to mass-produce them, also seemed to fit in well with the yeoman ideal, as well as other Progressive values. During the first two decades of the twentieth century, most American cities had come to be served by trolleys that offered extraordinary mobility and never cost more than a nickel. The network of interurban lines running between cities was so dense that at one point it was possible to travel clear across the country on traction lines, as some enthusiasts did. But like cable television companies in a later era, trolley operators had to win their franchises from local politicians, and the resulting bribery and constant scandals appalled the Progressive sensibility. Mass transit became associated in many people's minds with machine politics; autos, with yeoman-like individualism and freedom from corrupt government.

When combined with paved roads radiating out to the countryside, autos also promised to offer easier access to suburban living, which most Progressives favored. Cities at the time were extraordinarily dirty, infectious, overcrowded, and menaced by immigrant gangs. A Progressive Era American city was a dangerous place to raise a child and an ugly place to live. A "City Beautiful" movement emerged whose influence can be seen today in Washington, DC's monumental mall and the beautiful grounds of the Denver Public Library, for example. But the dominate Progressive impulse was to spread out and create segregated alternatives to city living.

As land use law professor Nicole Stelle Garnett has observed, the Progressives "believed that the busyness of urban life—characterized by the mixing of commercial and residential land uses—degraded human character and that changing the physical surroundings of a community to a single-use suburban model would nurture good citizens."[1] Here again, the yeoman ideal is at work, favoring homeownership and wholesome family life, this time on the expanding frontier of suburbia. To enforce this vision, Progressives invented zoning, adopting codes that insured large distances between homes, shops, and workplaces. Within such a landscape, mass transit was still feasible, as proven by the many "trolley suburbs" that emerged. Indeed, the typical suburb built during the Progressive Era was a perfect picture of what planners today call "smart growth," walkable communities with access to mass transit that were at the same time shady and safe. But auto driving was also more tempting, particularly after governments started pouring huge subsidies into road building, and the vision was lost.

Mental Accounting

"What subsidies?" many people might ask. Since the beginning of the twentieth century, road construction in the United States has been financed almost entirely by user fees, which causes many people to believe that roads and highways pay for themselves. By 1914, for example, every state had established motor vehicle licensing requirements, and roughly 90 percent of the revenue was earmarked for road "construction or maintenance." In 1919, Oregon became the first state to impose a gas tax, and by 1929, every state had done the same, using nearly all the revenue raised to build and improve roads. Later, the Interstate Highway System would be financed almost entirely by federal gasoline taxes.[2]

The earmarking of gasoline taxes for road building has over the years struck many Americans as fair and reasonable. A 1931 *Christian Science Monitor* editorial summarizes the popular view: "The great merit of the gasoline tax, from the standpoint of fairness, is that it accurately measures the proportions in which various motorists use the highways and assesses the cost of those facilities accordingly. But when part of the funds are turned to other purposes it loses its proper character as a use tax."[3]

From the beginning, however, people with a deeper understanding of politics and finance have seen through this specious reasoning. As chancellor of the exchequer in 1926, for example, Winston Churchill addressed the question of whether Britain should continue earmarking the torrent of revenue it was raising through gas taxes into road building, or consider it part of general revenues to be allocated by Parliament toward whatever the most pressing needs to the day might be. Churchill pointed out that other user fees did not automatically flow back to those who paid them:

> Entertainments may be taxed; public houses may be taxed; racehorses may be taxed; the possession of armorial bearings and manservants may be taxed—and the yield devoted to the general revenue. But motorists are to be privileged for all time to have the whole yield of the tax on motors devoted to roads. Obviously, this is all nonsense. . . . Such contentions are absurd, and constitute at once an outrage upon the sovereignty of Parliament and upon common sense.[4]

To put this in a modern context, imagine if all the revenue raised by alcohol taxes went for the construction of government liquor stores. Imagine if taxes on cigarettes were earmarked for the construction of cigarette factories. Imagine if all the proceeds raised by state lotteries went to fund the construction of more casinos. Outside of the realm of highway building and aviation, user fees rarely flow back automatically to those who pay them—and for good reason. Doing so would privilege certain forms of economic activity in the budget process and in so doing provide them with subsidies.

The highway lobby that formed in the teens and twenties understood this perfectly. An innocent might think that corporations with a financial stake in getting more people to drive—automakers, asphalt producers, tire companies—would organize to get general revenue subsidies for highway construction. That way the cost of highway building could be spread more thinly across the economy as a whole. But the highway lobby was far smarter than that. It knew it could gain far greater subsidy in the long run by using its influence to prevent state legislatures and Congress from using fuel excise taxes and registration fees for any purpose but road building. Their complete triumph came in 1956, when the Interstate Highway Act created a federal highway "trust fund" that formally granted highway builders the privilege of never having to compete for and justify highway expenditures against other social needs. Airlines achieved an equivalent triumph in 1970 with the creation of the Airport and Airway Trust Fund, which ensures that ticket taxes, taxes on air cargo, and other user fees flow back to the industry through government-financed airports and air traffic control, for example.

Why are so few people able to see through the myth that "highways pay for themselves" or that airlines don't receive subsidies? An insight comes from behavioral economists who have repeatedly demonstrated how humans value money differently, and often illogically, according to what "mental account" they assign it to. A story told about Dustin Hoffman by fellow actor Gene Hackman illustrates the phenomenon. One day when they were both young and out of work, Hoffman asked Hackman if he could borrow $5 so he could buy something to eat. Hackman, whose wife was working at the time, quickly agreed. He then walked into the kitchen of Hoffman's Pasadena apartment and was startled to find a line of mason jars, each with a label and all but one of them filled with money. "One says rent, one says entertainment, one says books, about five of them," Hackman recalls, "and they all had money in them, except the one that said 'food.'" When he confronted Hoffman about why he needed to borrow $5 when he had all this money, Hoffman explained that he couldn't use any of it for food, because he had budgeted it for other purposes, just as his father had told him to do.[5]

The way Hoffman viewed his mason jars is akin to the way the public views government trust funds. The money is "set aside" for a specific purpose, and it is simply wrong to "raid" the jar labeled "highways" or "aviation" and use the money for any other purpose, no matter how pressing. For any interest group, the ultimate victory is get the government to put its name on a jar. Ever after, they will be at an advantage over all other seekers of public money who lack their own jar—such as Amtrak, for example, which must battle for its funding every year, making long-term planning impossible. Better yet, much of the public won't even realize that the interest groups with jars have won an entrenched subsidy. Instead, they will accept the fiction that the money "belongs" to whoever's name is on the label.

What would the American transportation system look like without the distortions caused by earmarked taxes? Probably a lot like Europe's. Europeans love their cars, too. But in a country such as France, all taxes on motorists, as well on the users of other modes of transportation, flow to general revenues. That way there is no systematic bias favoring one mode of transportation over another. As a result, France enjoys a comparatively well-balanced transportation system, including a world-class high-speed passenger rail system that leaves the country well positioned to manage the challenge of rising energy prices and of meeting targets for reducing greenhouse gas emissions. France's Train à Grand Vitesse, or TGV, also provides its riders with a civilized alternative to the increasing indignities and delays of airline travel. Travel time from Paris to Bordeaux, roughly the same distance between Los Angeles and San Francisco, is 2 hours and 56 minutes at speeds up to two hundred miles per hour. Recent technological improvement will make future speeds much faster once the necessary infrastructure is in place.

The United States is the only advanced country in the world not committed to high-speed rail, and its overall transportation system is the least energy-efficient and least integrated of any modern nation's. The reason is not market logic, much less engineering necessity, but special interest politics, most of which the public and the press have barely ever perceived or understood. Yet transportation is the next big policy frontier, connecting all the big issues of the day: health care, energy, and the financial crisis caused by Wall Street betting the country on rising real estate values in auto-dependent suburbs. And so we continue our crash course on how today's transportation system came to be so broken.

Sidetracked

In 1950, the United States enjoyed the finest transportation system in the world. It had its problems, to be sure. But paved farm-to-market and postal roads connected virtually every hamlet. States were busy building toll roads, like the Pennsylvania Turnpike, which expanded options for motorists but without disguising the cost of driving. The country had already lost much of its trolley infrastructure, due in no small measure (as revealed by federal prosecutors in 1949) to a conspiracy led by General Motors, Standard Oil, and other auto interests to buy up trolley lines and convert them to buses. But at least bus service was still widely available.[6]

Meanwhile, railroads, temporarily flush with the profits earned during World War II, still operated thousands of intercity trains, many of them shiny new aerodynamic streamliners. Newly ordered diesel-electric locomotives were geared to run at 119 miles per hour. Midsized cities in the heartland thrived with fast, frequent rail service connecting them to larger population centers. In Lynchburg, Virginia, where today it is nearly impossible to fly anywhere within a thousand-mile radius without changing planes at least once and consuming most of a day, a constant parade of passenger trains offered direct service to Washington and New York, Norfolk and Cincinnati, St. Louis and Chicago, Atlanta, Birmingham, and New Orleans. To reach most of these destinations, it was possible simply to board a Pullman car in the evening and awake at one's destination.[7]

Unlike today, midsized cities were also served by fast-speed mail and express package trains, and so they suffered little or no logistical disadvantage in commerce compared to coastal cities. Places that later became disconnected "fly-over" zones, like Lynchburg, or Utica, or Des Moines, could still thrive.

This rational balance of different transportation modes, however, would not be allowed to hold, mostly for reasons of politics. Railroads continued to face ruinous regulation by the ICC, as well as rising labor costs enforced by state and federal labor protection legislation. Diesel-electric locomotives achieved great efficiencies over steam engines but still by law had to carry a fireman as if stoking the engine was still necessary, as well as up to four other unneeded crew members. The federal government would never allow railroads to take a strike, and in arbitrating rail labor disputes, federal officials consistently refused to take on costly work rules, which, for example, paid rail crews a full days pay for every hundred miles they traveled. The *Denver Zephyr*, a train capable of traveling nonstop from Chicago to Denver in 13½ hours at speeds up to 113 miles per hour, had to stop instead ten times for crew changes with the crews sharing ten days of wages. As one expert testified to Congress, "This type of labor agreement has loaded wage costs so heavily on the passenger train that these costs alone have often been the decisive factor necessitating the discontinuance of the operation of trains."[8]

Mandatory contributions to a federally administered pension fund for railroaders further skewed the balance between rail and other modes. Few truckers even had pension coverage, let alone the duty to support drivers long since retired. Few airline employees had pension coverage, either, and those who did were typically young. But under the Railroad Retirement Act of 1934, railroads had to pay (and still do) a stiff payroll tax to fund generous pensions. Because of the generosity of the pensions, which replaced up to 125 percent of a worker's income in retirement, and because of the falling ratio of workers to retirees as the industry contracted, railroad retirement payroll tax rates went up and up, climbing from an original 6 percent before reaching 33.3 percent by the 1980s. By then, the Bangor and Aroostook Railroad, for example, was paying twice as much in railroad retirement taxes as it did for diesel fuel. Amtrak, while in business for little more than a decade, was seeing a full 23 percent of its personnel costs go toward retirement, compared to the 3.1 percent that is typical of firms that offer pensions.[9]

Here is another important example of how rail passenger trains have been hobbled by politics and boneheaded regulation. In 1947, to eliminate the threat posed to airlines by trains traveling 119 miles per hour on short- to medium-distance routes, aviation interests pulled a coup. They succeeded in securing a federal legislation that prohibited, and still prohibits, passenger trains from moving faster than 79 miles per hour unless they have installed costly and, at the time, unworkable automatic train control devices. The same law held, and still holds, passenger trains running in unsignaled territory to a mere 60 miles per hour, even though for decades before this law, passenger trains routinely ran at 90 to 100 miles per hour while still being, overwhelmingly, the safest form of travel.[10]

Government, under the thrall of special interests, seemingly did everything it could to kill off railroads. As the cost of government rose after World War II, municipal tax collectors hiked up property taxes on railroads, which unlike competing modes, owned and maintained their own right-of-ways and terminals. By 1956, the New York Central had become the single-biggest taxpayer in New York City, paying $6.6 million in taxes on Grand Central Terminal alone. Throughout the country, rising railroad property taxes went to build new airports and highways, forcing rail executives to guess how much more they would have to pay to benefit their competitors.[11]

Under the influence of highway and aviation interests, government also made sure that rail passengers themselves would pay a stiff 15 percent excise tax on their tickets. Originally passed during World War II as a way to suppress civilian travel, the excise tax remained in effect after the war, adding $1.4 billion to the federal treasury just between 1945 and 1953. "The additional 15 percent added to the cost of rail transportation has often been the deciding factor in the choice of the private automobile over the rail service," declared a 1954 regulatory commissioner report.[12] The money went to general revenues, unlike excise taxes on airline passengers, which since their initiation in 1970 have been earmarked for airport construction and other subsidies to the airline industry.

Chevy to the Levy

Liberals in this era had a strange blind spot when it came to understanding how excessive public spending on highway and aviation undermined the Progressive/liberal tradition and its political coalition. At the moment of what looked to be liberalism's ultimate triumph, President John Kennedy described a "New Frontier" that included bold talk about moon shots, supersonic transports, and interstate highways. But the New Frontier, as well as Lyndon Johnson's Great Society, would barely lift a finger to preserve America's rapidly deteriorating transit systems, on which millions of working-class Americans depended. Nor would most liberals in this era worry a bit about the hardship imposed on rural America and heartland cities by the decline of America's intercity passenger rail service.

When President Johnson signed the first Urban Mass Transportation Act into law on July 9, 1964, it offered a paltry $375 million in capital assistance over three years. By comparison, the federal government would spend more than eight times that amount on airline subsidies and thirty-two times more on highways.[13] Many liberal Democrats were more than happy to do the bidding of rail and transit union bosses, supporting featherbedding work rules and unfunded pension bonuses, but never made balanced transportation a liberal cause. It would fall to Republican Richard Nixon, who never achieved his childhood dream of becoming a train engineer, to save the last vestiges of America's intercity rail system by creating Amtrak in 1971.

Nor did liberals of the era seem to understand how urban freeways and subsidies for suburban homeowners would encourage "white flight" and thereby contribute to the downward spiral of decaying urban schools and soaring crime rates. Perversely, the liberal blind spot on transportation issues contributed mightily to liberalism's downfall, as more and more Americans who tried to hold on in the cities found themselves "mugged by reality" and turned reactionary. Think of Archie Bunker.

Perhaps liberals in the 1960s and 1970s, more than they knew, were under the influence of that old yeoman tradition that ran through the Progressive Era—the one that hated railroads, hated cities, celebrated frontier life and the freedom of the open road. A few pointy-headed intellectuals, like Lewis Mumford or Jane Jacobs, might mock the suburbs and the emerging auto culture. But mainstream liberal politicians seemed persuaded, though they never used the term, that the America's yeomanry didn't care if the passenger train no longer stopped in town, or if the emerging new transportation system would leave them gazing up at contrails and isolated in fly-over America.

It was a strange disconnect. Perhaps, too, liberals of this era understood half-consciously that the New Deal had failed to protect America's yeomanry from economic marginalization, and that therefore liberalism needed to offer displaced yeoman at least an ersatz version of the lost dream—in the form of a suburban homestead and a sleek horseless carriage to wash and wax on the weekends. Since the New Deal, liberals had come to believe that large-scale production in both agriculture and industry, when guided by government and counterbalanced by a strong labor movement, could lead to greater efficiency, rationalization, standardization, and increased purchasing power for consumers. The program created an economics of abundance. Yet it also created a world of restless "organization men" stuck in corporate bureaucracies, of bored assembly line workers and homemakers increasingly left without productive function, who all had to give up the yeoman dream of true independence. To displaced yeoman, midcentury liberalism said in effect, "We offer you a bungalow, free television and highways, and a new Chevrolet to see the USA."

However it was, the abuse of America's once-magnificent rail system continued on and on without most liberals ever seeing the harm. When railroads discovered ways to lower costs, by using lighter, larger "Big John" hopper cars, for example, the ICC, under pressure from barge companies and truckers, refused to allow them to pass the savings on to shippers. The Post Office canceled the last of its major rail contracts in 1967 and switched to trucks and airlines. This rendered a death blow to what intercity passenger trains still remained and left small towns and heartland cities with much slower and less reliable postal service. Even as trucks picked off their mail and freight business, and subsidized highways and airlines lured passengers away, railroads were forced into the 1970s to continue running vast fleets of now money-losing commuter trains, as if they owed the public some sort of penance for the dastardly deeds of nineteenth-century robber barons. By 1980, all the major railroads of the Northeast were bankrupt, and the industry was in extremes.

End of the Line

Yet by then it was clear to everyone paying attention that a transportation system so heavily dependent on highways and aviation could not meet the needs of the future. Highways, at least until they became chocked with traffic, could whisk suburbanites into downtown cities, but where could they park? Beautiful cities like New Orleans became marred by acres of parking lots and garages where muggers often lurked, and still there was not enough parking space to accommodate burgeoning auto traffic. Highway planners did a reasonably good job of keeping ahead of congestion until the early 1970s, but their projections were undone once large numbers of women entered the workforce and began commuting by car, both to work and to child care facilities. The growth of malls, five-thousand-student high schools, and suburban office parks created unexpected traffic moving in all directions that planners had no idea how to tame.

Meanwhile, fuel and excise taxes didn't begin to cover the real cost of driving—not even the cost of highway maintenance. In 1983, the Mianus River Bridge on Interstate 95 collapsed, killing three people and providing a stark symbol of a new era in highway transportation marked by crumbling bridges and roads and ever-worsening congestion. In 2007, the catastrophic failure of the I-35W Minneapolis–St. Paul Mississippi River bridge, which killed thirteen, clued many Americans into the dimensions of the country's highway infrastructure deficit. America's interstates were built on the cheap and began wearing out even before the system was completed. Just preventing further deterioration of highway infrastructure will require $41 billion in spending through 2024, according to the Federal Highway Administration.[14]

The artificially low cost of driving and the lack of transportation alternatives in most areas also sent false price signals that caused millions of Americans to make economic decisions that ultimately worked against them. The young couple contemplating a first home would find they could get "more house for money" in a distant suburb not served by mass transit. But living there meant they needed two cars, which in any economic season are rapidly depreciating assets. Meanwhile, gas prices rose, congestion worsened, and more and more houses were built just like theirs for people making the same miscalculation.

Even before the housing bust, appreciation was much slower in areas lacking alternatives to driving. Today, the foreclosure signs dominating the landscape of auto-dependent edge cities like Stockton, California, make it questionable if they are even economically viable in an era of high energy costs and worsening congestion.[15]

In his magnificent book *Train Time*, written shortly before the housing bubble burst, John Stilgoe noted presciently, "Americans now live in what appears to be the final, sickly sweet blossoming of the automobile and airliner, and the related real estate development. A frantic energy masks the desperation of real estate developers terrified that people will not buy the last of the structures built according to automobile thinking."[16] Mortgage lenders failed to take into account how not just the cost of a house but also the combined cost of housing and transportation would affect homebuyers' ability to repay their loans. As it turns out, you may "get more house for the money" in sprawling areas not served by mass transit, but after the cost of auto transportation is figured in, the cost of living in sprawlville is actually much higher, particularly after accounting for disappearing home equity.[17]

America has made a staggering misinvestment. Retrofitting today's suburbia with mass transit lines and connecting cities and suburbia with high-speed passenger and freight rail will create jobs, ameliorate highway and airport congestion, reduce pollution, save energy, give parents more time with their children, and reduce the leading cause of dying young: auto accidents. But if those are not reasons enough, it might also, by boosting the value of depressed suburban real estate, help avert another Great Depression.

Only a more rational, balanced transportation system can save property values in most of the developments we have built over the last generation. When Al Gore championed "smart growth" in 1999, many who rallied to the banner seemed to be elitists who couldn't care less about the needs of working-class families for affordable homeownership. And many were indeed snobbish about the displaced yeomen of sprawling suburbia. But now comes a day when preserving the home values of the broad middle class and saving the suburbs have become the best argument for overhauling America's transportation system. This is no longer a question of aesthetics or environmental NIMBYism. It's a question of hard economics.

CHAPTER 11

Steel Wheel Solutions

B Y DEFINITION, unsustainable trends don't last. Already, the American transportation system is undergoing a brutal readjustment. Trucking is in big trouble. In the first quarter of 2008 alone, two thousand large trucking firms folded. As for owner-operators, *Traffic World* reports that "hundreds or thousands . . . have lately gone to unmarked graves."[1]

High fuel prices may come and go, but mounting congestion and increasing effective competition from freight railroads leave the industry unable to raise wages enough to retain sufficient drivers. According to the American Transportation Research Institute, the industry lost 243 million man-hours in 2004 due to traffic congestion, which is equivalent 88,000 full-time drivers each logging 2,750 driving hours annually.[2] In the coming decade, America's overall labor force will stop growing, making recruitment even more difficult.

This staggering loss of labor productivity, combined with trucking's inherent energy inefficiency when compared to rail, puts the future of long-distance trucking very much in doubt. Likely policy changes, such as cap-and-trade system for carbon emission or the imposition of carbon taxes, would further erode the long-haul trucking's dwindling comparative advantages.

The future of aviation is in question, too. Between January and August 2008, eleven U.S. airlines went out of business, including ATA and Air Midwest, and the industry on the whole was on track to lose $10 billion for the year despite record ticket prices. By the end of 2008, the number of domestic flights contracted 9.3 percent compared to the previous year. The list of small and medium-sized cities that have lost all scheduled passenger service in recent years runs into the hundreds, but among the more notable are four state capitals: Olympia, Washington; Dover, Delaware; Salem, Oregon; and Trenton, New Jersey.

Rich people will always be able to fly, but now industry experts seriously doubt whether commercial aviation can continue to serve a mass market if energy prices return to pre-recession levels, particularly for flights of under four hundred miles. As John Heimlich, chief economist of the Air Transport Association summed up in 2008, "We simply can't afford to carry every passenger who wants to fly."[3]

The readjustment in housing, of course, has also been brutal. Eventually, the effects of speculation and irresponsible lending will work their way through the housing market. But much of the nation's residential stock will remain in locations that are becoming less and less desirable places to live due to the rising cost of transportation, measured in both money and time. Americans may love their cars, but not so much that they will bid up real estate in places that make residents slaves to their automobiles. The cost of gas may ease, but the cost of congestion won't without alternatives to driving. Indeed, lower gas prices and more fuel-efficient cars would make suburban congestion worse, while not even necessarily reducing total energy consumption.

That's one lesson of this decade, which saw new hybrid technology deployed in bigger, heavier SUVs, with no net savings in fuel use or miles driven. The potential benefits of any new, more efficient engine technology can easily be more than erased by people taking advantage of that efficiency to drive more miles in heavier cars.

We applaud proposals, such as those made by the New America Foundation's Lisa Margonelli, to offer "smash credits" to people who scrap their current energy-guzzling cars and trucks and buy a smaller, more efficient vehicle. Absent other changes, however, simply improving the average vehicle's fuel efficiency does not solve congestion or relieve the stress and danger of long auto commutes. And if improved engine efficiency causes people to buy heavier cars than they otherwise would and drive them more, then total emissions and fuel consumption will not fall and may well increase—as has been the pattern in the past. By contrast, offering credits to people who insulate their houses or buy more energy-efficient appliances, furnaces, hot water heaters, or computers makes lots of sense because such measures do not induce more energy use.

Changes in demographics also do not bode well for sprawling, auto-dependent developments. Between 2010 and 2025, according to Census Bureau projections, the country's population will increase from 310 million to 357 million. This is a robust increase that will put great strains on our transportation system across the board. Many people fail to realize, however, that fully half of this growth will be among the population sixty-five and older, whose ranks are expected to swell from forty million to nearly sixty-four million.[4]

As people grow older, they often become less willing or able to drive, which makes it a great hardship for them to live in areas lacking alternative modes of transportation. More than one in five Americans age sixty-five and older does not drive. Still more should not drive. For each mile they are behind the wheel, drivers age eighty-five and over face a risk of being killed in a crash that is nine times higher than for drivers age twenty-five to sixty-nine. Sadly, many aging baby boomers will wind up stranded in sprawling suburbs that lack mass transit, but those who can escape will, thereby depressing property values in the developments they leave behind.[5]

It's possible to do nothing about these trends, but the cost to ordinary Americans would be extraordinary. A vastly expanded elderly population would contend with lack of mobility and increased social isolation, with all its attendant health risks. Property values would remain distressed across much of the American landscape, raising the cost to taxpayers of working out bad loans assumed with Wall Street's bailout. Highway congestion would worsen, relieved only by the falling number of Americans who can afford to drive and by the rising number who are too old to do so. Traveling long distances for family reunions and vacations would no longer be a middle-class prerogative without cheap gas and affordable flights. An overstrained logistical system would slow down every sector of the economy and raise the price of just about everything we consume, especially food. Again, the rich would do just fine, but for just about everyone else, we would be at a turning point marking the end of the American Dream. Fortunately, this decline is not inevitable if only we open our eyes and minds.

Steel Wheel Interstate

Most people hardly give a thought to freight logistics, except perhaps to curse the semis they must contend with on the interstates. It's a dreary-sounding subject, we know. But applying new thinking to how we move cargo around the country is a key to solving nearly all the major energy and environmental challenges facing the country, and much else as well. Once you realize the upside potential for all realms of life offered by more sensible freight logistics, the subject becomes exciting indeed.

Let's start with a literally concrete example to show the possibilities. Interstate 81 starts at the Canadian border in upstate New York and runs south by southwest along the eastern slope of the Appalachian Mountains into Tennessee. Mostly it traverses rural areas, and what cities lie along its route are only midsized and generally slow growing: Syracuse, Scranton, Harrisburg, Hagerstown, and Roanoke, for example.

Still, truck traffic on I-81 is staggering, accounting for roughly one out of every four vehicles on the four lanes through Virginia. They are there for a reason. Most of the trucks are on long hauls and are using I-81 to escape the tolls and congestion on I-95. That interstate, running from Maine to Florida through the eastern seaboard's major cities, is so overcrowded that truckers find it worth their while to drive hundreds of extra miles just to avoid it as long as possible.

This is bad news for just about everyone. Even truckers have to deal with an increasingly overcrowded, dangerous I-81, and for motorists it's a white-knuckle terror. Because much of the road is hilly, they find themselves repeatedly having to pass slow-moving trucks going uphill, only to see them looming large in the rear-view mirror on the down grade. For years, state transportation officials have watched I-81 get pounded to pieces by tractor-trailers—which are responsible for the almost all non-weather-related highway wear and tear. Making matters worse are projections that traffic will rise by 67 percent in just ten years.

The conventional response to this problem would be simply to build more lanes. It's what highway departments do. But at a cost of $11 billion, or $32 million per mile, Virginia cannot afford to do that without installing tolls, which might have to be set as high as 17 cents per mile for automobiles. When Virginia's Department of Transportation proposed doing this early last year, truckers and ordinary Virginian's alike set off a firestorm of protest. At the same time, just making I-81 wider without adding tolls would make its truck traffic problems worse as still more trucks would divert from I-95 and other routes.

Looking for a way out of this dilemma, Virginia transportation officials have settled on an innovative solution: use state money to get freight off the highway and onto rails. As it happens, running parallel to I-81 through the Shenandoah Valley and across the Piedmont are two mostly single-track rail lines belonging to the Norfolk Southern Railroad. Known as the Crescent Corridor, these lines have seen a resurgence of trains carrying containers, just like most of the trucks on I-81 do. The problem is the track needs upgrading and there are various choke points, so the Norfolk Southern cannot run trains fast enough to be time-competitive with most of the trucks hurtling down I-81. Even before the recent financial meltdown, the railroad couldn't generate enough interest from Wall Street investors to improve the line.

The railroad has long been reluctant to accept government investment in its infrastructure out of fear of public meddling, such as being compelled to run money-losing passenger trains. But now, like most of the industry, it has changed its mind, and it happily accepted Virginia's offer last year to fund a small portion—$40 million—of the investment needed to get more freight traffic off I-81 and onto the Crescent Corridor. The railroad estimates that with an additional $2 billion in infrastructure investment, it could divert one millon trucks off the road, which is currrently carrying just under five million. State officials are thinking even bigger. A study sponsored by the Virginia DOT finds that a cumulative investment over ten to twelve years of less than $8 billion would divert 30 percent of the growing truck traffic on I-81 to rail. That would be far more bang for the state's buck than the $11 billion it would take to add more lanes to the highway, especially since it would bring many other public benefits, from reduced highway accidents and

lower repair costs to enormous improvements in fuel efficiency and pollution. Today, a single train can move as many containers as 280 trucks
using one-third as much energy, and that's before any improvements
to rail infrastructure.

This is an important precedent that opens the mind to much larger
possibilities. Rail lines parallel nearly all the major interstates, and interstates themselves have meridians in which additional rail lines could be
built. In the West, where most shipments are long-haul and rail lines
were comparatively well maintained during the dark days of the 1960s
and 1970s, railroads have succeeded in capturing back much of the
business they once lost to trucks. But elsewhere, particularly in the East
where cities are closer together and where rail infrastructure is in worse
repair, railroads have been less successful. To make rail freight more
time-competitive with trucks along the I-95 corridor, for example,
costly tunnel projects would have to be undertaken, including replacing the Howard Street tunnel in Baltimore, which is so antiquated that
it has been listed on National Register of Historic Places since 1973.
It's a choke point like many others that severely retards the nation's
desperately needed transition to a more energy-efficient and cleaner
transportation system.

So we offer a proposal: a national "Steel Wheel Interstate System," designed to replace the current, crumbling, overcrowded,
energy-inefficient, rubber wheel interstates as the nation's primary
means of moving long-haul and intermediate-distance freight.[6]

Why don't the railroads just build the new tracks, tunnels, switch-
yards, and other infrastructure they need? America's major railroad companies are publicly traded companies answerable to often mindless, or
predatory, financial Goliaths. While Wall Street was pouring the world's
savings into underwriting credit cards and subprime mortgages on over-
valued tract houses, America's railroads were pleading for the financing
they needed to increase their capacity. And for the most part, the answer
that came back from Wall Street was no, or worse. CSX, one of the
nation's largest railroads, spent much of 2008 trying to fight off two
hedge funds intent on gaining enough control of the company to cut
its spending on new track and equipment in order to maximize short-
term profits.

So the industry, though gaining in market share and profitability after decades of decline, is starved for capital. While its return on investment improved to a respectable 8 percent by the beginning of this decade, its cost of capital outpaced it at around 10 percent—and that was before the credit crunch arrived. This is no small problem, since railroads are capital-intensive, spending about five times more just to maintain remaining rail lines and equipment than the average U.S. manufacturing industry does on plant and equipment.[7] Increased investment in railroad infrastructure would produce many public goods, including fewer fatalities from truck crashes, which kill some five thousnad Americans a year. But public goods do not impress Wall Street. Nor does the long-term potential for increased earnings that improved rail infrastructure would bring, except in the eyes of Warren Buffet—who is bullish on railroads—and a few other smart, patient investors.

The alternative is for the public to help pay for rail infrastructure. Actually, it's not much of a choice. Unlike private investors, the government must either invest in shoring up the railroads' overwhelmed infrastructure or pay in other ways. Failing to rebuild rail infrastructure will simply further move the burden of ever-increasing shipping demands onto the highways, the expansion and maintenance of which does not come free. The American Association of State Highway and Transportation Officials (hardly a shill for the rail industry) estimates that without public investment in rail capacity, $450 million tons of freight will shift to highways, costing shippers $162 billion and highway users $238 billion (in travel time, operating, and accident costs) and adding $10 billion to highway costs over the next twenty years. "Inclusion of costs for bridges, interchanges, etc., could double this estimate," its report adds.[8]

Choke Points

Let's start with the small-scale stuff that needs doing. There are many examples around the country where a relatively tiny amount of public investment in rail infrastructure would bring enormous social and economic returns. Why is I-95 so congested with truck traffic that drivers divert to I-81 and overwhelm that interstate as well? One big reason is that railroads can capture only 2 percent of the container traffic traveling up and down the eastern seaboard because of obscure choke points, such as the Howard Street tunnel in downtown Baltimore. When the tunnel shut down in 2001 due to a fire, trains had to divert as far as Cincinnati to get around it. Owner CSX has big plans for capturing more truck traffic from I-95 and for creating room for more passenger trains as well, but it can't do so until it finds the financing to fix or bypass this tunnel and make other infrastructure improvements down the line. In 2007, it submitted a detailed plan to the U.S. Department of Transportation to build a steel wheel interstate from Washington to Miami, but no federal funding has been forthcoming.[9]

The Howard Street tunnel is the worst of some seventy rail choke points in the Mid-Atlantic region alone. According to a study commissioned by the I-95 Corridor Coalition, a group of transportation officials along the highway's route, fixing these choke points would cost $6.2 billion and return twice that amount in benefits. The returns would include $2.9 billion in reduced freight transportation costs, $6.3 billion in direct savings due to reduced highway congestion for vehicles still on the road, and $3.7 billion in indirect economic benefits generated throughout the economy by these transportation savings. Importantly, rail capacity can often be improved substantially by relatively low-cost measures such adding signals, occasional switches, and new, computerized train control devices, whereas with rubber wheel interstates, the only way to add to capacity is to add lanes. This is another reason why the social rate of return on rail investment is much higher than on most highway projects.

Another notorious set of choke points is in Chicago, America's rail capitol, which is visited by some 1,200 trains a day. Built in the nineteenth century by noncooperating private companies, lines coming from the East to this day have no or insufficient connections with those coming from the West. Consequently, thousands of containers on their way elsewhere must be unloaded each day, "rubber wheeled" across the city's crowded streets by truck, and reloaded onto other trains. It takes forty-eight hours for a container to travel five miles across Chicago, longer than it does to get there from New York. This entire problem could be fixed for just $1.5 billion, with benefits including not just faster shipping times and attendant economic development, but drastically reduced road traffic, energy use, and pollution.

Wind Trains

Once kinks like these have been ironed out of the system, we can focus on the big picture—most important, the electrification of America's major rail lines. Today, most other industrial countries make extensive use of electric locomotives, and for good reason. They are 2.5 to 3 times more efficient than diesels, more powerful, and cheaper to maintain. They also last longer, accelerate faster, and have much higher top speeds. Trains carrying containers at 100 mph are more than possible. Powered by an overhead wire or third rail, electric locomotives don't have to lug the weight of their own fuel around with them. Another remarkable feature is that when electric locomotives brake, they generate electricity that is fed back into the grid and used to power other trains. An electric locomotive braking down one side of a mountain, for example, sends energy to trains struggling up the other side. With all these advantages, electric railroads are fully twenty times more fuel-efficient than trucks.[10]

Rail electrification also offers significant opportunities for zero-emission freight and passenger transportation. Heirs to the Milwaukee Road's hydropowered line could traverse the Great Plains powered by the region's wind farms. In fact, there is probably no more practical use for wind than using it to power "wind trains" running across the heartland. Most wind farms are and will be concentrated near rail lines in any event, because the large size of windmills makes them difficult and expensive to move by truck. There is also no loss of energy in transmission when windmills power passing trains—a big problem in other applications. Some companies are already exploring the possibilities: BNSF Railway, which traverses many wind zones, is investigating a deal in which it would lease space for power lines along its right-of-ways to utilities in exchange for access to discounted wind power for its trains.

In a study recently presented to the National Academy of Engineering, the Millennium Institute, a nonprofit known for its expertise in energy and environmental modeling, calculated the likely benefits of a

$250 to $500 billion expenditure on improved rail infrastructure. It found that such an investment would get 83 percent of all long-haul trucks off the nation's highways by 2030, while also delivering ample capacity for high-speed passenger rail. If high-traffic rail lines were also electrified and powered in part by renewable energy sources, that investment would reduce the nation's carbon emissions by 39 percent and oil consumption by 15 percent. By moderating the growing cost of logistics, it would also leave the nation's economy 10 percent larger by 2030 than it would otherwise be.

Much of the electrification could start almost immediately. In the 1970s, the National Academies of Science and many others concerned about that decade's energy crisis did extensive work in mapping out the specific lines most suitable to electrification. In 1977, at one of the many technical conferences on the subject, Milton J. Shapp, then governor of Pennsylvania, spoke for many of the visionaries involved when he observed that "particularly in view of the energy crisis, it is essential to the well being of our nation that our major railroads electrify." A temporary fall in oil prices and an abundance of short-term thinking killed almost every last project, but we still have benefit of all the studies sitting on shelves.

The work involved in constructing overhead wires, or catenary, requires unique skills, but one can imagine laid-off construction workers taking to it far better than, say, to nursing, and with less retraining. Current studies indicate that labor and construction costs would come to about $2 million per mile, maybe less if steel prices continue to sink. Wiring the thirty-six thousand miles of mainline track on the nation's high-density routes would thus come in at around $72 billion. Completing such a project could take as little as six years, according John Schumann of LTK Engineering.

Additional funds would be needed, of course, for new locomotives and generating capacity. But building or retrofitting locomotives to operate under the new grid could put lots of laid-off autoworkers back to work. General Motors, until it sold off its Electro-Motive Division in 2005 to private investors, was long the nation's dominate diesel-electric locomotive maker. The spinoff company is still headquartered in LaGrange, Illinois, though most production has shifted to London,

Ontario. General Electric, which remains a world leader in locomotive building, with a big plant in hard-pressed Erie, Pennsylvania, could also use the business and would bring much expertise to it.

If the public helps railroads make such investments in electrification and other infrastructure improvements, it will of course earn the right to demand important quid pro quos. Railroads, for example, would be required to apportion a certain amount of their increased capacity to public use, such as for commuter trains, which the railroads might or might not operate themselves. (Some show interest.) It should also be possible to negotiate open access to publicly financed rail infrastructure, so that outside companies can rent the rails and run their own freight or passenger trains on them, which is a good way to check any tendency toward monopoly pricing. In Great Britain, for example, a subsidiary of Virgin Airlines, called Virgin Trains, operates passenger trains over publicly financed infrastructure, as do other private passenger and freight companies. Most American railroads are wary of the open-access model, but with the promise of enough public capital and the threat of reregulation, deals can be struck.

For example, there is no reason we cannot again have fast, efficient express freight service of the kind the Railway Express Agency once provided. For cities as far apart as New York and Chicago, trains can beat planes on next-day mail service. As consulting engineer Alan Drake points out, when passengers and express freight or mail are borne by the same train, the economics of passenger rail improve dramatically, making possible far wider service. We also have the chance to reduce drastically the cost and the huge carbon footprint caused by using trucks and planes almost exclusively to ship perishables across the country. Until the 1970s, railroads handled nearly all fresh food movement from California and Florida, and they could again, making healthy winter fruits and vegetables cheaper and less hard on the planet.

Another potential use would be auto trains. Today, Amtrak offers a service that allows motorists to drive their cars onto special auto racks that are attached to the back of a passenger train. The train runs daily between northern Virginia and central Florida, saving users 855 miles of driving down I-95. The service is particularly popular among northern "snow-birds" who spend the winter in Florida and want to have their cars with them. For now, this is a specialty market, and it is not cheap because of the energy required to haul the weight of the automobiles. But with the potential energy efficiency of the steel wheel interstate system we've been describing, auto trains could make sense in many markets.

A similar service might also appeal to remaining independent long-haul truckers(we'll still need some for transport of time-sensitive cargo to and from remote locations)In Europe, a company called HUPAC offers a service known as "the rolling highway." By attaching a coach to the end of its container trains, it allows drivers to rest as they and their rigs traverse the Alps. Truckers in this country, before exceeding their daily legal maximum of eleven hours behind the wheel, could load their rigs onto a rolling highway and get some nine hundred miles down the road while they took their mandatory ten hours of rest.

Finally, the proposal has an additional political advantage: it doesn't involve pricing or guilt-tripping people out of their automobiles. Electrifying and otherwise improving rail infrastructure would indeed facilitate the coming of true high-speed rail passenger service to the United States, a goal Obama committed to as a candidate. But its success wouldn't depend on persuading a single American to take the train instead flying or driving. Indeed, with its promise of making driving more enjoyable and less dangerous, the proposal bridges the divide between auto-hating, Euroland-loving enviros and those who see access to the open road as an American birthright. What could be more post-1960s? Mr. President, this is change we can believe in.

Middle Seat Blues

The next big piece is rationalizing the airline industry. For U.S. aviation, the future can only go either one of two ways. If, as seems highly unlikely, we return to a long era of cheap energy prices, the demand for air travel will be high, but its supply will be tightly limited by competition for airspace and airport congestion. Both have become extreme at major hubs. In March 2007, only 72 percent of all U.S. flights arrived on time.[11]

If, in the more likely scenario, the effective price of oil remains in the $100-a-barrel range or higher (due to market forces carbon taxes, and/or restrictions on carbon emissions), airline travel will remain uneconomical for all but long hauls. Airlines consume a tremendous about of fuel on takeoff, which means their energy cost per passenger-mile is very high unless they travel long distances. Airlines are shedding short hauls because they cannot command ticket prices high enough to cover their energy costs, even after charging for baggage, imposing new fees, and ripping out kitchens and movie monitors to reduce weight. If airlines charged what it cost them to fly routes under four hundred miles, few people would find it worth the expense and would cancel their trip, drive, or, where possible, take the train.

So whether because of the capacity constraints on air travel, or because of the low energy efficiency of airplanes on routes under four hundred miles, or both, the case for building high-speed rail passenger lines in many corridors is overwhelming. The increasing amounts of time and money air travelers must spend to get to airports, plus the long dwell times and indignities they must endure to pass security, plus the increasing restrictions and costs attached to baggage handling, plus the very high carbon footprint caused by air travel, all just add to the case for giving travelers a better alternative.

America already has one high-speed rail lane—sort of. That's Amtrak's Northeast Corridor line running from Boston to Washington, DC. It is a legacy, incidentally, of the Reconstruction Finance Corporation, which during the Great Depression provided the Pennsylvania Railroad with the loans needed to electrify the line south of New York—a rare but important twentieth-century precedent for public investment in private rail infrastructure. Without this investment in electrification, passenger service on this route might well have so dwindled by the 1960s that highway builders would have long since paved the right-of-way over, but fortunately the corridor survived that era.

Today, under Amtrak's ownership, the Northeast Corridor is seeing continuing surges in ridership. On this line, even before the big run-up in air fares, Amtrak enjoyed 85 percent market share in competition with airlines.[12] It's flagship Acela trains are smooth, quiet, roomy, and have no middle seats. They also offer a feature particularly attractive to business travelers, college students, and kids alike: electrical outlets at each seat to allow for continuous use of laptops, cell phones, and GameBoys. (There's a "quiet car" for those who can't stand cell phone chatter.) Some seats are configured face-to-face with a table in between, which allows business travelers to conduct meetings as they travel and parents to play card and board games with their children. A pub-style café car serves sandwiches and beverages, and in first class, a steward serves full meals that can no longer be had at any price on competing airlines, as well as complimentary alcoholic beverages (which can sometimes make the trip a little too jolly).

Yet though the Acela trains briefly run as fast as 135 miles per hour, this is not true high-speed rail. In 1949, the Advanced Merchant's Limited, pulled most of the way by a steam engine, covered the leg from Boston to New York in just four hours, a mere twenty-seven minutes longer than the current schedule.[13] On the curvy route through Connecticut and western Rhode Island, Acela cannot even begin to get up to full speed for a reason redolent with historical irony. This segment was original owned by the New Haven Railroad, which once acquired the real estate for a straighter line. But, strapped for cash in the 1950s, the New Haven felt compelled to sell the land to the government, which used it to build the Connecticut Turnpike, now a key link in I-95. The profits the railroad earned hauling building material for the turnpike were the last it ever made.

So today, Acela just chugs along in comparison to France's TGV's or China's spanking new Beijing-Tianjin line, where trains run at 217 miles per hour. Congress has never granted Amtrak the funding necessary to smooth the curves and improve the tunnels that currently keep the Northeast Corridor trains from running at their full potential and, perversely, keeps hammering Amtrak for not making a profit! The French railway system, by contrast, due to adequate public investment in its infrastructure, turned in an operating profit of over a $1 billion in 2007.

Elsewhere in the country, Amtrak trains often offer spectacular scenery and have also seen sharp rises in ridership, often to the point that many trains are frequently sold out these days, particularly sleeper cars. In a sign of the times, it is not uncommon to meet people on board who have booked a sleeper for a three-and-a-half-day journey across the continent just so they can go "off grid" and be sure that by the time they arrive they will have completed a major project without interruption, whether a computer program or a television script. But the trains are generally limited to seventy-nine miles per hour, and because of aging equipment and the need to share tracks with freight trains, service is often unreliable. Outside the Northeast Corridor and a few travel lanes like Los Angeles–San Diego and Chicago-Milwaukee, intercity passenger trains barely figure in most transportation markets, and in vast swaths of the country, they don't even run.

California Dreamin'

In the Next Progressive Era, if it is to be progressive, the nation will at last join the ranks of other advanced industrial nations in committing to true, high-quality, high-speed passenger rail. Once it was argued that that the United States outside the Northeast Corridor lacked the population density required to make high-speed rail economically feasible. But this is clearly no longer the case.

California, for example, a state that once committed itself more than any other to the automobile, is now well along in developing plans for a high-speed rail system that can offer quick, clean travel alternatives between the state's major and intermediate cities—downtown Los Angles to downtown San Francisco, for example, in just two hours and thirty-eight minutes. The cost of building the system, according to studies, is just one-half to one-third of what would be required to accommodate California's population growth with more highway and airport construction, even if enough land could be found. A single highway lane can provide transportation for only about three thousand people an hour before choking; a single high-speed railroad track, by contrast, can handle forty thousand passengers per hour.

The proposed system fits nicely with the state's commitment, led by its Republican governor, Arnold Schwarzenegger, to reduce greenhouse gas emissions (GHG) and promote energy efficiency. According the California High Speed Rail Commission, the system would reduce dependence on foreign oil by more than twelve million barrels per year and reduce greenhouse gases by twelve billion pounds annually, while requiring no operating subsidies. Its ability to reduce intermediate-length airline trips makes it particularly beneficial to the environment, since high-altitude GHG emissions create 2.7 times the warming effect of those made on the ground. How much GHG the electrified, high-speed rail system will itself produce depends entirely on how the power for it winds up being generated, but if the source is any combination of wind, solar, hydro, or nuclear, it will produce no emissions at all.[14] Sadly, California faces a deep budget crisis, brought on in no small measure by its overreliance on automobiles and the related collapse in suburban home prices. But on November 4, 2008, California voters passed the ballot initiative necessary to set the high-speed rail system in motion, and there would be no better way for the Obama administration to stimulate the economy and create jobs. The Golden State will rapidly tarnish without it.

Florida Fiasco

To see California's future without high-speed rail, visit Tampa Bay. After more than ten years of planning, Florida was near breaking ground on a Tampa-Orlando-Miami high-speed line until Governor Jeb Bush threw his weight behind a misleadingly worded 2004 referendum to defund it. The plans are still waiting to be pulled off the shelf, and as Florida's tourism industry continues to be hammered by the high cost of driving, recession, and the breakdown of the commercial aviation, the case for building the system grows more overwhelming every day.

In the summer of 2008, Longman returned to Tampa, where he had worked as a business reporter during much of the 1990s. He discovered that the local economy was so depressed he could rent a compact car at the airport for just $25 a day, half of what he'd paid in the early 1990s, and stay in a luxury downtown hotel for just $100. Yet it was no bargain. Just two trips to the beach, through a maze of new highway construction, burned up $60 worth of gas. To this day, there is no public transportation, not even a bus, between Tampa and its sister city, St. Petersburg. Tampa sports a new light rail line, but it connects with neither the airport nor the railroad station, making it nearly as useless as Jacksonville's notorious "people mover," which goes 2.5 miles from nowhere to nowhere.

Clearwater, once a suburb of St. Pete, is now so isolated by traffic congestion that it might as well be a hundred miles away. Though the rails are still intact, neither city has seen a passenger train since the early 1970s. Tampa has a beautifully restored downtown rail station and abundant rail infrastructure leading to it, but it still lacks a single commuter train.

It is no coincidence that Tampa Bay is among the regions hardest hit by the foreclosure crisis (home prices are off 26 percent from their peak as of this writing) or that its tourist industry is declining. Tourists visiting Orlando now face a two-hour-plus white-knuckle drive down I-4 and through the stop-and-go sprawl of North Tampa should they want to brave a side trip to Busch Gardens. Predictably, attendance there in 2007 was down 12 percent compared to 2000. Whereas a high-speed train could by now be whisking tourists from Orlando's theme parks to St. Pete's or Clearwater's beaches in less than hour, the trip now takes at least three hours of hellacious driving with no place to park when you get there. Because of its sprawling, auto-dependent development, the cost of living throughout Florida is soaring far more than in areas better served by mass transit, even as real estate values plunge. Florida, always a bellwether state, provides an object lesson on the hazards of not building a balanced transportation system.[15]

Other well-studied, federally designated potential high-speed corridors include Washington-Charlotte-Atlanta, New York–Albany–Buffalo, and corridors linking Chicago with the many major midwestern cities that surround it within a radius of several hundred miles, including Detroit, Indianapolis, St. Louis, and Milwaukee. In response to a question during the 2008 presidential campaign, Barack Obama offered a succinct and amusing case for the potential of high-speed rail in the Midwest. He pointed out that flight times between most midwestern cities are only about forty-five minutes, except that

by the time you get to the airport, take off your shoes, get to the terminal, realize that your flight's been delayed two hours, go pay $10 for a cup of coffee, and a sandwich for another $10, come back, you get on the plane, you're sitting on the tarmac for another 25 minutes, you finally take off, you're circling above the

city for another half hour, when you land they can't find your lug-
gage, and then you get to where you're going—by the time it's all
done it's a five-hour trip! . . . So the time is right now for us to
start thinking about high-speed rail as an alternative to air transportation, connecting all these cities, and think about what a great
project that would be in terms of rebuilding America.[16]

Realistically, however, high-speed rail needs presidential leadership of
the kind Eisenhower and Kennedy gave to the interstate highway system.
And it needs dedicated federal tax revenue streams just like highways
and aviation enjoy. These might be financed by carbon taxes or by carbon credits under a cap-and-trade system. Creation of a national infrastructure bank could also attract global capital flows, which would be
fitting enough. The original canals and railroads that built America's
industrial greatness were mostly financed by European investors, which
points up how smart infrastructure eventually pays for itself by creating
jobs and stimulating the economy. Why wait?

In Transit

The final piece is rationalizing local trips. This is no small issue for the
nation's energy future. If Americans used public transportation at the
same rate as Europeans—for roughly 10 percent of their daily travel
needs—the United States would reduce its dependence on imported
oil by more than 40 percent, or nearly the amount of oil we import
from Saudi Arabia each year, while also achieving dramatic reduction
in greenhouse gases.[17]

It is also a quality-of-life issue. Most Americans will always want
and need a car. But that does not mean they want and need to fight
traffic, guzzle gas, and wear down their vehicles on every daily trip they
make.

As many others have said, a big part of the answer is more sensible
land use. Zoning that prohibits homes, stores, schools, and offices from
being within short distances of each other should be, and in many communities is being, rethought. "Walkable" communities offer substantial
benefits to public health, as we already seen. More compact develop-

ment also makes it much easier to configure convenient and economically feasible transit system.

What form those transit systems should take depends almost entirely on local conditions, including population density, existing travel and growth patterns, and available budgetary resources. In some places, car pools and vans will be the only feasible alternative for years. But a few precepts apply universally.

The first is that mass transit should not be an indignity. Over the years, most have been operated with poor people in mind, and it shows. Yet when the first New York subways were built, some trains offered parlor cars, and some stations were graced with potted plants and artwork. By offering first-class service on light rail, commuter, and subways lines, mass transit can break its long-established association with the downscale masses.

Frankly, too, an important reason why many people choose to drive is that it allows them to preserve their zone of privacy. They don't have to listen to other people's raucous conversations or worry about a drunk or a wolf sitting down next to them. An indication of just how important such considerations are to some people comes from the business class service Amtrak offers on many of its conventional trains. Ostensibly, business class riders don't get much over regular coach riders: a slightly larger seat, a free newspaper, and nonalcoholic beverages, which they most often have to fetch for themselves. Yet business class tickets command up to a 50 percent premium over regular coach and are usually sold out. Travelers will pay a lot for the chance to self-segregate, including the hassles of driving if there are no other options.

The ability to reserve seats on commuter trains, subways, and buses can also go a long way toward easing the anxiety that many commuters feel when using public transit. It is asking a lot of people to run the risk of being a straphanger for the whole duration of their commute. To the greatest extent possible, mass transit should be operated so that few people are ever forced to stand and so that people who are willing to pay for it are always guaranteed a seat. Offering reserved parking at stations is a good idea for the same reason.

A second precept is to avoid false thrift. Mass transit needs to be fast, frequent, and go lots of places for it to work on the scale we need.

Miami's twenty-one-mile, heavy rail, elevated Metrorail system, begun in 1984, is smooth, clean, and well engineered, but it has also acquired the local nickname, Metrofail. Why? Because it doesn't go where most people want to go. It fails to serve, for example, the city's bustling Seaport, trendy South Beach, and, most egregiously, Miami International Airport, which it approaches but just misses, reportedly due to the power of Miami's taxi medallion owners. (At long last, an extension to the airport is at least planned, and we understand some dirt is being pushed around.) For years, critics of mass transit have pointed to Metrorail as kind of reductio ad absurdum argument for why passenger rail can't work, but the real lesson of Metrorail is that half-built routes to nowhere don't draw passengers (and don't save any energy, either). We need to stop taking a crimped view of mass transit. To provide the scale and amenities it needs to work requires a national commitment at least as large as that given to the automobile for the last half of the twentieth century.

A third, seemingly small-bore but important precept is to empower riders with information. Few experiences make you feel more like a chump than standing at a bus stop wondering when the bus is ever going to come. (Urban bus rider lore: light a cigarette and it comes immediately.) Unless urban buses run on dedicated right-of-ways, they can almost never keep to a schedule. They tend to bunch up, so that instead of one bus coming every ten minutes, three come every thirty minutes. With today's technology, it is easy to offer electronic displays at bus stops that let people know how far away the next bus is and its estimated time of arrival. And it is even easier yet to let people use their cell phones and mobile Internet access devices to find out how long the wait will be, as some transit systems are starting to do. It is the sense of not knowing, of not being in control, that irritates so many people about mass transit and keeps them in the cars. Timely information, as well as effective law enforcement and ways for passengers to self-segregate, are all important but often overlooked means of improving the mass transit experience.

Another key is pricing. Given the role transit riders play in reducing pollution, congestion, and energy consumption, they deserve compensation from people who choose to drive instead. Using today's smart card technology, this would be easy to do. For example, people who could establish through the data collected on their smart cards that they regularly used mass transit (defined as, say, two trips per work day or more) could be made eligible to receive a $1,000 tax rebate. Drivers would finance the cost through new electronic tolls placed in areas served by mass transit.

A final precept should be so obvious that we are almost embarrassed to state it, yet it is too important not to mention. We are now a generation behind in rationalizing all our transportation modes because, uniquely among advanced nations, we let ourselves be duped by the low market price of energy during the late 1980s and throughout all the 1990s. This could well happen again. The long-term trend in oil production is as predictable as the tides. But in the short term, oil prices have already plunged due to the combination of a global recession and the bursting of a speculative bubble in oil futures. The key challenge for public policy is to ensure that one way or another we are not lured into inaction by such a dip. For example, it would be smart public policy to establish a flexible gas tax formula to ensure that the price of gasoline at the pump will never again be below $3.50 a gallon. With that certainty, individuals, car companies, alternative energy entrepreneurs, and state and local urban planners would all be encouraged along the track we need to take to establish energy independence, cleaner air, and a higher and sustainable quality of life.

CHAPTER 12

Yeoman's Work

I F THE ORIGINAL Progressives could see today's America, what would they make of it? Those with a bent for efficiency and conservation would be appalled by the lack of thrift. They would be puzzled, too, by a health care system that builds on their commitment to scientific medical education but barely approaches anything like scientific management. Some would be cheered, and others alarmed, by the decline of racial segregation and the entry of most mothers into the paid workforce. Progressives surely would not be pleased, either, to see a nation that has simultaneously become overdependent on automobiles while forgetting how to make cars. In the Progressive Era, America was a manufacturing giant that had no fear of Japan or China except for their exports of impoverished "coolies."

But what would perhaps perplex and depress Progressives the most is our loss of even the concept of an American yeomanry. They would see factions in our society divided against each other that in their own time were natural allies because of a shared allegiance to the yeoman ideal. They would wonder at the mutual contempt between Christian fundamentalists and reform-minded experts, between red states and blue states, between Hillary Clinton's "embittered" working-class supporters and Barack Obama's legions of college-educated "progressive" activists. They would ask, What kind of a progressivism is this that doesn't know how to talk to the yeomen or even know that yeomanry still endures as the unifying essence of the American character?

Let's try to place ourselves in the frame of the yeoman tradition, as the original Progressives would do in looking at their great-great-grand-children. There have always been, and still are, two essential types among America's yeomanry. One is the striving strain—materialistic, acquisitive, and set on rising in the world. From the beginning, this type included the entrepreneurial farmer on the frontier who behaved more like a real estate developer, rapidly clearing acreage only to sell up and move on. It also included the sort of individual Woodrow Wilson approvingly referred to as "the man on the make"—who would prove his entrepreneurial prowess if only government would give him the opportunity to do so by investing in good public schools, land grant colleges, farm-to-market roads, and protection from monopolists.

In contrast, there has always been what might be called the spiritual strain of yeomanry, made up of individuals who deny themselves opportunities to enjoy a rising material standard of living in order to cling stubbornly to their independence. Among this type were the mountain men of West Virginia and Tennessee, who in the 1920s could have easily found jobs on Detroit's assembly lines but who stayed put in their cabins, determined to maintain their traditional way of life. There were also the small-town storeowners, who could have gained economic security by going to work at the new A&P in the same era but who held on, preferring to be their own boss. And there were innumerable craftsmen and artisans—furniture makers, boat builders, jewelers—who took deep pride in their work and persevered, even as the rise of industrial production ensured that they would never get rich and would quite likely go broke.

By the 1930s, both types seemed to be on the verge of extinction. "In the coming upheavals of the 20th Century," writes Rex Burns, "the yeoman's ghost would be heard, but faintly and uneasily, and—like the flute music in Death of a Salesman—with a sense of profound loss."[1] President Eisenhower would give a nod to the importance of entrepreneurialism by calling for the creation of the Small Business Administration in 1953. By then, however, it seemed as if the triumvirate of Big Business, Big Labor, and Big Government would rule the future. No longer did opinion leaders see a strong American yeomanry as essential to either liberty or prosperity. Accordingly, talk of yeomanry simply slipped out of the American political vocabulary. FDR was the last president to evoke the term, when he stated during the Depression, "In our national life, public and private, the very nature of free government demands that there must be a line of defense held by the yeomanry of business and industry and agriculture."[2]

In the postwar vision, individual freedom, such as it might be, would be maintained not by yeomanry but by what the economist John Kenneth Galbraith characterized as a system of "countervailing power" in which giant institutions—unions, corporations, the mass media, government—held each other in check. Economic growth would not depend on entrepreneurial energy from below but would derive from macro forces: stimulative fiscal and monetary policies, government and corporate investment in research and development, mass media advertising, and "planned obsolescence" to pump up aggregate demand.[3]

Consumers were the new heroes on the expanding frontier of mass consumption. If they lacked freedom and independence, they could at least console themselves with their bungalows, finned automobiles, and more stuff bought on store credit than their parents had ever dreamed of owning.

Yet still the yeoman ideal would not die. Many baby boomers, as they reflect back on the arc of their lives, may see in their experience various reconnections to the yeoman tradition. For example, those who, beginning in the 1960s and 70s, rejected the colossal institutions of postwar American life, proclaimed "Small Is Beautiful," and yearned to dedicate their lives to such "countercultural" pursuits as organic farming, handcraft production, or the running of small bookstores are direct descendents of the spiritual strain of American yeomanry.

So are those who may be hostile to the sixties but who have willfully sacrificed wage income to enjoy the independence of being small-scale contractors, hobby shop owners, owner-operator truckers, commercial fishermen, or part-time ranchers. For the spiritual yeoman, meaning derives not just from the nature of the work itself but also from the opportunity to make a living, no matter how modest, in tight-knit small towns or places of great natural beauty where wage jobs are few.

Other boomers may recognize more of themselves in the striving strain of American yeomanry. By the late 1970s, the ruling coalition of Big Business, Big Labor, and Big Government that had prevailed since the late New Deal hit a wall, producing high unemployment and stagflation. Into the economic void came the high-tech start-ups—companies founded as often as not by college dropouts in their parents' garages and funded by credit cards—whose "creative destruction" pushed the American economy out of its lethargy. Yet if Bill Gates started out as a classic striving "man on the make," the sort of yeoman who would have stirred Woodrow Wilson's heart, he soon enough became a monopolist. This, in short order, defines the central economic dilemma of today's America: how to once again preserve the yeoman's interest in an era of rising inequality and vast concentrations of capital.

The New Yeomanry

We now live in a world in which, for increasing numbers of Americans, there are few alternatives to some form of yeomanry. The grand bargain struck between industrial labor and large manufacturers in the postwar era, which allowed even automobile assembly line workers to own their own cars and homes, send their kids to college, and look forward to comfortable retirement, is now a dead letter. Similarly, the option of becoming an "organization man," securely entrenched in a rule-bound corporate bureaucracy, is rapidly disappearing.

Between 1983 and 2006, median job tenure (time in one job) declined by 38 percent among men aged thirty-five to forty-four and by 37 percent among men aged forty-five to fifty-four. When displaced workers find new jobs, they often take a sharp drop in pay, a phenomenon that during the last recession (2001–2003) was most pronounced for highly educated individuals, whose typical earnings loss was about 21 percent.[4]

Global competition, which increasingly affects white-collar as well as blue-collar workers, is partly to blame for the declining economic power of employees. So are automation and an aging workforce, in which there are fewer and fewer workers to support the "legacy cost" of each retiree, and in which older workers face increasing age discrimination due to the soaring cost of their employer-provided health care. Taken together, these and other trends have increased the power of large holders of capital and caused a rewriting of the social contract.

Its new terms are roughly these. The corporation is answerable only to its stockholders. Attempts to strengthen unions, limit outsourcing, or control immigration meet strong corporate resistance. Many contingent workers, meanwhile, become not only slaves without masters but also slaves without health care benefits or pensions.

Under this contract, too, the cost of obtaining credentials, such as a college degree, is escalating, while the rewards in economic security are diminishing. Between 2000 and 2005, tuition and fees at four-year private colleges increased by 25 percent and at four-year public colleges by 46 percent.[5] Yet during the same period, men with college degrees, according to the U.S. Census Bureau, saw a 7 percent drop in their real median income. By 2005, men with professional degrees earned 2.6 percent less as a group (adjusted for inflation) than they did in the recession year of 1992—and this despite the baby boom generation aging into positions of seniority. The earnings trends for educated women look better when compared to their mothers, but only because more women have gravitated to traditionally male fields.[6] Entry-level wages for college-educated women fell by 1.7 percent between 2000 and 2007.[7]

In the face of these trends, the downsized executive becomes a "consultant," the overstressed mother becomes a "mompreneur," the unemployed journalist a "blogger." At the same time, however, many of the new yeomen/yeowomen are remarkably successful. Between 1995 and 2004, the family net worth of salaried workers barely moved, from a median of $60,300 to $67,200 (in 2004 dollars). Meanwhile, the median family net worth of the self-employed jumped from $191,800 to $335,600![8] No wonder, then, that some 70 percent of today's teenagers aspire to own their own business, compared to only 25 percent who aspire to work for a large company.[9] The return of yeomanry is a triumph for those who have the ambition, capital, smarts, and good luck to realize its many opportunities. Wouldn't it be truly "progressive" if government policy bent itself toward putting that opportunity within the reach of far more people?

Localization

Looking to the future, we see many trends in technology, demography, the cost of logistics, and consumer preference that will offer up new opportunities for yeomanry, specifically for small-scale, localized production. Food production is a good first example. The two big trends in food production have long been industrialization (factory farms) and globalization (winter strawberries rushed by jetliner from Chile). Yet there are strong signs that these trends have reached their limits and are beginning to reverse.

An inevitable return of high energy prices will dramatically increase the cost of transporting food long distances. At the same time, fear about the safety and quality of the food supply is a becoming a global phenomenon. In Japan, fear of mad cow disease led to a three-year ban on U.S. beef, and supermarkets there still don't stock it because consumers shun it as a disease vector. In Europe, public rejection of "Frankenfood" has effectively banned U.S. grain exports.

Public trust in industrial agriculture is greater in the United States but fading fast. As the recent alarms in the United States about spinach, tomatoes, and chiles tainted with *E. coli* bacteria illustrate, the opportunity to buy food labeled "organic" or "natural" in Wal-Mart will not be sufficient to assuage the public's growing uneasiness about the food supply. Industrial-scale agriculture, whether organic or not, fails to the extent that it succeeds. The bigger its division of labor, and the longer its supply and distribution chains, the less the consumer feels he or she can trust the safety and quality of its products.

Terrorist threats to the food chain, or just the fears thereof, are also likely to drive future demand for locally grown or homegrown food. When Tommy Thompson stepped down as U.S. health secretary in 2004, he delivered a stark warning: "I, for the life of me, cannot understand why the terrorists have not attacked our food supply, because it is so easy to do."

After falling for generations, the number of small farms in the United States is rising. According to the latest available national statistics, while the total number of farms in the United States declined by 86,894 between 1997 and 2002, the number of small farms (ten to forty-nine acres) shot up by 32,870.[10] Despite gigantic forces stacked against him, even the yeoman farmer is making a comeback. For the first time since the 1970s, it is now possible to become a successful small farmer without inheriting land. The trend draws strength from the expansion of a highly educated, affluent, upper-middle class whose members have the luxury and sophistication to fret about what traces of pesticides their children may ingest or whether their roast chicken once enjoyed a chance to range freely. The aging of the population also causes a rising proportion of society to be preoccupied with health and therefore with the quality of food.

The rising use of ethanol and other forms of energy derived from biomass is also likely to drive up the cost of commercially produced food, thereby building a better case for growing your own or buying from a neighbor. Much farmland currently used to feed humans is being diverted to "feeding" their cars instead, causing more upward pressure on food prices. At the same time, publications like *Mother Earth News* already contain many ads for what might be called personal biodiesel distillers—small-scale products that allow for the home production of biodiesel fuel using lawn clippings, leaves, and other organic material.

What happens to foreclosed McMansions, many built on lots of five or more acres of once-prime farmland? High transportation and food prices may render many sprawling suburbs more like the "garden cities" Lewis Mumford once hoped they would be, as organic yeoman farmers move in to take advantage of broad new opportunities. One imagines a day when erstwhile McMansions will have their three-car garages converted to aquaponic greenhouses, in which tilapia and catfish produce the nitrogen needed to grow lush yields of vegetables. In other neighborhoods, rundown McMansions with three-story cathedral ceilings will make great structures for stacking hay bales, roosting chickens, or displaying produce to local customers.

Global Aging

Population aging, both here and abroad, is also working as a force toward localization and an expansion of yeomanry. Within the United States, population aging leaves an increasing fraction of the workforce facing the effects of age discrimination and of atrophied and obsolete skill sets. Already, the laid-off fifty-year-old executive who sets up a "consultancy" in a spare bedroom is a common enough phenomenon to be a cliché. In the future, an aging population will produce many more people who have been displaced from wage employment well before they can afford retirement. These people will be looking for ways to earn money in their own homes and garages.

Population aging, combined with low fertility, low marriage, and high divorce rates, has also greatly expanded the ranks of Americas approaching old age with weak family support systems. Nearly 20 percent of the baby boom generation never had children. Another 17 percent only had one. Weak family support systems, in turn, combined with general inadequate retirement savings, will provide large demand for alternative, communal living arrangements sustained by home or local production. Such communes may or may not grow all of their own food, but they will look for ways in which their members can sustain themselves as much as possible through mutual aid, communal food preparation, elder care, and transport. Organizing such communes offers tremendous opportunities to yeoman entrepreneurs.

Meanwhile, all of our major trading partners face rapidly contracting labor forces, due to low fertility rates. Japan's working-age population has been shrinking since 1995 and is expected to account for less than half of the country's total population within twenty-five years.[11] Europe faces severe manpower shortages as well. China's working-age population will peak somewhere around 2015 before beginning a very rapid decline. This will create what Chinese demographers described as a 4-2-1 society, in which one child is responsible for supporting two aged parents and four grandparents. In every region of the world, birthrates are falling and even throughout most of the developing world are now below replacement levels.[12]

It is difficult to know all of the ramifications of such a sea change in global demographics, but when combined with other trends, one implication is clear. The current global trading system based on high, credit-driven mass consumption in the United States and low-cost, surplus labor and capital abroad has already passed its limits. Most American consumers are tapped out on their credit, know they need to save more and have begun to do so. Labor costs in China, meanwhile, are already rising quickly due to the slowing growth of its labor force. A return to pre-recession energy prices will vastly increase the cost of transporting goods across the Pacific.

Meanwhile, Japan, Germany, China, Russia, and other large creditor nations will need to repatriate much of the capital they have invested in the United States to pay for the cost of their burgeoning elderly populations. Because of population aging, the McKinsey Global Institute Project projects that the rate of household financial wealth accumulation in industrial nations will fall 36 percent between 2005 and 2025.[13] Today's high-savings nations—Japan, Germany, China—will begin to "dis-save" as more and more of their population ages into retirement, contributing to profound structural dislocations in the world's financial system that may well already be upon us. Advances in automation may smooth some of the challenges created by an aging global workforce, but here, too, trends in manufacturing technology favor small-scale, local production.

Personal Fabrication

The emergence of so-called rapid prototyping devices is an example to watch. These are computer-driven machines, some dating back to the 1980s, that are currently used in industrial settings to build models, prototypes, and sometimes very small production runs of parts. Typically, these machines start with a design made on a computer and then use digital commands to "print" the product by spraying cross sections of plastic or other materials until an entire three-dimensional form emerges. Other rapid prototype machines take the opposite approach: instead of adding up layers of materials, they use computer-driven lasers to cut or subtract them away. By 2007, rapid prototyping had become a $1.1 billion industry, with sales expected to double by 2012.[14]

Leading technologists believe that in much the same way yesterday's mainframe computers morphed into today's personal computers, today's rapid prototype machines will morph into tomorrow's personal fabricating devices. As with personal computers, the size and cost of these machines (currently starting at around $18,000) will drop quickly even as their power and potential expand. Today, it is already possible to use a 3-D scanner, such as the ZScanner 700, to create a digital blueprint of, say, a BMW tail light, and then simply print a replica for a cost of a few cents in materials.

Or you can use computer-assisted design software to create your designs, or buy or barter for someone else's designs for, say, eyeglasses, jewelry, or a laptop computer, and then print them out in 3-D. Without the development of any new technology, it will also soon be possible to print houses and other structures, as has been demonstrated by Behrokh Khoshnevis of the University of Southern California and the Center for Rapid Automated Fabrication Technologies.[15] Adding to the low price and likely rapid diffusion of the personal fabricator is its potential to reproduce itself.

Another example suggestive of how technology is evolving to empower small-scale production comes from a place you might not think to look: toy stores. Available at toy stores everywhere for about $240 is the Lego "Mindstorm" kit—developed by the Massachusetts Institute of Technology. It comes with some five hundred familiar plastic Lego bricks and gears. More significantly, it also comes with a small microprocessor that plugs into tactile and visual sensors. The microprocessor runs on open-source software that any user can modify. The kit thus allows the user to construct, for example, a robot that can see and feel its environment and that can be programmed to perform desired tasks, including, at least theoretically, mixing up a batch of soap or building a copy of itself.

The kit is advertised as appropriate for children age ten and up, but it turns out most sales are to grown-ups. Working with the Center for Bits and Atoms at MIT, Ken Paul, a process engineer for the United States Postal Service, has used Lego Mindstorm kits, for example, to model workflow patterns in large Postal Service sorting facilities. MIT graduate students use them routinely to build prototypes of various inventions, including a three-axis fabrication tool that can both construct and deconstruct or "recycle" parts.[16]

The Mindstorm kit represents a point in the development of personal fabrication that is perhaps equivalent to the introduction of the Altair 8800 personal computer kit in January 1975. Its primary appeal is to geeky hobbyists, its software is primitive, and there is not much practical use the average person can make of it. Another similarity is that its revolutionary potential may be easily overlooked. In 1977, the president of the Digital Equipment Corporation famously said, "There is no reason for any person to have a computer in their home." Many people may similarly be at a loss to think of what they would do with a personal fabricator, even one that could, for example, be easily programmed to make common household items. But this is simply a failure of vision.

The personal fabrication revolution is arriving just as consumer preference is more and more favoring goods and services that are not mass produced. In addition to locally produced food, they include handcrafted furniture, original art, custom-fitted clothes, as well as "homemade" journalism, commentary, and entertainment in the form of blogs and websites. Just as the blogosphere allows for the home production and distribution of personal opinions, ideas, as well as plagiarized text and video, an emerging "Legosphere" allows for the home or small business production and distribution of material inventions, whether original in design or not.

Yeomanry and the Next Social Contract

Yet yeomanry also means taking risks that more often than not do not work out. Every year, about a half million small firms go under.[17] The yeoman's high exposure to risk predictably leads to deep political resentments and populist outbursts. Yeomen are often griping characters, especially when down on their luck, and deeply suspicious of unseen forces. Precisely because they do not work in institutions, they tend to be prickly about their social status and about their relationship to government.

For example, though often highly dependent on public spending for suburban and rural roads, schools, Social Security, water projects, crop subsidies, state universities, securities regulation, and the like, the yeoman, whether a farmer or a striving dot-com entrepreneur, is likely to deny his dependence. What he lacks, he likely thinks someone took from him, whether it is monopolies like Microsoft and

ConAgra, or activist judges, pointy-headed bureaucrats, or welfare cheats.

Since yeomen are likely to stay close to home, whether they are small storeowners in Topeka or freelance computer programmers in Seattle, it also matters a lot to them to have like-minded neighbors. This can have a negative effect when it comes to accepting true diversity of opinion and values.

The yeoman also tends to have a streak of anti-intellectualism—or at least a distrust of experts. Many who are religious take a dim view of credentialed professionals ensconced in large institutions who variously contradict their belief in creationism, in the humanity of an embryo, or in the constitutionality of school prayer. Similarly, many organic farmers and progressive entrepreneurs place more faith in crystals than in God, but they will not stand still to hear experts contradict their fears of genetically modified food, nuclear power, and overpopulation. The yeoman is happy to have experts agree with him but often undeterred when they do not.

The yeoman is therefore not an easy individual to lead, which explains his historical association with personal freedom and limited government. Yet what if we looked at today's expanding ranks of yeomen as Thomas Jefferson would? Remember his insight that the opportunities open to the yeomen of his time were vital to the interests of urban wageworkers. So long as the frontier remained open, employers had to contend with the fact that their workers always had the option "to quit their trades and go to laboring the earth." The same is figuratively true today. The more opportunities today's Americans have to flourish (or even just to subsist) by engaging in modern forms of yeomanry, the more pressure that puts on employers to treat wageworkers well; for else they, too, will just go laboring, if not the earth, then the new frontiers of cyberspace.

Even spiritual yeomen who cling to their antiquated and seemingly inefficient crafts for the sheer joy of it—farriers, glassblowers, potters, as well as poets, playwrights, street performers, antique dealers, breeders, vintners, quilters, hardwood artisans, printmakers, and community fest promoters—all play an important and often overlooked role in benefiting the larger economy, despite their apparent low efficiency. By withholding their labor from the wage system, they thereby force employers to treat their remaining workers just that much better.

Small Dealers and Worthy Men

If we accept the social value of America's reemerging yeomanry, what public policies would best encourage and protect its members? We have already discussed many: asset-building strategies, protection from predatory lenders, a safer, more efficient, effective and affordable health care system, a rationalized transportation system. Yet this is not all.

In this age of giant international corporations and agribusinesses, of global supply chains and secretive hedge funds, there is also, as in the Progressive Era, a role for much stronger government regulation of Big Business. This includes rigorous prosecution of monopolies even when they are efficient. Populists and Progressives worked to defend the interests of small farmers and businessmen without much concern about what scale of production would offer the "best deal" for shoppers. Writing for the majority in an 1897 opinion against tariffs favoring large-volume shippers, U.S. Supreme Court justice Rufus Peckham took the typical Progressive view: even when big combinations of capital could deliver lower prices, they should be opposed because they threatened to put "small dealers and worthy men" out of business. If small-scale farming, manufacturing, transport, and retailing had built-in inefficiencies that led to higher prices, so be it. That was the price of liberty. As Senator Henry Teller of Colorado observed in 1889, "I do not believe that the great object in life is to make everything cheap."[18]

Today, we might add, corporate concentration causes suppliers to be so hounded for cost cuts that they cannot afford to engage in research and development or maintain quality. Have you had the experience of having a new laptop or television fail only because its on/off switch jammed, or the glove compartment door fall off in a new car? The pressure on suppliers to make a 25-cent part for 5 cents makes such failures common, even with consumer items costing thousands of dollars.

Competition policy should also consider the interests of "small dealers and worthy men" on a wide range of other issues—farm policy, land use for big-box stores, allocation of broadband spectrum—even if that involves what at first seems like countenancing willful inefficiency. Established broadcasters, for example, may be able to make efficient use to their spectrum rights in rolling out high-definition television and cell phone networks. Yet the lack of "open access" to these networks is a direct threat to the Internet's yeomanry—including not only small-scale providers of communications services but everyone trying to run a small business with a faulty cell phone and overpriced wireless Internet connection.[19]

Similarly, a new Wal-Mart may at first offer nominally cheaper prices to consumers but at an unacceptable long-term cost, including decaying downtowns and increased pressure on suppliers to cut wages, cut corners, and outsource. Wal-Mart, for now, is highly efficient and is not a monopoly. It is, however, like many other global corporations, what economists call a monopsony, due to its ability to dictate price to its suppliers. As New America fellow Barry Lynn explains, "The ultimate danger of monopsony is that it deprives the firms that actually manufacture products from obtaining an adequate return on their investment. . . . Over time, it tends to destroy the machines and skills on which we all rely."[20]

Food production is another area in which low prices should not be the only standard. Deeply subsidized agribusiness produces an American diet that is relatively cheap in price but expensive in cost, not only to consumers' health but to the environment. Junk food is not an inevitable market outcome. Reducing subsidies to agribusiness would result in higher food prices, to be sure. But it would also promote both the biological and the political health of the population, thereby making the real cost of food lower. As Jefferson would remind us, the benefits of yeomanry extend to such intangibles as the promotion of civic culture, wholesome, sustainable production, and a check on the rapacious practices of Big Business in collusion with Big Government.

It also should be remembered that consolidation is often inherently inefficient in many realms, especially those involving creativity. As long ago as the 1940s, Hollywood discovered that the hierarchal studio system was inferior to a model in which free agency played a much larger role.[21] Similarly, in the computing industry, the tendency is away from the button-downed, monopolistic IBM of the 1960s toward production based on collaborative networks of free agents, many of whom literally work at home in their pajamas.[22] As more and more of the economy evolves toward similar networks of small-scale, often home-based producers, the question becomes how to adjust the social contract so that the new yeomen get the seed money, health care, pensions, and infrastructure they need.

Encouraging local, small-scale production, whether in agriculture, manufacturing, or services, also promises to produce many other benefits we are prone to overlook. These include less pollution and anomie caused by excessive auto commuting; more chances for women, minorities, and older workers to escape prejudice in the workplace through self-employment; and more opportunities to harmonize paid work with caring for children or aging parents.

The Nurturing Sector

When it comes to family, we would also do well to consider the views of Progressive Era maternal feminists like Mother Jones, who tried to preserve the yeoman ideal by campaigning to prevent corporations from devouring family life. Today, the market system has penetrated and distorted nearly all aspects of home economics and human nurture. As a rule, the adults who sacrifice the most to create and mold precious human capital retain only a small share of the public good they create. Those who devote themselves full-time to raising their children receive no wages and no additional support from government in old age. Daycare workers take home less pay than hotel maids. Elementary school teachers could easily make more money as casino dealers. Camp counselors could raise their income by taking a cashier job at the mall. High school teachers would receive more money if they taught stock or real estate seminars. The highest-paid college professors are those who teach the least. Among doctors, pediatricians generally receive far less compensation than specialists dealing with adult illnesses.

To take another example, most states require a prospective nursery school teacher to have earned at least an associate's degree, with a major in childhood development, to have passed a certification exam, and to have served as a student teacher. Nonetheless, the average annual wage of preschool teachers in 2007 was just $25,800. By comparison, the average wage for animal trainers, according to the Bureau of Labor Statistics, was $30,390.

These are the actual terms of the contemporary social contact as it applies to those involved in raising and educating the next generation. The system has benefited both Big Business and Big Government in a self-reinforcing cycle. As the human capital that the family creates is effectively taxed away, the family discovers it needs two or more incomes, plus ever-increasing debt loads, to sustain itself. Mothers join fathers in the paid workforce, thereby providing employers with new workers and the government with new taxpayers, which helps replace the workers and taxpayers who are not being born because of the increasing tax on parenthood. The economy at least appears to grow, because while the work a woman performs as a mother and homemaker does not count in estimates of GDP growth, the work she performs as a paid employee in any field does. The harried, two-paycheck family, moreover, creates increased market demand for a broad range of fully taxable products—processed foods, business attire, takeout service, an extra car.

If we were in the habit of thinking of the family, as Progressive Era maternal feminists did, not merely as a private consumption unit but as the sector of the economy most responsible for human capital formation, we would not allow it to be starved for resources while the value it creates is consumed by employers and other, less productive sectors. A society that creates more and more disincentives to invest in children, while also undercompensating parents and other caregivers for the increasingly essential human capital they create, is living beyond its means.

These circumstances do not require a return to the "family wage" model championed by Progressive Era maternal feminists, with its explicit wage discrimination against women. But they must be mitigated by reducing the direct and opportunity costs of parenthood. One helpful step would be to offer increased Social Security pensions to parents, who are the ones who ultimately fund the system. Another would be to join the ranks of other advanced nations in offering paid maternity/paternity leave, including for the self-employed. It would also be a good idea if institutions of higher learning and employers would stop discriminating against people who have used their young adult years to start families. Here is a new civil rights issue for the age.

The Next Progressive Era

Such ideas are neither liberal nor conservative, but they are truly Progressive in the original sense and consistent with the yeoman ideal that more than any other defines the American creed. Because of the long hold and widespread appeal of the yeoman ideal on the American political imagination, a politics that pays honor to this tradition has the potential to bridge the country's cultural divides, just as occurred during the last Progressive Era.

The yeoman's association with liberty, family, and patriotism may ring loudest with heartland conservatives; his distrust of large institutions and engagement in small-scale, sustainable production may resonate most with today's urban professionals. Yet his true appeal, as always, is in being beyond Left and Right. The yeoman is committed to free enterprise but adamant that government provide grants of free soil, public education, or (coming soon, let's hope) health care; in favor of regulating Big Business to prevent monopoly and enforce product safety; but also a furious defender of the rights and privileges of small-scale ownership. If American "exceptionalism" has a face, it belongs to the yeoman.

Celebration of the yeoman ideal can also help us feel connected to a distinctively American past even as we face withering economic and social changes that challenge our identity as Americans. The yeoman, even when beat down and betrayed by banks, middlemen, politicians, thin soil, or a bad Internet connection, has a dignity and independence of mind nearly all Americans want to, and should, recognize in themselves.

Introduction

1. Christopher L. Peterson, "Predatory Structured Finance," *Cardozo Law Review* 28, no. 5 (2007).

2. Robert F. Bruner and Sean D. Carr, *The Panic of 1907: Lessons Learned from the Market's Perfect Storm* (Hoboken, NJ: Wiley, 2007).

3. P. S. Mead et al., "Food-Related Illness and Death in the United States," *Emerging Infectious Disease* 5, no. 5:607–625.

4. Cited by Mikael Skurnik, "Viruses vs. Superbugs: A Solution to the Antibiotic Crisis?" *Journal of the American Medical Assocaition* 297 (2007):644–645.

5. Theda Skocpol, *Protecting Soldiers and Mothers* (Cambridge, MA: Harvard University Press, 1992), xx.

6. "What Is Meant by Conservation?" *Ladies Home Journal* 28 (November 1911), pp. 23–95. Reprinted in David Strading, ed., *Conservation in the Progressive Era: Classic Texts* (Seattle: University of Washington Press, 2004), 34.

7. Elizabeth Sanders, *Roots of Reform: Farmers, Workers, and the American State, 1877–1917* (Chicago: University of Chicago Press, 1999).

Chapter 1

1. CNN/You Tube debate, Charleston, South Carolina, July 23, 2007, http://edition.cnn.com/2007/POLITICS/07/23/debate.transcript/.

2. John Dewey and James Hayden Tufts, *Ethics* (New York: Holt, 1908), 4. See also Wilson Carey McWilliams, "Standing at Armageddon: Morality and Religion in Progressive Thought," in *Progressivism and the New Democracy*, ed. Sidney M. Milkis and Jerome M. Mileur (Amherst: University of Massachusetts Press, 1999).

3. Cited by Michael Kammen, *A Machine That Would Go of Itself: The Constitution in American Culture* (Edison, NJ: Transaction, 2006).

4. Walter Lippmann, *Drift and Mastery* (New York: Mitchell Kennerley, 1914), 276.

5. Our thanks to what Jared Bernstein for coining this useful phase. See his book, *All Together Now: Common Sense for a Fair Economy* (San Francisco: Berrett-Koehler, 2006).

6. Matt Bai, *The Argument: Billionaires, Bloggers, and the Battle to Remake Democratic Politics* (New York: Penguin Books, 2007), 298.

7. Herbert David Croly, *The Promise of American Life* (New York: Macmillan, 1911), 409.

8. *Buck v. Bell*, 274 U.S. 200, 47 S.Ct. 584, 71 L.Ed. 1000 (1927). Upholding a Virginia law authorized the forced sterilization of "feeble-minded" persons, Justice Oliver Wendell Holmes wrote for the majority. "It is better for all the world, if instead of waiting to execute degenerate offspring for crime or to let them starve for their imbecility, society can prevent those who are manifestly unfit from continuing their kind. The principle that sustains compulsory vaccination is broad enough to cover cutting the Fallopian tubes. . . . Three generation of imbeciles are enough."

9. Frederic Clemson Howe, *The Confessions of a Reformer* (Kent, OH: Kent State University Press, 1988), 16.

10. Cited by William Strauss and Neil Howe, *Generations: The History of America's Future, 1584 to 2069* (New York: HarperCollins, 1991), 256.

11. William English Walling, *Socialism as It Is: A Survey of the World-wide Revolutionary Movement* (New York: Macmillan, 1912), 33.

12. Richard Hofstadter, *Age of Reform* (New York: Vintage Books, 1955).

13. Eldon J. Eisenach, *The Lost Promise of Progressivism* (Lawrence: University Press of Kansas 1994), 6.

14. Gabriel Kolko, *The Triumph of Conservatism: A Re-interpretation of American History, 1900–1916* (Glencoe, IL: Free Press, 1963); Christopher Lasch, *The True and Only Heaven: Progress and Its Critics* (New York: Norton, 1991).

15. Eldon J. Eisenach, *The Lost Promise of Progressivism* (Lawrence: University Press of Kansas, 1994), 21, fn. 19.

16. David W. Southern, *The Progressive Era and Race: Reform and Reaction, 1900–1917* (Wheeling, IL: Harlan Davidson, 2005).

17. "The Negro Crisis: Is the Separation of the Two Races to Become Necessary?" *American Magazine* (1907), cited by Southern, *The Progressive Era and Race*.

18. Robert J. Glennon Jr., "Justice Henry Billings Brown: Values in Tension," *University of Colorado Law Review* 44 (1973):553–604.

19. Cited by Michael J. Klarman, *From Jim Crow to Civil Rights: The Supreme Court and the Struggle for Racial Equality* (Oxford: Oxford University Press 2006), 66.

20. Booker T. Washington, the 1895 Atlanta Compromise Speech, in *Ripples of Hope: Great American Civil Rights Speeches*, ed. Josh Gottheimer and Bill Clinton (New York: Basic Civitas Books, 2003), 134.

Chapter 2

1. Small Business Administration, *The Small Business Economy for Data Year 2006* (Washington, DC: U.S. Government Printing Office, 2007), table 1.3.

2. Internal Revenue Service, *SOI Tax Stats —Integrated Business Data* (Washington, DC: Author, [2003]), table 1, www.irs.gov/taxstats/bustaxstats/article/0,,id=152029,00.html. For a popular discussion of this phenomenon, see Daniel H. Pink, *Free Agent Nation: How America's New Independent Workers Are Transforming the Way We Live* (New York: Warner Books, 2001).

3. U.S. Government Accountability Office, *Employment Arrangements: Improved Outreach Could Help Ensure Proper Worker Classification*, GAO 06-656 (Washington, DC: Author, July 2006); *Defining the Independent Workforce: What Is It, Why Is It Expanding, and What Are Its Challenges?* Independent Workforce Issue Brief, Freelancers Union, www.freelancersunion.org/advocacy/issue-briefs/what-is-the-independent-workforce.pdf, retrieved September 24, 2008.

4. Lawrence Mishel, Jared Bernstein, and Heidi Shierholz, *The State of Working America, 2008–2009*, Economic Policy Institute, executive summary, www.stateofworkingamerica.org/index.html, retrieved September 18, 2008.

5. Hector St. John de Crèvecoeur, *Letters from an American Farmer* (1782; repr., New York: Dutton, 1957), 51.

6. Thomas Jefferson, *Notes on the State of Virginia* (1787; repr., Richmond, VA: J. W. Randolph, 1853), 176.

7. "Letter to Mr. J. Lithgow," Washington, DC, January 4, 1805.

8. Marion Mills Miller, ed., *Great Debates in American History* (New York: Current Literature Publishing, 1913), 42.

9. Frederick Jackson Turner, *The Frontier in American History* (New York: Holt, 1920), 62.

10. Quoted by Julian E. Zelizer, *The American Congress: The Building of Democracy* (Boston: Houghton Mifflin, 2004), 271.

11. *Transactions of the Illinois State Historical Society for the Year 1901* (Springfield, IL: Phillips Brothers State Printers, 1901), 39.

12. "Annual Message to Congress," December 3, 1861, reprinted in *Appleton's Annual Cyclopaedia and Register of Important Events* (New York: Appleton, 1867), 610.

13. Henry Louis Gates Jr., "Forty Acres and a Gap in Wealth," *New York Times*, November 18, 2007, op-ed page.

14. Quoted in Rosanne Currarino, "The Politics of 'More': The Labor Question and the Idea of Economic Liberty in Industrial America," *Journal of American History* 93, no. 1 (June 2006), www.historycooperative.org/cgi-bin/

justtop.cgi?act=justtop&url=http://www.historycooperative.org/journals/jah/
93.1/currarino.html, retrieved November 7, 2008.

15. Paul R. Ehrlich, Anne H. Ehrlich, and Gretchen C. Daily, "What It Will
Take," *Mother Jones* (September/October 1995).

16. Cited in Dale Fetherling, *Mother Jones, The Miners' Angel: A Portrait*
(Carbondale: Southern Illinois University Press, 1979), 164.

17. Allan Carlson, *The American Way: Family and Community in the Shaping of American Identity* (Wilmington, DE: ISI Books, 2003).

18. Linda Gordon, "Social Insurance and Welfare Assistance: The Influence
of Gender in Welfare Thought in the United States, 1890–1935," *American
Historical Review* 97 (February 1992):48 (emphasis added); cited in Carlson,
The American Way, 63.

19. Cited in Mimi Abramovitz, *Regulating the Lives of Women: Social Welfare Policy from Colonial Times to the Present* (Boston: South End, 1988), 224.

20. Wilson's campaign speech at Lincoln, Nebraska, delivered on October 5,
1912.

21. Mishel et al., *The State of Working America, 2008–2009*.

Chapter 3

1. Joseph Conrad, *Chance* (London: Dent, 1921), 74.

2. Arthur Henry Chamberlain and James Franklin Chamberlain, *Thrift
and Conservation: How to Teach It* (Philadelphia: Lippincott, 1919), 7.

3. "Thrift Education," the report of the national conference on thrift education, Washington, DC, June 27 and 28, 1924, under the auspices of the
Committee on Thrift Education of the National Education Association and the
National Council of Education; Library of Congress, *Prosperity and Thrift: The
Coolidge Era and the Consumer Economy, 1921–1929*, testimony of C. E. Fleming, YMCA, Washington, DC, secretary of the local thrift committee.

4. William Hannibal Thomas, *The American Negro: A Study in Racial
Crossing* (New York: Macmillan, 1901), 81, 5.

5. S. W. Straus and Rollin Kirby, *History of the Thrift Movement* (Philadelphia: Lippincott, 1920), 108.

6. Helga Schmidt-Hackstock, "Economy," *Milwaukee Railway System
Employees' Magazine*, May 1918, cited in Chamberlain and Chamberlain, *Thrift
and Conservation*, 23.

7. Anonymous, cited in Chamberlain and Chamberlain, *Thrift and Conservation*, 42.

8. Cited in Chamberlain and Chamberlain, *Thrift and Conservation*, 45.

9. Ibid., 49.

10. Institute for American Values, Institute for Advanced Studies in Culture, New American Foundation, et al., *For a New Thrift: Confronting the Debt*

Culture (New York: Commission on Thrift, 2008), citing Rolf Nugent, "The Loan-Shark Problem," in *Law and Contemporary Problems* (Durham, NC: Duke University School of Law, 1941), 5.

11. Clarence W. Wassam, *Salary Loan Business in New York City* (New York: Russell Sage Foundation, 1908), 81.

12. Institute for American Values et al., *For a New Thrift*, 42, citing Roy F. Bergengren, *CUNA Emerges* (Madison, WI: Credit Union National Association, 1935), 56.

13. Ibid., 48.

14. Scott E. Carrell and Jonathan Zinman, "In Harm's Way? Payday Loan Access and Military Personnel Performance," Federal Reserve Bank of Philadelphia, Working Paper No. 08-18, August 1, 2008, www.phil.frb.org.

15. "Thrift Education."

16. Ibid., testimony of John W. Stout, vice president, Educational Thrift Service, Inc.

17. Ibid., testimony of H. R. Daniel, secretary, American Society for Thrift.

18. James Terry White, *Character Lessons in American Biography for Public Schools and Home Instruction* (New York: Character Development League, 1909), 65.

19. "Thrift Education,: statement of Miss E. A. Shelton, representing the Camp Fire Girls.

20. Ibid.

21. Cited by John Kobler, *Ardent Spirits: The Rise and Fall of Prohibition* (New York: Putnam's, 1973).

22. David M. Graber, "Review of Bill McKibben's *The End of Nature*," *Los Angeles Times Book Review*, October 22, 1989, p. 9.

23. Lendol Calder, *Financing the American Dream: A Cultural History of Consumer Credit* (Princeton, NJ: Princeton University Press, 1999), 206. We are particularly indebted to Calder for his excellent history of American consumer finance.

24. Jean Bethke Elshtain, "'You Kill It, You Eat It' and Other Lessons from My Thrifty Childhood," www.saveafarm.org/news-farm-economics.html#Elshtain, retrieved November 7, 2008.

Chapter 4

1. *Talkin' 'bout My Generation: The Economic Impact of Aging U.S. Baby Boomers* (Washington, DC: McKinsey Global Institute, June 2008), executive summary, exhibit 4, p. 14.

2. Ibid., exhibit 5, p. 15.

3. John Kenneth Galbraith, *The Affluent Society* (Boston: Houghton Mifflin, 1958), 201; Daniel Bell, *The Cultural Contradictions of Capitalism: 20th*

Anniversary Edition (New York: Basic Books, 1996), 21. For an excellent history of credit in the United States, see Laonal Calder's book, *Financing the American Dream: A Cultural History of Consumer Credit* (Princeton, NJ: Princeton University Press, 1999).

4. Nancy Coleman and Karen Conner, *The State of Working America 2002–2003*, Economic Policy Institute, www.epi.org/content.cfm/newsroom_releases_swa090102.

5. José García, *In the Red or in the Black?* (New York: Demos, 2008), 4.

6. Story reported by Brigid Schulte, "The Pain of Foreclosure," *Washington Post*, December 21, 2007, p. B1.

7. Christopher L. Peterson, "Usury Law, Payday Loans, and Statutory Sleight of Hand: Salience Distortion in American Credit Pricing Limits," *Minnesota Law Review* 92 (2008):1111.

8. Robin A. Morris, "Consumer Debt and Usury: A New Rationale for Usury," *Pepperdine Law Review* 15 (1988):151–154.

9. We are grateful to Demos: A Network for Ideas and Action, and Professor Elizabeth Warren of the Harvard Law School for their data and analysis of credit cards in America.

10. Christopher L. Peterson, "Predatory Structured Finance," *Cardozo Law Review* 28, no. 5 (2007). See also Kenneth A. Snowden, "Mortgage Securitization in the United States: Twentieth Century Developments in Historical Perspective," in *Anglo-American Financial Systems: Institutions and Markets in the Twentieth Century*, ed. Michael D. Bordo and Richard Sylla (New York: New York University Solomon Center, 1995), 261–298.

11. Matthew Haggman, Rob Barry, and Jack Dolan, "Thousands with Criminal Records Work Unlicensed as Loan Originators," *MiamHerald.com*, www.miamiherald.com/static/multimedia/news/mortgage/originators.html, retrieved November 7, 2008.

12. This idea has also been promoted by scholars Michael S. Barr, Sendhil Mullainathan, and Eldar Shafir in a New America Foundation report entitled "Behaviorally Informed Financial Services Regulation," October 17, 2008, www.newamerica.net/files/naf_behavioral_v5.pdf.

13. Project on Student Debt, "Policy Agenda to Address Rising Student Debt," http://projectonstudentdebt.org/index.php.

14. Jessica Silver-Greenberg and Ben Elgin, "The College Credit-Card Hustle," *Business Week*, July 28, 2008, p. 38.

Chapter 5

1. Robert DeYoung, William C. Hunter, and Gregory F. Udell, "The Past, Present, and Probable Future for Community Banks," paper presented at "Whither the Community Bank?" a conference prepared by the Federal Reserve

Bank of Chicago and the Journal of Financial Services Research, March 13–14, 2003, p. 31, http://chicagofed.org/news_and_conferences/conferences_and_events/files/whither_the_community_bank_deyoung_hunter_udell_conf.pdf.

2. Ben S. Bernanke, "The Financial Accelerator and the Credit Channel," speech to the Credit Channel of Monetary Policy in the Twenty-first Century Conference, Federal Reserve Bank of Atlanta, Atlanta, GA, June 15, 2007, www.federalreserve.gov/newsevents/speech/Bernanke20070615a.htm

3. "Small Banks' Competitors Loom Large," Southwest Economy, Federal Reserve Bank of Dallas, January/February 2004,www.dallasfed.org/research/swe/2004/swe0401b.html.

4. Robert DeYoung, "Community Banks at Their Best: Serving Local Financial Needs," 2004 Annual Report, Federal Reserve Bank of Chicago, 2004.

5. Grace Abbott, *The Immigrant and the Community* (New York: Century, 1917), 84.

6. For more information on this proposal, see Phillip Longman and Ellen Seidman, "To Save America's Finances, Bring Back Community Banks," New America Foundation, Big Ideas Series, November 2008, www.newamerica.net.

Chapter 6

1. Story from "Families Saving and Building Hope: 2007 Report on the Graduates of the Assets for All Alliance," www.siliconvalleycf.org/docs/assetsForAll.pdf.

2. Michael Sherraden, *Assets and the Poor: A New American Welfare Policy* (Armonk, New York: Sharpe, 1991).

3. Reid Cramer, Rourke O'Brien, and Alejandra Lopez-Fernandini, "The Assets Report: A Review, Assessment, and Forecast of Federal Assets Policy," New America Foundation, Washington, DC, March 12, 2008.

4. Lillian Woo and David Buchholz, "Subsidies for Assets: A New Look at the Federal Budget, Federal Reserve System/CFED Research Forum on Asset Building," paper first presented at the 2006 Assets Learning Conference in Phoenix, Arizona, revised February 2007; www.cfed.org/imageManager/assets/subsidiesforassets.pdf, retrieved November 8, 2008.

5. Howard E. Shuman, *Politics and the Budget: The Struggle between the President and Congress* (Englewood Cliffs, NJ: Prentice Hall, 1984), 105.

6. Phillip Longman, *The Return of Thrift* (New York: Free Press, 1996), 177. See also the classic formulation by Stanley S. Surrey, *Pathways to Tax Reform: The Concept of Tax Expenditure* (Cambridge, MA: Harvard University Press, 1973), and Christopher Howard, *The Hidden Welfare State: Tax Expenditures and Social Policy in the United States* (Princeton, NJ: Princeton University Press, 1999).

7. "Agrarian Justice, 1797," retrieved from Social Security Online, www.socialsecurity.gov/history/tpaine3.html.

8. Under the UK's Child Trust Fund, implemented in 2005 but backdated to all children born as of September 1, 2002, the government issues parents/guardians a £250 (U.S.$488) voucher upon a child's birth. Children from lower-income households receive an additional £250. The parent/guardian then takes the voucher to a bank and uses the voucher to open an account on behalf of the child. (Parents/guardians can choose to open a savings account or an account that invests in shares. This decision depends, in part, on their appetite for risk.) If the parent/guardian does not redeem the government-issued voucher after one year, an account is automatically opened on behalf of the child. All accountholders receive a top-up of £250 on their seventh birthday, and accountholders from low-income families receive an additional £250 top-up at this age. Over three million accounts have been opened thus far. For more information about this and other asset-building programs throughout the world, see Jamie Zimmerman, Jeff Meyer, and Ray Boshara, *Child Savings Accounts: Global Trends in Design and Practice* (Washington, DC: New America Foundation, 2008).

9. For a recent summary of research on asset effects, see Signe-Mary McKernan and Michael Sherraden, eds., *Asset Building and Low-Income Families* (Washington, DC: Urban Institute Press, 2008).

10. Babylon Today National Debt Clock, www.babylontoday.com/national_debt_clock.htm.

11. Peter R. Orszag, "Long Term Budget Outlook Redux," Director's Blog, Congressional Budget Office, June 17, 2008, retrieved at http://cboblog.cbo.gov/?p=130, July 26, 2008. See also Congressional Testimony at www.cbo.gov/doc.cfm?index=9385.

12. Laurence J. Kotlikoff, "Drifting to Future Bankruptcy," *Philadelphia Inquirer*, October 22, 2006. See also Laurence J. Kotlikoff and Scott Burns, *The Coming Generational Storm* (Cambridge, MA: MIT Press, 2004).

13. Press release, "More Than Half of Americans Say They Are Not Saving Adequately," Wachovia, Consumer Federation of America, December 10, 2007.

14. Richard H. Thaler and Cass R. Sunstein, *Nudge: Improving Decisions about Health, Wealth, and Happiness* (New Haven, CT: Yale University Press, 2008), 108.

15. Ibid., 112–115.

16. James M. Poterba, *Annuity Markets and Retirement Security*, Fiscal Studies (London: Institute for Fiscal Studies, September 2001), 249–270.

17. See Martha Derthick's classic *Policy Making for Social Security* (Washington, DC: Brookings Institution, 1979).

18. "U.S. Interim Projections by Age, Sex, Race, and Hispanic Origin: 2000–2050," table 2a, and "Projected Population of the United States, by Age and Sex: 2000 to 2050," www.census.gov/ipc/www/usinterimproj/.

19. J. M. Keynes, "Some Economic Consequences of a Declining Population," *Eugenics Review* 29 (1937):1–5.

20. Congressional Budget Office, *The Long-Term Outlook for Health Care Spending* (Washington, DC: Author, November 2007), appendix D, figure D-1, www.cbo.gov/ftpdocs/87xx/doc8758/AppendixD.7.1.shtml.

Chapter 7

1. Cited by Frederick Lewis Alan, *The Big Change: America Transforms Itself 1900-1950* (New York: Harper, 1952), 202.

2. RAND Corporation, *The First National Report Card on Quality of Health Care in America* (Santa Monica, CA: Author, 2004), 1, www.rand .org/pubs/research_briefs/RB9053-2/index1.html.

3. Congressional Budget Office, *The Long-Term Outlook for Health Spending* (Washington, DC: Author, November 2007).

4. World Health Organization Statistical Information System, accessed August 8, 2008; data are for 2005.

5. J. P. Bunker et al., "Improving Health: Measuring Effects of Medical Care," *Milbank Quarterly* 72 (1994):225–258.

6. William Dean Howells, *A Hazard of New Fortunes*, Project Gutenberg EBook 4600, www.gutenberg.org/files/4600/4600.txt.

7. "Achievements in Public Health, 1900–1999: Healthier Mothers and Babies," *Morbidity and Mortality Weekly Report*, Centers for Disease Control, 48, no. 38 (October 1, 1999):849–858, www.cdc.gov/mmwr/preview/ mmwrhtml/mm4838a2.htm.

8. Paul Starr, *The Social Transformation of American Medicine* (New York: Basic Books, 1982), 193, citing Stanley Joel Reiser, "The Emergence of the Concept of Screening for Disease," *Health and Society* 56 (Fall 1978): 403–425.

9. Ibid., 192, citing Michael Marks Davis, *Dispensaries* (New York: Macmillan, 1918), 12–17; Michael Marks Davis, *Clinics, Hospitals and Health Centers* (New York: Harper, 1927), 15–17.

10. Ibid., 192.

11. Suellen M. Hoy, *Chasing Dirt: The American Pursuit of Cleanliness* (New York: Oxford University Press, 1995), 133.

12. Philip J. Cook, *The Costs and Benefits of Alcohol Control* (Princeton, NJ: Princeton University Press, 2007), 24, table 2.2.

13. "The Craze for Health Care," reprinted in the *Saturday Evening Post: Reflections of a Decade* (Indianapolis, IN: Curtis, 1980), 140.

14. J. P. Bunker, H. S. Frazier, and F. Mosteller, "Improving Health: Measuring Effects of Medical Care," *Milbank Quarterly* 72 (1994):225–258.

15. Willard Gaylin, "Faulty Diagnosis," *New York Times*, June 12, 1994, section 4a, p. 1.

16. "The Futurists: Looking toward A.D. 2000," *Time*, February 25, 1966, p. 29.

17. Mark Schlesinger, "A Loss of Faith: The Sources of Reduced Political Legitimacy for the American Medical Profession," *Milbank Quarterly* 80, no. 2 (2002).

18. "Climate Change Poses a Huge Threat to Human Health," *Science Daily* www.sciencedaily.com– /releases/2008/01/080124190814.htm.

19. Jerome Goodman, "Superbugs," *New Yorker*, August 11, 2008, pp. 46–55; Wen-Chien Ko et al., "Community-Acquired *Klebsiella pneumoniae Bacteremia*: Global Differences in Clinical Patterns," Centers for Disease Control, *Emerging Infectious Diseases* 8, no. 2 (February 2002).

20. RAND, *The First National Report Card*, figure 4.

21. Majid Ezzati et al., "The Reversal of Fortunes: Trends in County Mortality and Cross-County Mortality Disparities in the United States," *PLoS Medicine*, April 2008, 5.

22. For a good popular discussion of the relationship of health and wealth, see Elizabeth Gudrais, "Unequal America: Causes and Consequences of the Wide—and Growing—Gap between Rich and Poor," *Harvard Magazine*, July/August 2008, cover story.

23. William H. Lucy, "Mortality Risk Associated with Leaving Home: Recognizing the Relevance of the Built Environment," *American Journal of Public Health*, September 2003, 1564–1569; Alan Ehrenhalt, "The Deadly Dangers of Daily Life," *Governing*, August 2002.

24. Surface Transportation Policy Project, *Mean Streets* (Washington, DC: Author, 2004), www.transact.org/PDFs/ms2002/MeanStreets2002.pdf.

25. Ibid.

26. M. Wei et al., "Relationship between Low Cardio Respiratory Fitness and Mortality in Normal-Weight, Overweight, and Obese Men," *Journal of the American Medical Association* (1999):1547–1553.

27. U.S. Department of Health and Human Services, Public Health Service, Office of the Surgeon General, *The Surgeon General's Call to Action to Prevent and Decrease Overweight and Obesity* (Washington, DC: Author, 2001), www.surgeongeneral.gov/topics/obesity/calltoaction/CalltoAction .pdf.

28. Centers for Disease Control, "Lower Direct Medical Costs Associated with Physical Activity," press release, www.cdc.gov/nccdphp/dnpa/pr-cost.htm.

29. "Urban Sprawl and Public Health," *Public Health Reports* 117, www.publichealthgrandrounds.unc.edu/urban/frumkin.pdf.

30. J. S. House, K. R. Landis, and D. Umberson, "Social Relationships and Health," *Science* 241 (1988):540–545.

31. Robert Putnam, *Social Capital: Measurement and Consequences* (Paris: Organization of Economic Co-operation and Development, March 19, 2000), www.oecd.org/dataoecd/25/6/1825848.pdf.

Chapter 8

1. Steven Asch et al., "Who Is at Greatest Risk for Receiving Poor-Quality Health Care?" *New England Journal of Medicine* 354 (2006):1147–1156, http://content.nejm.org/cgi/citmgr?gca=nejm;354/11/1147.

2. Reed Abelson, "Heart Procedure Is off the Charts in an Ohio City," *New York Times*, August 18, 2006, Business section, p. 1.

3. Peter Orzag, director of the Congressional Budget Office, "Health Care and Behavioral Economics," speech presented to the National Academy of Social Insurance, May 2008; Rehnardt as quoted by both Orzag and Gina Kolata, "Sharp Regional Incongruity Found in Medical Costs and Treatments," *Women's Health*, January 30, 1996, www.nytimes.com/specials/women/warchive/ 960130_1576.html.

4. A. K. Jha et al., "Effect of the Transformation of the Veterans Affairs Health Care System on the Quality of Care," *New England Journal of Medicine* 348 (2003):2218–2227.

5. Institute of Medicine, *To Err Is Human: Building a Safer Health System*, www.iom.edu/CMS/8089/5575.aspx.

6. J. E. Wennberg and A. M. Gittelsohn, "Variations in Medical Care among Small Areas," *Science*, December 14, 1973, pp. 1102–1108.

7. Eliot Fisher et al., "The Implications of Regional Variations in Medicare Spending, II: Health Outcomes and Satisfaction with Care," *Annals of Internal Medicine* 138 (2003):288–298.

8. N. Gibbs and A. Q. Bower, "What Scares Doctors? A: Being the Patient," *Time*, May 1, 2006, cover story.

9. See, for example, Jonathan Perlin et al., "The Veterans Health Administration: Quality, Value, Accountability, and Information as Transforming Strategies for Patient-Centered Care," *American Journal of Managed Care* 10, no. 11, pt. 2:828–836; U.S. Congressional Budget Office, *The Health Care System for Veterans: An Interim Report* (Washington, DC: Author, 2007); A. Oliver, "The Veterans Health Administration: An American Success Story?" *Milbank Quarterly* 85, no. 1 (2007):5–35.

10. Denis Protti and Peter Groen, "Implementation of the Veterans Health Administration VistA Clinical Information System around the World," *Electronic Healthcare* 7, no. 2 (2008).

11. See Phillip Longman, *Best Care Anywhere: Why VA Health Care Is Better Than Yours* (San Francisco: PoliPoint, 2007).

12. Roger Maduro, *VistA® and Open Healthcare News* 3, no. 1 (May 22, 2008), www.imm7.com/clients/vista/VistANews.

13. Paul Starr, *The Social Transformation of American Medicine* (New York: Basic Books, 1982), 201.

14. Ibid, 111, citing F. H. Todd, "Organization," *Journal of the American Medical Association* 39 (October 25, 1902):1061.

15. Cited by Larry R. Kirkland and Charles S. Bryan, "Osler's Service: A View of the Charts," *Journal of Medical Biography* 15, suppl. 1 (2007):50–54.

16. Cited by Max Lerner, *America as a Civilization*, vol. 2 (New York: Simon & Schuster, 1967), 124.

17. Cited by Kirkland and Bryan, "Osler's Service," 50–54.

18. Ibid.

19. John Carey, "Is Heart Surgery Worth It?" *Business Week*, July 18, 2005, www.businessweek.com/magazine/content/05_29/b3943037_mz011.htm.

20. For a useful summary of this sad chapter in American medicine, see H. G. Welch, "Presumed Benefit: Lessons from the American Experience with Marrow Transplantation for Breast Cancer," *British Medical Journal* 324 (2002):1088–1092. For a more general discussion of overtreatment and mistreatment in American medicine, see Shannon Brownlee, *Overtreated: Why Too Much Medicine Is Making Us Sicker and Poorer* (London: Bloomsbury, 2007).

21. *The Principles and Practice of Medicine*, 4th ed. (New York: Appleton, 1901), 109, 420.

22. Ibid., 109.

23. Shannon Brownlee, "Newtered," *Washington Monthly*, October 2007, www.washingtonmonthly.com/features/2007/0710.brownlee.html.

24. Tom Daschle, *Critical: What We Can Do about the Health-Care Crisis* (New York: St. Martin's, 2008), 175, citing Atul Gawande, *Complications: A Surgeon's Notes on an Imperfect Science* (New York: Picador, 2002), 78.

25. Melody Petersen, *Our Daily Meds: How the Pharmaceutical Companies Transformed Themselves into Slick Marketing Machines and Hooked the Nation on Prescription Drugs* (New York: Farrar, Straus, & Giroux, 2008).

Chapter 9

1. A. Q. Mowbray, *Road to Ruin* (Philadelphia: Lippincott, 1969), 34–35.

2. "Realizing the Potential: Expanding Housing Opportunities Near Transit," Federal Transit Administration and the U.S. Department of Housing and Urban Development, Report CA-26-6004, 2007.

3. "S&P/Case-Shiller Home Price Indices," June 2008, www2.standardandpoors.com/portal/site/sp/en/us/page.topic/indices_csmahp/0,0,0,0,0,0,0,0,0,1,1,0,0,0,0,0.html.

4. "Weighing the Evidence," *New York Post*, November 26, 1911.

5. Stephen B. Goddard, *Getting There: The Epic Struggle between Road and Rail in the American Century* (Chicago: University of Chicago Press, 1994), 52–53; Marc Levinson, *The Box: How the Shipping Container Made the World Smaller and the World Economy Bigger* (Princeton, NJ: Princeton University Press, 2006), 153.

6. Environment Protection Agency, *A Glance at Clean Freight Strategies: Intermodal Shipping*, http://epa.gov/smartway/transport/documents/carrier-strategy-docs/intermodal%20shipping.pdf.

7. Charles F. Adams Jr., "A Chapter of Erie," *North American Review*, July 1869, p. 53. For a description of Adams's motives for writing the essay, see Thomas K. McCraw, *Prophets of Regulation* (Cambridge, MA: Harvard University Press, 1984), 5.

8. The Pennsylvania Railroad, for example, which enjoyed only minor competition from the Baltimore & Ohio in Pittsburgh but which competed head to head with three major truck lines for through traffic between New York and Chicago, charged more to ship grain from Chicago to Pittsburgh and from Chicago to New York. Similarly, thanks to the fierce competition from fast clipper ships, railroads set comparatively low rates for transcontinental shipments to San Francisco after the opening of the Overland Route, but high rates for shipments to Denver and other landlocked cities. Rates were particularly high, on a per-mile basis, for grain shipments from Iowa and other granger states, owing not only to a general lack of competition from waterways but also to the thin flow of traffic on many rural branch lines, which created high average costs. Morrell W. Gaines, "Reasonable Regulation of Railroad Rates," *Yale Review*, July 1912, pp. 657–677.

9. "Railroad Inflation," *North American Review*, January 1869, p. 159, quoted by McCraw, *Prophets of Regulation*, 11.

10. John R. Stilgoe, *Train Time: Railroads and the Imminent Reshaping of the United States Landscape* (Charlottesville: University of Virginia Press, 2007), 43–49, 72–73.

11. "Famous Firsts," *Stevens Indicator*, Spring 1963, p. 16.

12. "Roads Could Save $1,000,000 a Day," *New York Times*, November 22, 1910, p. 6.

13. Albro Martin, *Enterprise Denied: Origins of the Decline of American Railroads, 1897–1917* (New York: Columbia University Press, 1971), 213.

14. "An Old New Gospel," *Philadelphia North American*, November 29, 1910, page not shown, clipping from the papers of Frederick Taylor, Stevens Institute, Hoboken, NJ.

15. *New York Times*, November 2, 1914, p. 11.

16. John F. Stover, *History of the Baltimore and Ohio Railroad* (Purdue, IN: Purdue University Press, 1987), 234.

17. Quoted by William J. Cunningham, *American Railroads: Government Control and Reconstruction Policies* (New York: Shaw, 1922), 11–13.

18. John W. Barringer, *Super Railroads for a Dynamic American Economy* (New York: Simmons-Boardman, 1955).

19. Martin, *Enterprise Denied*, 349.

20. Levinson, *The Box*, 153.

21. Surface Transportation Board, "Surface Transportation Board Calculates Rail Industry's Cost of Capital & Revenue Adequacy for 2007," press release, September 26, 2008.

Chapter 10

1. Nicole S. Garnett, "Save the Cities, Stop the Suburbs?" Notre Dame Legal Studies Paper No. 06-10, http://ssrn.com/paper=908248.

2. Richard E. Wagner, "State Excise Taxation: Horse-and-Buggy Taxes in an Electronic Age," Tax Foundation Background Paper, No. 48 (May 2005).

3. "Road Use for a Road Tax," *Christian Science Monitor*, January 2, 1931.

4. James A. Dunn Jr., *Miles to Go: European and American Transportation Policies* (Cambridge, MA: MIT Press, 1981), 103–4.

5. "Dustin Hoffman and Gene Hackman: Together at Last!" (pt. 2 of 2), available on YouTube, 4:50 minutes. Also see Richard H. Thaler and Cass R. Sustein, "Dustin Hoffman's Mental Accounting," http://nudges.wordpress .com/2008/05/27/dustin-hoffmans-mental-accounting/, retrieved August 25, 2008.

6. Stephen B. Goddard, *Getting There: The Epic Struggle between Road and Rail in the American Century* (Chicago: University of Chicago Press, 1994), 127, 134–35.

7. John R. Stilgoe, *Train Time: Railroads and the Imminent Reshaping of the United States Landscape* (Charlottesville: University of Virginia Press, 2007), 43–49, 72–73; Peter T. Maiken, *Night Trains: The Pullman System in the Golden Years of American Rail Travel* (Baltimore: Johns Hopkins University Press, 1989), 395–97.

8. Mark Reutter, "The Lost Promise of the American Railroad," *Wilson Quarterly*, Winter 1994; Maury Klein, *Unfinished Business: The Railroad in American Life* (Lebanon, NH: University Press of New England, 1994), 158.

9. Phillip Longman, "The Great Train Robbery: How the Railroad Retirement System Swindles Taxpayers, Robs Younger Workers, and Derails Amtrak," *Washington Monthly*, December 1987.

10. Stilgoe, *Train Time*, 73; and Reutter, "The Lost Promise."

11. Reutter, "The Lost Promise."

12. Ibid.

13. Federal Transit Administration, *The Beginnings of Federal Assistance for Public Transportation*, www.fta.dot.gov/about/about_FTA_history.html; Office of Management and Budget, *Budget of the United States Government, Fiscal Year 2009*, Historical Tables, table 3.2, "Outlays by Function and Subfunction," www.whitehouse.gov/omb/budget/fy2009/pdf/hist.pdf.

14. Federal Highway Administration, *Status of the Nation's Highways, Bridges, and Transit 2006: Conditions and Performance*, chap. 7, executive summary, www.fhwa.dot.gov/policy/2006cpr/, retrieved August 24, 2008.

15. David Streitfeld, "Ruins of an American Dream," *New York Times*, August 24, 2008, Business section, p. 1.

16. Stilgoe, *Train Time*, 8.

17. The Center for Neighborhood Technology and the Brookings Institution's Urban Markets Initiative have done fine work in mapping the combined cost of housing and transportation in different markets across the country. For an example of their work, see http://htaindex.cnt.org.

Chapter 11

1. William Hoffman, "Shippers Battle Rising Costs: Fast Rising Prices, Slow Economy Push Logistics Spending to $1.4 Trillion," *Traffic World*, June 23, 2008, p. 8.

2. Joe White, "Too Much Freight, Not Enough Drivers?" *Traffic World*, August 25, 2008, p. 6.

3. John Heimlich, VP and Chief Economist, Air Transport Association of America, "Reformulating Commercial Aviation," PowerPoint presentation, August 22, 2008; and Heimlich, "Commercial Aviation: The Brakes Are On," November 5, 2008, www.airlines.org/airlines_fuel.pdf.

4. U.S. Census Bureau, Population Division, *2008 National Population Projections*, table 2, "Projections of the Population by Selected Age Groups and Sex for the United States: 2010 to 2050," www.census.gov/population/www/projections/2008projections.html, retrieved August 25, 2008.

5. Linda Bailey, *Aging Americans: Stranded without Options* (Washington, DC: Surface Transportation Policy Project, April 2004).

6. To our knowledge, David L. Foster, executive director of Rail Solutions, coined this phrase, and he has certainly done compelling writing on the concept behind it. Rail Solutions has been active in the fight to win a rail alternative to the expansion of I-81. See its website at www.railsolutions.org.

7. American Association of State Highway and Transportation Officials, *Freight-Rail Bottom Line Report*, http://freight.transportation.org/doc/Freight RailReport.pdf, p. 2

8. Ibid., 17.

9. U.S. Department of Transportation Corridors of the Future Program Application, the Southeast I-95 Corridor, applied for by CSX Corporation, May 25, 2007, http://www.vhsr.com/system/files/CSX+CFP+Submission.pdf.

10. Alan Drake, "Stop Ignoring Rail, America," *EV World*, reprinted from the Association for the Study of Peak Oil and Gas (ASPO)–USA *Peak Oil Review*, July 9, 2007.

11. Daniel Machalaba, "Crowds Heed Amtrak's 'All Aboard': Improved Service, Air Woes Lure Travelers in Northeast; Long Hauls Still Suffer," *Wall Street Journal*, August 23, 2007, p. B1.

12. "Aviation Planning at the Leading Edge, Short-Haul Transportation to and from New York: The Effect of Airport Congestion on Mode Choice," presentation to the FAA Forecast Conference, March 11, 2008.

13. Peter E. Lynch, *New Haven Passenger Trains* (Minneapolis, MN: MBI, 2005), 31.

14. National Surface Transportation Policy and Revenue Study Commission, Passenger Rail Working Group, *Vision for the Future: U.S. Intercity Passenger Rail Network through 2050*, December 6, 2007, p. 15. According to the study, altitude-adjusted aviation emissions range from 0.49 kilogram per passenger-mile for long flights to 0.65 for short flights, compared with just 0.20 for Amtrak (diesel, 0.196; electric, 0.20–0.215).

15. For a picture of what might have been Florida's high-speed rail future, see Phillip Longman, "Florida's Dream Train Revived?" (proposed Miami-Tampa-Orlando high-speed rail line), *Florida Trends*, January 1993, www.highbeam.com.

16. Speech delivered August 5, 2008, in Youngstown, OH.

17. Robert J. Shapiro, Kevin A. Hassett, and Frank S. Arnold, *The Benefits of Public Transportation Conserving Energy and Preserving the Air We Breathe* (Washington, DC: American Public Transportation Association, 2002).

Chapter 12

1. Rex Burns, *Success in America: The Yeoman Dream and the Industrial Revolution* (Amherst: University of Massachusetts Press, 1976), 176.

2. Address at the Texas Centennial Exposition, Dallas, June 12, 1936, the American Presidential Project, www.presidency.ucsb.edu/ws/index.php?pid=15302, as quoted by Michael Lind, "The Smallholder Society," *Harvard Law and Policy Review* 1, no. 1 (2007). Subsequent presidents would often use such phrases as a "yeoman's job" in their public speeches, but a digital search of presidential papers and speeches turned up no references to the "yeoman ideal" after 1936.

3. John Kenneth Galbraith, *American Capitalism: The Concept of Countervailing Power* (Boston: Houghton Mifflin, 1952).

4. Federal Reserve Bank of San Francisco, "Economic Letter," June 1 2007.

5. College Board, *Trends in College Pricing 2007*, table 3b, www.collegeboard.com, retrieved September 19, 2008.

6. U.S. Census Bureau, *Current Population Survey, Annual Social and Economic Supplements*, table P-16, www.census.gov/hhes/www/income/histinc/p16.html.

7. *State of Working America, 2008–2009*, executive summary, www.state-ofworkingamerica.org/swa08_00_execsum.pdf, retrieved September 19, 2008.

8. "Recent Changes in U.S. Family Finances: Evidence from the 2001 and 2004 Survey of Consumer Finances," *Federal Reserve Bulletin*, 2006, p. A23, www.federalreserve.gov/pubs/bulletin/2006/financesurvey.pdf.

9. CNN/*USA Today*/Gallup Survey, April 2005, http://http-download .intuit.com/http.intuit/CMO/intuit/futureofsmallbusiness/SR-1037_intuit_ SmallBiz_Demog.pdf.

10. *2002 Census of Agriculture*, vol. 1, chap. 1, U.S. National Level Data Table 1, "Historical Highlights: 2002 and Earlier Census Years," United States Department of Agriculture, www.nass.usda.gov/census/census02/volume1/ us/index1.htm.

11. Population Division of the Department of Economic and Social Affairs of the United Nations Secretariat, *World Population Prospects: The 2006 Revision and World Urbanization Prospects: The 2005 Revision*, http://esa.un.org/ unpp, retrieved September 4, 2008.

12. Richard Jackson and Neil Howe, *The Graying of the Middle Kingdom: The Demographics and Economics of Retirement Policy in China* (Washington, DC: Center for Strategic and International Studies, 2004), 4. See also Phillip Longman, *The Empty Cradle: How Falling Birthrates Threaten World Prosperity and What to Do about It* (New York: Basic Books, 2004).

13. McKinsey Global Institute, *The Coming Demographic Deficit: How Aging Populations Will Reduce Global Savings* (San Francisco: Author, 2005). See also Richard Jackson and Neil Howe, *The Graying of Great Powers: Demography and Geopolitics in the 21st Century* (Washington, DC: Center for Strategic and International Studies, Global Aging Initiative, 2008).

14. Wohlers Associates, *Wohlers Report 2008* (Fort Collins, CO: Author, May 2008), www.wohlersassociates.com/press46.htm, retrieved September 19, 2008.

15. See www.contourcrafting.org for a video demonstration. At the same time, personal fabrication machines will put dangerous new powers in the hands of malicious individuals—the ability to rapidly manufacture assault rifles and bombs, for example, as well as yet undreamed-of weapons of mass mayhem. This reality will require social controls of the type that are only possible within small, tight-knit communities.

16. Neil Gershenfeld, address to the Third International Fab Lab Forum and Symposium on Digital Fabrication, Pretoria, South Africa, June 29, 2006, http://cba.mit.edu/events/06.06.ZA/symposium.html, 21:32.

17. This statistic applies to firms with fewer than twenty workers. See Small Business Administration, *Small Business Economy for Data Year 2005*, table A.8, "Employer Firm Births, Deaths, and Employment Changes by Employment."

18. Quoted in Richard C. Schragger, "The Anti–Chain Store Movement: Localist Ideology, and the Remnants of the Progressive Constitution,

1920–1940," University of Virginia Law School Public Law and Legal Theory Working Paper, 2005, p. 21.

19. For more information on this issue, visit the New America Foundation's Wireless Future Program website at www.newamerica.net/programs/wireless_future#programtabs-2.

20. Barry C. Lynn, "Breaking the Chain: The Antitrust Case against Wal-Mart," *Harper's Magazine*, July 2006, p. 30, http://harpers.org/archive/2006/07/0081115, retrieved November 10, 2008.

21. *United States v. Paramount Pictures, Inc.*, 334 U.S. 131 (1948); Society of Independent Motion Picture Dealers, "The Hollywood Antitrust Case," research database, www.cobbles.com/simpp_archive/1film_antitrust.htm.

22. For a discussion of the transition from IBM's old "closed system" to its "open system" of production in computing, see Michael H. Best, *The New Competitive Advantage: The Renewal of American Industry* (New York: Oxford University Press, 2001), 46, 79.

ACKNOWLEDGMENTS

WE HAVE many people to thank for their ideas, suggestions, and influences, starting with those connected to the New America Foundation, a nonpartisan think tank in Washington, DC, where Phil Longman is a senior fellow and Ray Boshara is vice president and director of the Asset Building Program. Though too numerous to mention in total, New American colleagues to whom we are particularly grateful include Shannon Brownlee, Jeff Meyer, Steve Coll, Reid Cramer, Michael Lind, Barry Lynn, Sherle Schwenninger, Frank Micciche, and Bernard Schwartz. Ellen Seidman, director of Financial Services Policy at New America and formerly director of the Office of Thrift Supervision, played a key role in formulating our ideas on debt and bank reform, particularly those found in chapter 5. California-based fellow T. A. Frank also played an important role in the reporting and writing of that chapter.

We'd also like to thank the Ford, Rockefeller, Charles Stewart Mott, Annie E. Casey, F.B. Heron, and Citi Foundations, whose generous support of New America made the writing of this book possible.

We'd like to thank Peter Barnes and Pam Carr of the idyllic Mesa Refuge in Point Reyes, California, where Boshara completed most of his writing for this book, and whose ideas were enriched through lovely evening dinner conversations with fellow Mesa writers-in-residence Mark Hertsgaard and Eric Tipler.

We are also grateful to David Blankenhorn and Barbara Whitehead of the Institute for American Values for their important work in researching and promoting the idea of thrift and for their chronicling the role of "antithrift" institutions in modern-day America.

Paul Glastris, editor in chief of the *Washington Monthly*, played a vital role in helping us craft our ideas and set them down on paper. We

231

are also grateful to our editor at PoliPoint, Peter Richardson, for his deft use of his pencil to improve our prose. We deeply appreciate as well PoliPoint publisher Scott Jordan's commitment to this project long before we quite knew where it—and the country's political direction—was heading.

Sandra Longman, a deep student of American history and intellectual life, played a key role in formulating the book's arguments, as well as in sustaining her scribbling husband's emotional life during its composition. Their son, Sam, deserves credit, too, for his patience with a father who too rarely emerged during a long summer from his basement office.

Boshara cannot begin to adequately thank his wife, Lora L. Iannotti, and their three children—Arianna, Isabella, and Eli—for their unflinching love, support, and especially good humor not just during the writing of this book but in every aspect of his life. He also would like to recognize a dear, lifelong friend, Bill Zavarello, whose commitment to social justice inspired his own. Finally, Boshara would like to express his love and gratitude to his parents—Corky Boshara of Akron, Ohio, and Ray and Liz Boshara of Las Vegas, Nevada. They taught him the values of saving, hard work, independence, and family, for which he is forever grateful.

Phillip Longman is a Schwartz Senior Fellow at the New America Foundation and also research director of its Next Social Contract Project. He is the author of numerous articles and books on demographics, health care, economics, and social change. His work has appeared in such publications as the *Atlantic, Der Spiegel,* the *Financial Times, Foreign Affairs, Foreign Policy, Fortune,* the *Harvard Business Review,* the *National Review,* the *New Republic,* the *New Statesman,* the *New York Times Magazine,* the *Wall Street Journal,* and the *Washington Monthly.* His book *The Empty Cradle: How Falling Birthrates Threaten World Prosperity and What to Do about It* (Basic Books, 2004, was reissued in paperback in 2006). It examines how the rapid yet uneven fall in birthrates around the globe is affecting the balance of power between nations and influencing the global economy and culture. He is also the author of *Best Care Anywhere* (PoliPoint, 2007), which chronicles the quality transformation of the Veterans Administration's health care system and applies its lessons to a plan for reforming the U.S. health care system as a whole. Mr. Longman's other books include *Born to Pay: The New Politics of Aging in America* (Houghton Mifflin, 1987) and *The Return of Thrift* (Free Press, 1997).

Formerly a senior writer and deputy assistant managing editor at *U.S. News & World Report,* Mr. Longman has won numerous awards for his business and financial writing, including UCLA's Gerald Loeb Award and the top prize for investigative journalism from Investigative Reporters and Editors in 1990. He is a graduate of Oberlin College and was also a Knight-Bagehot Fellow at Columbia University. He lives in Washington, DC, with his wife, Sandy, and son, Sam.

Ray Boshara is vice president of the New America Foundation. He has advised the Clinton and George W. Bush administrations and several presidential candidates, testified before the U.S. Congress, and given speeches all over the world on strategies to build savings, financial security, and wealth for low- and moderate-income persons. Many of his ideas to promote financial security have been included in bipartisan legislation or become law, including legislation to create savings accounts at birth for every child born in America. He has written for the *Washington Post*, the *New York Times*, the *Atlantic*, *Esquire*, the *New York Daily News*, and the Brookings Institution, and he has appeared on CNBC, C-SPAN, and several radio programs across the nation. He is a member of the National Academy of Social Insurance and serves on many national commissions and advisory boards, including the Commission on Thrift. He also serves as a consultant to the Committee on Domestic Justice and Human Development of the United States Conference of Catholic Bishops. Prior to joining New America, he worked for the Select Committee on Hunger in the U.S. Congress, the United Nations in Rome, CFED (Corporation for Enterprise Development), and the Aspen Institute. He began his career as a certified public accountant, working for Ernst & Whinney (now Ernst & Young).

Mr. Boshara is a graduate of Ohio State University, Yale Divinity School, and the John F. Kennedy School of Government at Harvard. He was named a PaceSetter at Ohio State and a Littauer Fellow at Harvard for outstanding scholarship and leadership. In 2002, he was selected by *Esquire* magazine as one of America's Best and Brightest. He was born in Akron, Ohio, and now lives in Washington, DC, with his wife, Lora Iannotti, and their three children—Arianna, Isabella, and Eli.

The Blue Pages: A Directory of Companies Rated by Their Politics and Practices
Helps consumers match their buying decisions with their political values by listing the
political contributions and business practices of over 1,000 companies. $9.95, paperback.

Rose Aguilar, *Red Highways: A Liberal's Journey into the Heartland*
Challenges red state stereotypes to reveal new strategies for progressives. $15.95,
paperback.

Dean Baker, *Plunder and Blunder: The Rise and Fall of the Bubble Economy*
Chronicles the growth and collapse of the stock and housing bubbles and explains
how policy blunders and greed led to the catastrophic—but completely predictable—
market meltdowns. $15.95, paperback.

Jeff Cohen, *Cable News Confidential: My Misadventures in Corporate Media*
Offers a fast-paced romp through the three major cable news channels—Fox CNN,
and MSNBC—and delivers a serious message about their failure to cover the most
urgent issues of the day. $14.95, paperback.

Marjorie Cohn, *Cowboy Republic: Six Ways the Bush Gang Has Defied the Law*
Shows how the executive branch under President Bush has systematically defied the
law instead of enforcing it. $14.95, paperback.

Marjorie Cohn and Kathleen Gilberd, *Rules of Disengagement: The Politics and
Honor of Military Dissent*
Examines what U.S. military men and women have done—and what their families and
others can do—to resist illegal wars, as well as military racism, sexual harassment, and
denial of proper medical care. $14.95, paperback.

Joe Conason, *The Raw Deal: How the Bush Republicans Plan to Destroy Social Security and the Legacy of the New Deal*
Reveals the well-financed and determined effort to undo the Social Security Act and
other New Deal programs. $11.00, paperback.

Kevin Danaher, Shannon Biggs, and Jason Mark, *Building the Green Economy:
Success Stories from the Grassroots*
Shows how community groups, families, and individual citizens have protected their
food and water, cleaned up their neighborhoods, and strengthened their local
economies. $16.00, paperback.

Kevin Danaher and Alisa Gravitz, *The Green Festival Reader: Fresh Ideas from
Agents of Change*
Collects the best ideas and commentary from some of the most forward green thinkers
of our time. $15.95, paperback.

Reese Erlich, *Dateline Havana: The Real Story of U.S. Policy and the Future of Cuba*
Explores Cuba's strained relationship with the United States, the island nation's evolving culture and politics, and prospects for U.S. Cuba policy with the departure of Fidel Castro. $22.95, hardcover.

Reese Erlich, *The Iran Agenda: The Real Story of U.S. Policy and the Middle East Crisis*
Explores the turbulent recent history between the two countries and how it has led to a showdown over nuclear technology. $14.95, paperback.

Steven Hill, *10 Steps to Repair American Democracy*
Identifies the key problems with American democracy, especially election practices, and proposes ten specific reforms to reinvigorate it. $11.00, paperback.

Markos Kounalakis and Peter Laufer, *Hope Is a Tattered Flag: Voices of Reason and Change for the Post-Bush Era*
Gathers together the most listened-to politicos and pundits, activists and thinkers, to answer the question: what happens after Bush leaves office?
$29.95, hardcover; $16.95 paperback.

Yvonne Latty, *In Conflict: Iraq War Veterans Speak Out on Duty, Loss, and the Fight to Stay Alive*
Features the unheard voices, extraordinary experiences, and personal photographs of a broad mix of Iraq War veterans, including Congressman Patrick Murphy, Tammy Duckworth, Kelly Daugherty, and Camilo Mejia. $24.00, hardcover.

Phillip Longman, *Best Care Anywhere: Why VA Health Care Is Better Than Yours*
Shows how the turnaround at the long-maligned VA hospitals provides a blueprint for salvaging America's expensive but troubled health care system. $14.95, paperback.

Phillip Longman and Ray Boshara, *The Next Progressive Era*
Provides a blueprint for a re-empowered progressive movement and describes its implications for families, work, health, food, and savings. $22.95, hardcover.

Marcia and Thomas Mitchell, *The Spy Who Tried to Stop a War: Katharine Gun and the Secret Plot to Sanction the Iraq Invasion*
Describes a covert operation to secure UN authorization for the Iraq war and the furor that erupted when a young British spy leaked it.
$23.95, hardcover.

Susan Mulcahy, ed., *Why I'm a Democrat*
Explores the values and passions that make a diverse group of Americans proud to be Democrats. $14.95, paperback.

David Neiwert, *The Eliminationists: How Hate Talk Radicalized the American Right*
Argues that the conservative movement's alliances with far-right extremists have not only pushed the movement's agenda to the right, but also have become a malignant influence increasingly reflected in political discourse. $16.95, paperback.

Christine Pelosi, *Campaign Boot Camp: Basic Training for Future Leaders*
Offers a seven-step guide for successful campaigns and causes at all levels of government. $15.95, paperback.

William Rivers Pitt, *House of Ill Repute: Reflections on War, Lies, and America's Ravaged Reputation*
Skewers the Bush Administration for its reckless invasions, warrantless wiretaps, lethally incompetent response to Hurricane Katrina, and other scandals and blunders. $16.00, paperback.

Sarah Posner, *God's Profits: Faith, Fraud, and the Republican Crusade for Values Voters*
Examines corrupt televangelists' ties to the Republican Party and unprecedented access to the Bush White House. $19.95, hardcover.

Nomi Prins, *Jacked: How "Conservatives" Are Picking Your Pocket –Whether You Voted for Them or Not*
Describes how the "conservative" agenda has affected your wallet, skewed national priorities, and diminished America—but not the American spirit. $12.00, paperback.

Cliff Schecter, *The Real McCain: Why Conservatives Don't Trust Him—And Why Independents Shouldn't*
Explores the gap between the public persona of John McCain and the reality of this would-be president.
$14.95, hardcover.

Norman Solomon, *Made Love, Got War: Close Encounters with America's Warfare State*
Traces five decades of American militarism and the media's all-too-frequent failure to challenge it. $24.95, hardcover.

John Sperling et al., *The Great Divide: Retro vs. Metro America*
Explains how and why our nation is so bitterly divided into what the authors call Retro and Metro America. $19.95, paperback.

Daniel Weintraub, *Party of One: Arnold Schwarzenegger and the Rise of the Independent Voter*
Explains how Schwarzenegger found favor with independent voters, whose support has been critical to his success, and suggests that his bipartisan approach represents the future of American politics. $19.95, hardcover.

Curtis White, *The Spirit of Disobedience: Resisting the Charms of Fake Politics, Mindless Consumption, and the Culture of Total Work*
Debunks the notion that liberalism has no need for spirituality and describes a "middle way" through our red state/blue state political impasse. Includes three powerful interviews with John DeGraaf, James Howard Kunstler, and Michael Ableman. $24.00, hardcover.

For more information, please visit www.p3books.com.